Party Politics in Alabama
From 1850 Through 1860

The Library of Alabama Classics,
reprint editions of works important
to the history, literature, and culture of
Alabama, is dedicated to the memory of

Rucker Agee

whose pioneering work in the fields
of Alabama history and historical geography
continues to be the standard of
scholarly achievement.

Party Politics in Alabama
From 1850 Through 1860

Lewy Dorman
With an Introduction by Leah Rawls Atkins

The University of Alabama Press
Tuscaloosa & London

Introduction copyright © 1995
The University of Alabama Press
Tuscaloosa, Alabama 35487-0380

Originally issued in 1935 by the Alabama State Department of
Archives and History, Historical and Patriotic Series No. 13

∞

The paper on which this book is printed meets the minimum requirements of American
National Standard for Information Science-Permanence of Paper for Printed Library Materials,
ANSI Z39.48-1984.

Library of Congress Cataloging-in-Publication Data

Dorman, Lewy, 1887–
    Party politics in Alabama from 1850 through 1860 / Lewy Dorman with an introduction
by Leah Rawls Atkins.
        p.   cm. — (Library of Alabama classics)
    Originally published: Montgomery, Ala. : Alabama State Department of Archives and
History, 1935, in series: Historical and patriotic series.
    Includes bibliographical references (p.) and index.
    ISBN 0-8173-0780-X (alk. paper)
    1. Alabama—Politics and government—To 1865. I. Title. II. Series.
F326.D7 1995
320.9761\09\034—dc20   94-35291

British Library Cataloguing-in-Publication Data available

CONTENTS

List of Maps   vi
Introduction by Leah Rawls Atkins   vii
Letter of Transmittal   5
Preface   7
Chapter
    1. Alabama in 1850   11
    2. Preliminary Survey of Parties, 1847–49   27
    3. The Secession Movement and the Disintegration
        of the Old Parties, 1850–51   43
    4. The Reorganization of Parties, 1851–52   65
    5. Democratic Party Sucessess, 1852–54   77
    6. The Know Nothing Campaign of 1855   101
    7. The Presidential Campaign of 1856   125
    8. Transition to the One-Party System
        in Alabama, 1857–59   137
    9. Disruption of the Democratic Party in 1860 154
  10. Conclusion   170

Appendix A. Tables of Election Figures
    Presidential Elections, 1848–60   176
    Congressional Elections, 1847–59   178
    Gubernatorial Elections, 1847–59   192
    For Delegates to the Secession Convention   194

Appendix B. Roll of Members of the Alabama Legislature
    The House   198
    The Senate   208

Maps and Charts, 1850–60   215
Bibliography   229
Index   236

LIST OF MAPS

Density Map of Alabama, 1850   215

Distribution of Slaves in Alabama, 1850   216

Native States of the People of Alabama, 1870   217

Presidential Election in 1848   218

Congressional Elections in 1851   219

Composition of the Lower House of the Legislature in 1851   220

Presidential Election in 1852   221

Vote in the Senate to Change from the White Basis Principle
  of Representation, 1854   222

Gubernatorial Election in 1855   223

Vote in the Lower House for United State Senator in 1855   224

Presidential Election in 1856   225

Presidential Election in 1860   226

Election for Delegates to the Secession Convention, December 1860   227

INTRODUCTION

by

Leah Rawls Atkins

The smoke from Alabama cotton set ablaze in 1865 to keep it from falling into Union hands had hardly cleared when the decade leading up to Alabama's decision to leave the Union on January 11, 1861, was being analyzed and the causes of secession and war debated. Walter L. Fleming was the first Alabama historian to write about the period in a major monograph; he specifically addresses the causes of the war in the introduction of his 1905 Columbia University dissertation, *Civil War and Reconstruction in Alabama*. Fleming had been a student of George Petrie at Auburn. After receiving his master's degree from what was then called the Agricultural and Mechanical College of Alabama, he entered Columbia to study under William A. Dunning, and the influence of Dunning is evident in his work.[1] In *Civil War and Reconstruction in Alabama*, Fleming concludes that the spread of abolitionist activity and such national political developments as the demise of the Whig party and the founding (as its northern successor) of the Republican party, which opposed the extension of slavery, had increased Alabama's support for the radical states'-rights position advocated by William L. Yancey.[2]

In 1926 Fleming was serving as head of the History Department at Vanderbilt University when a young man from Clayton, Alabama, Lewy Dorman, transferred his graduate credits from the University of Chicago and entered the Vanderbilt doctoral program. Fleming had no trouble interesting Dorman in Alabama topics, for the native of Barbour County had written his master's thesis at the University of Alabama on free blacks in Alabama and had been researching Alabama subjects at Chicago under William E. Dodd. Frank L. Owsley, Sr., another former student of Petrie at Auburn and of Dodd at Chicago, was also teaching at Vanderbilt and inspired Dorman.

The doctoral dissertation Dorman completed under the direction of Fleming and Owsley, *Party Politics in Alabama From 1850 Through 1860*, became the definitive monograph on politics in Alabama during the decade of the 1850s once it was published by the Alabama State Department of Archives and History in 1935.[3] Dorman's book has long been out of print, and existing copies at public and university libraries are frayed and worn, while those copies offered for sale infrequently by rare book dealers command high prices.

Lewy Dorman was born in Clayton, in Barbour County, Alabama, on September 12, 1887, the son of Alexander Alpheus Dorman and Martha Isabella

Slaughter. His father's family was from South Carolina and probably of Hugue-
not descent. They migrated to Alabama in 1831 and settled in Barbour
County, near Louisville, while his maternal grandparents located south of
Comer, also in Barbour County.[4] Dorman's father served in the Confederate
army in the Jeff Davis Legion, and Dorman grew up listening to stories of frontier days in Barbour County, of political stump debates and Civil War battles.

Dorman was educated in the public schools of Clayton and entered the
State Normal School at Troy in 1904. He financed his education by teaching in
the rural schools of Barbour County and occasionally working as a telephone
operator and carpenter's helper. His father, who farmed and occasionally
worked in a store, and two brothers assisted him financially when they could,
and in 1910 Dorman received his two-year education degree and began teaching full time in the Union Springs high school. He continued to study and
periodically returned to classes, eventually receiving his bachelor's degree in
1914 from the University of Alabama.

Dorman completed his master's in history at the University of Alabama in
1916; his thesis, " The Free Negro in Alabama from 1819 to 1861," was directed by Col. Thomas C. McCorvey. Dorman used the collections, especially
newspapers and manuscripts, of the Alabama State Department of Archives
and History in his research. The Alabama archives had been established in
1901 under the directorship of Thomas M. Owen, and it was rapidly increasing
its holdings. Using census data for 1840, 1850, and 1860, Dorman traced the
increase in the numbers of free blacks in the state, discussing the reasons for the
large concentration of free blacks in the city of Mobile, which had one-third of
the total number of free blacks living in Alabama in 1840 and nearly one-half
by 1860.[5]

Even before Dorman completed his requirements for his master's degree at
the University of Alabama, he began attending graduate school during summer
sessions at the University of Chicago, studying under William E. Dodd.
Dorman returned from Chicago in the fall of 1917 and was teaching history at
Daphne Normal School when he married Margaret (sometimes called Mar-
guerite) Long Thompson. The couple returned to Clayton where Dorman
taught at the high school, and in 1918 a son, Ralph, was born and two years
later a daughter, Gertha Pearl.[6]

In the fall of 1921, because of the recommendation of the University of
Alabama History Department, Dorman was offered a position teaching history
at the Woman's College of Alabama, now Huntingdon College in Montgomery.[7] He and his family moved to a faculty residence on Woodley Road, and
they became active in campus life.[8] In summer of 1924, Dorman taught for six
weeks at Jacksonville Normal School. He was a history professor at the

Woman's College until the spring of 1926, when he returned to graduate school at the University of Chicago; however, financial problems forced him to leave Chicago, return to the South, and accept a teaching fellowship at Vanderbilt University.[9] Dorman spent one year in residence at Vanderbilt during 1927–28, and developed "a real affection" for old Vandy and the history faculty.[10]

At Vanderbilt, Dorman studied under Fleming, Owsley, and William C. Brinkley. His dissertation, probably already begun at Chicago, was directed at Vanderbilt by Fleming until ill health curtailed the professor's activities and Owsley assumed the responsibility. Dorman used the summer months to conduct research at the archives in Montgomery, and by the spring of 1930, he had completed a draft. When Marie Bankhead Owen, who had succeeded her husband as director of the Alabama State Department of Archives and History, wrote Professor Owsley at Vanderbilt requesting articles on Alabama for the department's new publication, The Alabama Historical Quarterly, Owsley recommended Dorman's manuscript. While offering to submit an essay of his own as soon as he completed his study of Confederate diplomacy, Owsley praised Dorman's dissertation, "done for a degree at Vanderbilt University [and] something which simply *must* be published somewhere." Owsley called Dorman's work "a beautiful and penetrating study. No one else will ever do this work as painstakingly as he has done [it]."[11] At the time, Vanderbilt required that dissertations be published before degrees were conferred, so publication of the dissertation was critical.[12]

In 1928, while he was still working on the dissertation, Dorman accepted a professorship at Athens College and continued to polish his manuscript.[13] Early in 1930 Dorman's promising academic career ended when a cancerous growth was discovered on his larynx, and, in an operation performed in New Orleans, he lost most of his vocal cords. Margaret taught his classes at Athens during his operation in Louisiana and while he recuperated. But his teaching career, and to a large extent his future scholarship, was ended by the loss of his ability to lecture or speak much "above a whisper."[14] The family moved to live with Margaret's parents in Hurtsboro, where she taught high school to support her husband and two children.

Despite the loss of his ability to speak clearly, Dorman began research on a history of Barbour County and continued to work on having his dissertation published in order to complete the requirements for his doctoral degree. Dorman corresponded with the J. D. Burke Company of Macon, Georgia, and secured printing prices, but with the hard times of the Depression, he decided that "it would not be wise for me to put out any money" toward producing the dissertation, for "I shall never be able to teach again." The unsettled economic conditions made him especially wary of investing his "little income for disability from the life insurance companies."[15]

Finally in 1934, after receiving letters of endorsement from Albert B. Moore at the University of Alabama and from Owsley and Brinkley at Vanderbilt, Marie Bankhead Owen asked the board of trustees of the Department of Archives and History to approve publication of Dorman's study of Alabama politics in the 1850s. Meeting in the governor's office on November 27, 1934, the board resolved to accept the manuscript and pay for its publication from the state's printing fund.[16] From her correspondence with her brother, U.S. Senator John H. Bankhead II, who represented his district as a member of the board of trustees of the Alabama State Department of Archives and History, it is evident that Mrs. Owen was having some difficulty with Governor Benjamin Meek Miller, who was shortly to end his term in office. This may be one reason she encouraged her brother to make a special effort to come from Jasper for the meeting of the archives' trustees; however, if she feared that under the governor's influence the trustees might turn down her request to publish Dorman's dissertation, she did not indicate it specifically in her letters asking her brother to attend or thanking him for doing so. She wrote that "you will recall the antagonistic mood of the Executive at the meeting of 1931. Since that time, the Governor has come to realize that this Department is doing a practical and splendid work for the State."[17]

Mrs. Owen was pleased that the trustees approved her request, and Dorman was delighted with the state contract. It provided that his book would include his election maps, tables of elections, a bibliography, and an index, but he was disappointed that the cover would be softbound, in a format similar to Thomas P. Abernethy's dissertation on Alabama's formative period published by the archives in 1922. The contract price covered 1,000 soft-cover books for $700, but Dorman wrote Owsley that he planned to contract with the printer "to sew and bind in boards a hundred copies," probably the copies he would provide Vanderbilt in fulfillment of his degree. Brinkley wrote Dorman about technical details that needed to be worked out before printing the dissertation, and Dorman discussed these with Mrs. Owen and the printer.[18] The manuscript was printed in Wetumpka as part of the archives' Historical and Patriotic Series, and after its appearance, Vanderbilt awarded Dorman the doctoral degree on June 13, 1935.[19]

Dorman's work immediately became the standard reference on Alabama politics in the 1850s and, along with Thomas Perkins Abernethy's *The Formative Period in Alabama, 1815–1828*, Theodore Henley Jack's *Sectionalism and Party Politics in Alabama, 1819–1842*, and Clarence Phillips Denman's *The Secession Movement in Alabama*, was one of four works from the early decades of the twentieth century that became significant to the study of Alabama before 1860. When Albert B. Moore revised his 1927 history of Alabama for use as a college textbook, he strengthened his treatment of the "decade of crises" by drawing from Dorman's study.[20]

Dorman's work relies heavily on newspapers, something reviewer Ruth Ketring [Nuermberger] suggested was "an unfortunate fact, for the inner workings of politics were never revealed in the columns of the press."[21] Later when her study of the Clay family appeared, the Duke University curator of manuscripts noted in her bibliographical essay that "Dorman's insight into the workings of Alabama politics is on the whole good, although his style is pedestrian."[22] Dorman did use the manuscript holdings of the Alabama archives, and he read private collections of manuscripts, including the C. C. Clay papers before they were given to Duke University in 1931. In 1953 he sent Frank Owsley, now teaching at the University of Alabama in Tuscaloosa, "a batch of Clayton papers" to be deposited in the university's special collections library.[23]

Beyond the narrative history in *Party Politics*, its other valuable contributions to a study of Alabama in the 1850s are its summary of the political composition of the Alabama legislature beginning with the House of Representatives in 1847 and the Senate in 1849; legislative rolls by county identifying the party affiliation of each legislator; maps of Alabama showing settlement patterns, distribution of slaves, and party election returns by county; and tables of election figures by congressional district and county. Dorman's bibliographical annotations are valuable, especially his list of newspapers with holdings and party affiliations; unfortunately some of the newspapers he used are no longer available.

In 1936 Dorman renewed a childhood friendship with Lella Warren when she returned to Clayton to work on her novel, *Foundation Stone*, which is set in the frontier and antebellum periods of eastern Alabama and features a fictionalized life of her grandmother. Dorman, who had completed his history of Barbour County, agreed to serve as Warren's historical consultant for the novel.[24] He lent Warren his only typescript copy of his Barbour County history, and she took it with her when she returned to Washington to complete her novel.[25] Periodically, Warren would write Dorman asking for specific information, which the historian would supply.

When Warren's manuscript was complete in August 1938, she sent a draft to Dorman, who read it carefully and returned a detailed critique.[26] Although in her foreword Warren acknowledged "Professor Lewy Dorman of Hurtsboro, Alabama, who so generously shared his wealth of source material with me," her publishers were concerned that she had no formal agreement with him. Alfred A. Knopf insisted that Warren have Dorman sign a contract and that she agree to compensate him for the use of his information. She sent Dorman a contract, and after some changes, he reluctantly signed it.

Dorman was delighted at the success of Warren's novel following its publication in the summer of 1940. Perhaps pleased at the prospect of sharing her royalties, he advised her on Alabama promotions, suggesting that she contact Marie Bankhead Owen, who could give her "some help if she is so inclined. The club women have a high regard for her opinions."[27] As the novel met with more local and national success, Dorman wrote Warren in May 1941, inquiring about the "income to be expected from the sale of your book." A few weeks later Warren sent Dorman a check for $820, the first and last payment he received for his work with her, although the contract called for percentages of up to $5,000 from her royalties.[28]

Dorman's history of Barbour County, an 810-page typed manuscript collected in black loose-leaf notebooks, was deposited in the W. S. Hoole Special Collections Library at the University of Alabama by Dorman in 1956.[29] A narrative history that covers in short chapters such topics as Indians, early settlers, roads and rivers, churches, land sales and the growth of plantations, Dorman's study emphasized the antebellum period and devoted only one chapter to the period from 1900 to 1930. He relied heavily on newspapers and manuscripts but also drew upon "conversations" with older residents of the county, an example of an early use of oral history by an Alabama historian. Although the manuscript is well researched and seems to have been edited and corrected over a period of years, the writing is simplistic, and the work would need heavy editing if it were to be published.

During the late 1930s Dorman continued to research and write an Alabama history textbook, which he expected to submit to the state textbook commission in May 1937. His wife, Margaret, duplicated some of his material for her high school students, but the book was never printed, for reasons, Dorman wrote Owsley, that "would take you a week to read." But he wrote Lella Warren that his manuscript "would never be accepted" over Mrs. Owen's work, for she "has ambitions," strong political and family clout, and a monopoly on the elementary state history textbook market.[30] Although Warren offered to try to get Dorman's book published, Dorman declined to bother her, writing that "all I have is pretty light stuff, something which might be suitable for high school supplementary readings."[31]

Despite his disability, Dorman did try to find employment in a position where he could use his talents as a researcher and historian and his knowledge of Alabama history. He repeatedly sought a research appointment with the Alabama State Department of Archives and History and took the State Personnel Department examination for the position of Historical Materials Collector in 1943. But he was not confident he would be hired. Requesting a reference, he wrote Owsley, then in Nashville, that "through the Graves Era the system of getting state positions was simple. If you voted for Graves, you got a job; if you did not vote for him you never expected a job, and consequently, were never disappointed. Under the merit system, you fill a long, tiresome black [examination book], then worry your friends to give you a reference, possibly get on the eligible list, and then see the head of the department (Mrs. Owen in this case) select the person whom he or she would have selected without the merit system."[32]

The next year Dorman's cancer reappeared, and in his second operation in 1944 his remaining vocal cord was removed, leaving him unable to talk without the help of an electric larynx. He continued to work on his Alabama history and collected local history stories and tales of the Chattahoochee River and Barbour County. In 1946 Mrs. Owen wrote to him requesting that he fill out an Alabama author's form, and she told him that she was using his material on party politics in her book for which she would give him credit.[33] Dorman sometimes wrote essays for the local or Columbus, Georgia, newspapers and generously shared his knowledge of Alabama and Barbour County history with writers and historians. Anne Kendrick Walker, who wrote *Backtracking in Barbour County: A Narrative of the Last Alabama Frontier* (1941), and Weymouth T. Jordan, who wrote many articles and published *Ante-bellum Alabama: Town and County* in 1957, were just two of many historians who made the pilgrimage to Hurtsboro to discuss antebellum Alabama politics and Barbour County history with Dorman.

On January 23, 1965, Lewy Dorman died in Hurtsboro at the age of 77. In a letter to his parents Dorman once wrote that "the world has been so much better to me than I have been to it." Yet one wonders what he might have produced and how much his historical perspective might have broadened if his academic career had not ended so suddenly.

Since Dorman's death, two studies of Alabama's secession have appeared: William L. Barney's *The Secessionist Impulse: Alabama and Mississippi in 1860* (1974) and J. Mills Thornton's powerful and insightful *Politics and Power in a Slave Society: Alabama, 1800–1860* (1978).[34] In his comparative study, Barney uses statistical analyses of the supporters of presidential candidates Stephen A. Douglas, John Bell, and John C. Breckinridge to determine why some Alabamians were willing to support Breckinridge's radical stand while others were content to follow the more moderate Douglas and Bell positions. Barney determined that the secessionists in Alabama were younger men, in many cases planter-lawyers of recent wealth, who were more alarmed by restrictions upon the expansion of slavery and more threatened by the rhetoric of the abolitionists, than were the older planters, who supported the more moderate candidates Douglas and Bell.

Although Thornton's title indicates a sixty-year account, he emphasizes the same decade that Dorman studied but includes extensive background on the Jacksonian period and its effect on the way the state's electorate viewed the crises over slavery and northern political developments. While Barney barely mentions William L. Yancey's role in the secession crisis, and Dorman downplays Yancey's position in the Democratic party, Thornton analyzes at length both Yancey's political strategy and his growing prominence and power over the Alabama electorate.

Barney and Thornton are not at odds with Dorman's interpretation, which seems remarkably modern, but their work elaborates upon it and offers more detailed explanations. For instance, Dorman's work supports Thornton's challenge to Eugene Genovese's interpretation of an elite slavocracy's hegemony stressing, as he does, the political strength of the Democratic small farmers of north Alabama.

Dorman's *Party Politics in Alabama From 1850 Through 1860* gives the reader a sense of the flow of events and introduces the political leaders who vied for control and influence in the state. He explains the sectional rivalries and factional politics that flavored the Alabama political climate in the critical decade of the 1850s and provides the proper context and introduction to Thornton's many-layered, brilliant, and always provocative interpretation of these years.

NOTES

1. Thomas J. Pressly, *Americans Interpret Their Civil War* (1954; New York: Free Press, 1962), 172–78; Robert R. Rea, *History at Auburn: The First One Hundred Years of the Auburn University History Department* (Auburn, Ala.: Department of History, 1991), 10–11.

2. Walter L. Fleming, *Civil War and Reconstruction in Alabama* (New York: Columbia University Press, 1905).

3. Lewy Dorman, *Party Politics in Alabama From 1850 Through 1860* (Wetumpka, Ala.: Wetumpka Printing Company for the Alabama State Department of Archives and History, 1935).

4. Dorman family group sheet provided by Lewy Dorman's daughter, Gertha Pearl Dorman Long, and biographical memoranda form filled out by Lewy Dorman in 1946, Surname File, Roll #170, Alabama Department of Archives and History (ADAH), Montgomery.

5. Lewy Dorman, "The Free Negro in Alabama from 1819 to 1861," M.A. thesis, University of Alabama, 1916, 23.

6. Claudia Roberts, "The Dorman Boys of Clayton," *Montgomery Advertiser*, April 15, 1917, copy courtesy of Gertha Dorman Long.

7. Lewy Dorman to W. S. Hoole, April 1, 1957, Gift File, W. S. Hoole Special Collections Library, University of Alabama, Tuscaloosa.

8. Woman's College of Alabama, *Bulletin*, 1921–22, 1923-24, 1924–25, 1925–26, and *Wo-Co-Ala News*, January 10, 1924, Huntingdon College Archives, Huntingdon Library, Montgomery, Ala.

9. Gertha Dorman Long to Leah Rawls Atkins, November 22, 1993; *Wo-Co-Ala News*, May 25, 1924, Huntingdon College Archives, Huntingdon Library; Dorman, biographical memoranda form, Surname File, ADAH; clipping *Montgomery Advertiser*, July 31, 1960, Surname File, ADAH; clipping *Columbus Enquirer*, May 19, 1961, courtesy of Gertha Dorman Long. Dorman was enrolled at the University of Chicago during the summers of 1915, 1916, 1917, 1921, and 1922, and during the fall term of 1919 and spring term of 1927. Telephone interview with Dyan Evans, Registrar's Office, University of Chicago, April 27, 1994.

10. Lewy Dorman Alumni File, Record Group 935, Archives, Jean and Alexander Heard Library, Vanderbilt University, Nashville, Tenn., copies courtesy of Professor Jimmie Franklin.

11. Marie Bankhead Owen to Frank L. Owsley, Sr., April 15, 1930, and Frank L. Owsley, Sr., to Marie Bankhead Owen, April 18, 1930, Director's Office, Administrative files, 1930–, *Alabama Historical Quarterly* correspondence, ADAH.

12. Vanderbilt University, *Bulletin*, 1935, 74.

13. Dorman, Surname File, Roll #170, ADAH; and *The Maid of Athens*, 1929 yearbook Athens College, 18.

14. Marie Bankhead Owen to Frank L. Owsley, Sr., May 3, 1930, Director's Office, Administrative files, 1930–, *Alabama Historical Quarterly*, ADAH.

15. J. W. Burke Company to Lewy Dorman, September 13, 1932, Dorman Papers, W. S. Hoole Special Collections Library, University of Alabama, Tuscaloosa; Lewy Dorman to Frank L. Owsley, Sr., September 14, 1933, Frank L. Owsley, Sr., Papers, Jean and Alexander Heard Library, Vanderbilt University, Nashville, Tenn., copies courtesy of Mrs. Frank L. Owsley, Sr.

16. Minutes of the Board of Trustees, Alabama Department of Archives and History, November 27, 1934, ADAH.

17. Marie Bankhead Owen to Hon. John H. Bankhead, November 28, 1934, Director's Office, Administrative files, 1930–, ADAH.

18. Lewy Dorman to Frank L. Owsley, Sr., December 12, 1934, Owsley Papers, Vanderbilt. If a dissertation were published for sale by "a reputable publisher" then Vanderbilt required only three copies. The Department of Archives and History distributed the Dorman book free to libraries, state officers, and citizens. Vanderbilt University, *Bulletin*, 1935, 74.

19. Gertha Dorman Long to Leah Rawls Atkins, May 9, 1994.

20. Albert B. Moore, *History of Alabama and Its People* (University, Ala.: University Supply Store, 1934).

21. Ruth A. Ketring [Nuermberger], *Journal of Southern History* 2 (February 1936): 117–18.

22. Ruth K. Nuermberger, *The Clays of Alabama: A Planter-Lawyer-Politician Family* (Lexington: University of Kentucky Press, 1958), 327.

23. Lewy Dorman to Mr. [Weymouth ?] Jordan, December 7, 1953, and W. S. Hoole to Lewy Dorman, March 4, 1954, Gift File, WSH Library, UA.

24. Nancy G. Anderson, "Introduction" to reprint edition, Lella Warren, *Foundation Stone* (University: University of Alabama Press, 1986), xvii.

25. Lewy Dorman to Lella Warren, June 18, 1938, Warren Papers, Auburn University at Montgomery; and Lewy Dorman to Frank L. Owsley, Sr., December 17, 1953, Owsley Papers, Vanderbilt.

26. Lewy Dorman to Lella Warren, August 6, 1938, Warren Papers, AUM.

27. Lewy Dorman to Lella Warren, August 22, 1940, Warren Papers, AUM.

28. Lewy Dorman to Lella Warren, May 6, 10, and 28, 1941, and contracts, in Warren Papers, AUM; and Lewy Dorman to Frank L. Owsley, Sr., December 17, 1953, Owsley Papers, Vanderbilt.

29. Sarah A. Verner to Lewy P. Dorman, October 15, 1956, Gift File, WSH Library, UA; John S. Lupold, *Chattahoochee Valley Sources & Resources: An Annotated Bibliography The Alabama Counties* (Eufaula, Ala.: Historic Chattahoochee Commission, 1988), 1:1.

30. Lewy Dorman to Frank L. Owsley, Sr., December 17, 1953, Owsley Papers, Vanderbilt.

31. Lewy Dorman to Lella Warren, May 28, 1941, Warren Papers, AUM.

32. Lewy Dorman to Frank L. Owsley, Sr., September 8, 1943, Owsley Papers, Vanderbilt.

33. Marie Bankhead Owen to Lewy Dorman, April 27, 1946, Surname File, Roll #170, ADAH.

34. William L. Barney, *The Secessionist Impulse: Alabama and Mississippi in 1860* (Princeton, N. J.: Princeton University Press, 1974); and J. Mills Thornton III, *Politics and Power in a Slave Society: Alabama 1800–1860* (Baton Rouge: Louisiana State University Press, 1978).

Party Politics in Alabama
From 1850 Through 1860

TO

THE MEMORY OF

MY PARENTS

ALPHEUS ALEXANDER DORMAN

AND

MARTHA SLAUGHTER DORMAN

LETTER OF TRANSMITTAL

To His Excellency
Governor B. M. Miller,
Montgomery, Alabama.

Sir:

I have the honor to transmit herewith, recommending that it be published as Bulletin No. 13 of the Historical and Patriotic Series of the State Department of Archives and History, a manuscript entitled, "Party Politics in Alabama, From 1850 Through 1860." The author, Mr. Lewy Dorman, will receive his degree of Doctor of Philosophy from Vanderbilt University upon the publication of this dissertation.

This document has been prepared with great care by its author who has cited authorities for his historical statements. I deem it a valuable contribution to Alabama history and trust you will approve its publication as a State Bulletin.

Copies of this Bulletin will be placed, with the compliments of the Department of Archives and History, in all public libraries in Alabama and in the College and High School libraries of the State. Copies will also be presented to the great libraries throughout the United States having Alabama sections available to students. In addition to the foregoing, copies will also be presented to all public officials of the State. As long as the issue lasts, it will be subject to call by any student in Alabama, with the hope that a perusal of its pages will inspire the reader with a greater veneration for our past and a proper pledge of patriotic devotion for the future.

Very respectfully,

MARIE BANKHEAD OWEN,
Director.

PREFACE

Before the general secession movement can be understood, especially during the years from the Mexican War until the election of Lincoln, it is essential that a thorough and detailed study be made of the political history of each state. Such a study has local historical value aside from its bearing upon the secession of the South, for each state had its own history and its own peculiar problem during this stirring period. It is with an idea of portraying the political history of Alabama from 1850 to 1860, as well as presenting a segment of the secession movement during the decade, that this study was undertaken. The clash of intra-sectionalism—the jealousy between north Alabama and the southern pine belt section on one hand and the Black Belt on the other over representation and the general political control—is seen in full operation during this time. This sectionalism, begun before the slavery controversy and lasting to the present, is a familiar phenomenon also in the history of Virginia, North Carolina, South Carolina, and Georgia. While these intra-state clashes cut across parties prior to 1850, such a tendency was stronger during the ten years previous to the election of Lincoln than before because of the breakdown of political parties under the impact of the larger sectional contest between North and South. The Southern Rights Party, headed by W. L. Yancey in Alabama, and having its counterpart in every Southern state, demanded equal rights for the slavery interests in the territories. The Kansas-Nebraska Act, the organization of the Republican Party as a sectional and anti-Southern body, and the heightened violence of the abolition agitation which seemed to take root in the Northern mind during this time rapidly drove Alabamians, as well as the citizens of other Southern states, into the Southern Rights Party. The study of state and national elections over this period shows this change in process and gives concrete illustrations of the reaction of the Southern mind to the situation.

This study was begun as a dissertation for the degree of Doctor of Philosophy in Vanderbilt University under the late Professor Walter L. Fleming, and, after he was forced by illness to give up his duties, the work was supervised by Professor Frank L. Owsley, who gave me much valuable aid. I have also received many valuable suggestions from Dr. William C. Binkley and Dr. Carl S. Driver, of Vanderbilt University, as well as from Professor A. B. Moore, Head of the History Department of the University of Alabama, who gave me the benefit of his wide knowledge of Alabama History.

I am under obligations to several people for the loan of materials. Mrs. Bettie V. Adams, of Gurley, Mr. John G. Sanderson, of Courtland, and Mr. Emmett Seibels, of Montgomery, permitted me to use manuscript materials in their possession. Mr. R. F. Hudson and Mr. Grover C. Hall permitted me to use the files of the Montgomery Advertiser, and Miss Laura Elmore gave me access to the newspaper files of the Carnegie Library of Montgomery. Mrs. Marie B. Owen, Director of the Alabama State Department of Archives and History, gave me the full use of the materials in her department and showed me many courtesies. Miss Mattie Alexander, Miss Frances Hails, Miss Mary Mullen, and Mr. Peter A. Brannon, of the staff, all aided me in my research work in the department. To the late Dr. Thomas M. Owen, founder of the department, every student of Alabama History is deeply indebted. The splendid collection of materials which he made for the department makes possible research in Alabama History.

LEWY DORMAN.

Hurtsboro, Alabama,
February 27, 1935.

Dr. Lewy Dorman, c. 1920s
(Courtesy of Ralph Dorman)

CHAPTER I.

ALABAMA IN 1850

The decade from 1850 to 1860 was one of varied changes in Alabama. It was a time of unrest, both in state and national affairs, which wrought frequent changes in the political parties in the state. Differences in opinion regarding the slavery controversy in 1850-51 caused a disruption of the two old parties—the Whig and Democratic—and the formation of the Union Party and the Southern Rights Party, which differed over the acceptance or rejection of the compromise measures which Congress was debating in 1850. The Union Party won in the election of 1851, but it was not able to keep this advantage as the Democrats reorganized their old party, after the election, and by 1852 the two old parties were opposed to each other very much as they had been prior to 1850. The Whig Party gradually declined after 1852, and in 1855 a new party, known as the American Party, succeeded it as the opponent of the Democratic Party. This new party continued for only two years, and from 1857 there was no regularly organized party in opposition to the Democrats, although there were loosely organized groups which were usually spoken of as the Opposition Party.

The issues which separated the Whigs and Democrats in Alabama in 1850 were not always clearly defined. Both parties believed in the protection of Southern Rights from Northern aggressions, although they differed in the method of opposing the aggressions of the enemies of the South, and in the degree to which the opposition should be carried. Local factors, such as physical features, where the immigrants into Alabama came from and where they located, the transportation facilities, all these, caused sectionalistic conditions and party changes. Before entering into the details of the history of the parties, a description is given of these factors in order to explain the meaning of the party changes.

Alabama is divided into four geographical divisions, extending, in general, across the state from east to west. These areas are the

Tennessee Valley in the north, a hilly and mountainous area in the central part, then the Black Belt, and lastly the coastal area which extends to the state of Florida and the Gulf of Mexico.

The Tennessee Valley extends from Tennessee to the headwaters of the streams which flow into the Tennessee River from the south. The hilly and mountainous area consists of several mountain ranges and valleys and extends southward to the fall line of the rivers which flow southward. This line is marked by the falls of the Black Warrior River at Tuscaloosa, the Coosa River at Wetumpka, and the Tallapoosa River at Tallassee. The Black Belt extends from the fall line southward and includes the area drained by the Alabama and Tombigbee river systems. The coastal area of South Alabama is separated from the Black Belt by the water-shed between the Alabama River system and the streams which form the Choctawhatchee and Escambia river systems, and includes the counties drained by the two last named rivers and those in the basin of the Mobile River.

The Tennessee Valley in 1850 comprised nine counties which, geographically and economically, were divided into two groups. The six western counties had a moderately level surface, a planter class, and a large slave population; the three eastern counties were mountainous, had few plantations, and only small slaveowners. The difference is evident from a comparison of Lauderdale, Limestone and Madison—in the western group—with Jackson and De-Kalb, eastern counties. Lauderdale had one planter who owned three hundred slaves; in Limestone and Madison over one-half of the voters were slaveowners and each county had an average of more than twelve slaves for each slaveowner. Jackson and De-Kalb, eastern counties, had averages of only one-half as many slaves for each slaveowner.[1]

The mountain area consisted of about fifteen counties. It resembled the eastern counties of the Tennessee Valley both in surface and in being the home of small slaveowners. The western part of this area was drained by the upper Black Warrior and Cahaba rivers; the eastern part was drained by the upper Coosa and Tallapoosa rivers. These rivers were too small to furnish navigation through the mountainous counties, but their valleys offered

---

[1] U. S. Census, 1860.

the means of travel and transportation over dirt roads from the Tennessee Valley and from upper Georgia into the Black Belt in south Alabama. The lower counties of this area resembled the Black Belt counties on which they bordered.

The Black Belt consisted 'of about fifteen counties in which the slaves outnumbered the white population. The soil was fertile and adapted to the plantation system. It was predominantly the home of the large planters, many of whom owned more than one hundred slaves. In some of the Black Belt counties in 1860, seventy-five per cent of the voters were slaveholders in contrast with the white counties of the mountain area in which only ten per cent of the voters were slaveowners. Several of the Black Belt counties had an average of more than twenty slaves for each slave-owner.[2]

There were thirteen coastal counties in which the white population outnumbered the slaves in 1850. The eastern counties of this area were noted for a fine quality of wiregrass which produced such fine cattle that these counties were often designated the "Cow" counties by the newspapers of the fifties. Some of the counties of the Mobile River basin had a slaveholding system which resembled the Black Belt counties.

The Democratic Party in 1850 had its greatest strength in the eastern counties of the Tennessee Valley and in the mountainous and hilly counties of central Alabama. The greatest strength of the Whigs was in the Black Belt and in the western counties of the Tennessee Valley. In the counties which fringed the Black Belt on the north and in the "Cow" counties, the strength of the two parties was so evenly matched as to furnish fighting ground for the two parties. It was in these two groups of counties that most of the political changes occurred in the early fifties. Both parties had strong leadership in the Black Belt counties and the party contests there were usually closely and warmly contested.

There were great variations in density of population in the different divisions in 1850. In 1840 the most densely populated counties were those of the Tennessee Valley and the western Black Belt counties, situated in the basins of the Alabama and Tombigbee rivers. During the decade from 1840 to 1850, the greatest increase in population was in the lower basin of the Coosa and Tallapoosa

---

[2] U. S. Census, 1860.

rivers, in counties which had been organized from territory which the Creek Indians had ceded in 1832. From 1832 to 1840 nine counties had been formed in east Alabama from the territory of this cession.

Between 1850 and 1860 the greatest increase in slave population was in the hill counties of northeast Alabama and in the white coastal counties. This was due to immigration of slaveholders into these newer lands from other states and from other counties in Alabama, and also to a number of non-slaveholders becoming slaveholders during the decade. This extension of slave areas and increase in the number of slaves and slaveholders had an important political effect—it gradually universalized the system in Alabama and put the slaveholders more and more in political control of the state. In some of the counties which showed an increase in slave population, there was an increase in the political power of the Whigs, but for the most part the newer slaveholders became Democrats. The newer slaveholders owned only a few slaves and in general were more strongly in favor of the protection of slavery rights than were the older and larger slaveowners, who were chiefly Whigs and who were conservative with respect to the demands for the protection of slavery extension.

The earliest immigrants into Alabama located in the river basins where the land was more fertile and transportation was less difficult than in the upland areas. Most of the immigrants up to 1860 came from Virginia, North Carolina, South Carolina, Georgia and Tennessee. The Tennesseans came directly south and settled in the Tennessee Valley. The Georgians entered the state from the east and located, particularly after 1832, in the counties of the Creek cession. The people from the other seaboard states came down the valleys of the Appalachians and entered Alabama by way of the Tennessee Valley or through the valleys of the Coosa and Tallapoosa rivers. Many of the early settlers in east and north Alabama later made their way into the western Black Belt counties.

The immigrants usually retained the political attitudes which they brought with them from the older states. The Tennesseans, as a rule, were of the political faith of Andrew Jackson and, consequently, were Unionists when secession became an issue in the early fifties. The Virginians and Carolinians, to a great extent, became the large planters of the western Black Belt counties and became Unionists, although a number of South Carolinians who had studied in South Carolina College under the famous Dr. Thomas Cooper were strong advocates for Southern Rights. The Georgians, even those of the Black Belt, showed a strong preference for the Democratic party. It was this group which furnished most of the leadership for the Southern Rights movement in the early fifties and for secession in 1860.

The population of Alabama in 1850 was largely rural. There were only ten towns in the state in this year with a population as large as one thousand. Over one-half of the fifty-two counties had no towns with as many as five hundred population. Mobile with 22,000 population and Montgomery, which had been made the capital in 1846, with 5,000 population were the largest cities.

Most of the towns were located in the Tennessee Valley or in the Black Belt counties. The county seat was usually the largest and most important town in the county. Here lived the county officials and lawyers; both groups exercised an important part of the political leadership. The newspapers were usually printed in the county seats and played an important function as gatherers and disseminators of political news. The planters kept informed on political affairs by reading the papers or by making trips to town, either to look after their business affairs or to attend the sessions of the courts.

There were 7,638 people of foreign birth in Alabama in 1850 and the number increased to 12,352 by 1860, an increase of more than twice the per cent of increase of the native white population of the state. Most of the foreign population lived in the cities or the towns. Mobile in 1860 had over seven thousand foreigners, which was about one-fourth the population of the city; the proportion in Montgomery was much less.[3]

Prejudice against foreigners gave rise to a political movement in the middle of the fifties, when an issue was made against foreigners and Catholics, which resulted in the most interesting political campaign during the decade.

Occasionally some political aspirant attempted to array town against country in a campaign in order to get some advantage, but

[3] Eighth Census of the U. S., 1860, *Mortality*, p. lviii.

such efforts were usually futile. Except for Mobile and Montgomery, there was no commercial group separate from the planter group. The planters often lived in the towns and carried on their commercial transactions, leaving the immediate management of their plantations largely to the direction of their overseers.

The lack of uniformity in geographical features and the differences in traditions among the various groups of people who came into the state developed sectionalisms which produced many complications in the political parties in Alabama during the decade from 1850 to 1860. The state was only thirty years old in 1850 and had not developed a strong sense of state consciousness or state pride. As late as 1832 one-fourth of the area of the state was still in the hands of the Cherokee and Creek Indians.

The greatest geographical and political dissimilarity was between the Tennessee Valley and the Black Belt. During the decade there was a sentiment in north Alabama in favor of withdrawing from the state and uniting with the state of Tennessee, because, it was claimed, the interests of that section were more closely identified with Tennessee. In 1854 the *Florence Gazette* was advocating this change. Mobile at one time was threatening to secede from Alabama and to unite with Mississippi.

There was also a sectionalism between east and west Alabama, though not so marked as between north and south Alabama. The settlers who were so energetic in forcing the Indians from the eastern counties were different from the people of the older counties of west Alabama. The former were more radical in advocating resistance to Northern anti-slavery measures than were the people of west Alabama.

The development of means of transportation and communication during the fifties did much to remove the sectionalism. The principal means of communication during the decade were railroads, river transportation and dirt roads. The railroad was just being developed as a means of transportation by 1850 and, although interest in railroad building was high, the cost was so heavy and the difficulties of construction were so great that construction was slow.

At the beginning of the decade there were 132 miles of railroad in Alabama which represented a line from Tuscumbia to Decatur, and a line from Montgomery to West Point, Georgia, which gave

Montgomery a connection with Atlanta, Chattanooga, and the seaboard cities of Savannah and Charleston. During the decade many lines were chartered. The most important of the proposed lines was a road from Montgomery to reach the Gulf at either Pensacola or Mobile; one from Girard on the Chattahoochee River to Mobile; and a third road to connect Selma on the Alabama River with Gunter's Landing on the Tennessee River, going by way of Montevallo and Talladega.

Of this proposed railroad construction, only 743 miles were completed during the decade. The road from Montgomery to Mobile was almost completed by 1860; the Girard and Mobile road was completed only to Union Springs prior to the war; the Alabama and Tennessee was completed only to Talladega; the Memphis and Charleston was completed from Decatur through Huntsville into Chattanooga and gave communication throughout the Tennessee Valley.

River transportation was important but limited. The Tombigbee-Black Warrior system and the Alabama River system gave the interior counties an outlet to Mobile and the Gulf, and the Tennessee River gave transportation to the counties of the Tennessee Valley.

Most of the counties had to rely for transportation either wholly or partly on dirt roads, which, though bad and requiring slow movements for the most part, traversed every section of the state. These highways radiated from the most important towns in every direction. In 1854 Montgomery had two mail coaches daily to Mobile, which made the trip in thirty-five hours. This was a saving of time of ten hours as compared with the river steamers which required forty-five hours. The capital city was connected with the Tennessee River at Gunter's Landing by a daily coach and mail line which had a schedule of forty-nine hours. Montgomery had a half dozen other lines which gave it connection with Troy, Greenville, Selma, Wetumpka, Greensboro, and Tuskegee.

Selma had as good facilities for river transportation as had Montgomery, but did not have as good rail connection with the east as Montgomery had. This caused Selma to advocate the building of the Alabama and Tennessee road to get connection with the Tennessee River and with Rome, Georgia, and to favor the use of state funds and the credit of the state to finance the construction of this road. Montgomery opposed this aim of its rival. It also opposed the construction of the Girard and Mobile railroad as this road did not pass through the capital city.

The mountains made travel between north and south Alabama slow and difficult. Huntsville, Decatur and Tuscumbia could be reached from Montgomery by railway by 1855 but this necessitated a long trip through Atlanta and Chattanooga. The valleys, extending from northeast to southwest, gave the people of the Tennessee Valley access to the people in the Warrior and Cahaba basins. Tuscaloosa on the Black Warrior had stage connections with Gunter's Landing, Blountsville, Jacksonville and Florence—all in north Alabama.

The highways were of great importance during the decade in developing state unity. Over them newspapers were transported into all sections of the state. This made it easier for the political leaders to develop political solidarity within their party ranks through instruction of the voters. The roads were built at local expense and the appropriation of money for their construction did not become an issue in state politics. The building of the railroads, however, was an important political issue during the fifties and exercised an important influence upon the parties, particularly in the middle of the decade.

The press was a great unifying agency during the decade of the fifties. In 1850 there were sixty newspapers in Alabama. Of these, six were dailies, five were tri-weeklies, one was a semi-monthly, and forty-eight were weeklies. The total annual circulation of these papers was more than two and one-half millions of copies. The average circulation of the weeklies was over six hundred for each issue; that of the dailies was a little less than five hundred.[4]

The papers were unequally distributed among the counties of the state. About thirty, or more than one-half of them, were printed in the fourteen Black Belt counties; the others were about equally distributed among the Tennessee Valley counties, the mountainous counties, and the city of Mobile. There was only one paper in the six white counties which bordered on the state of Florida. The city of Montgomery and Dallas County each had as

---

[4] U. S. Census, 1870, p. 482 ff.

many papers as had the fifteen mountainous counties. Of the fifty-two counties of the state in 1850, more than one-half did not have a newspaper.

Newspapers of the fifties were more transitory than are those of the present time. This was particularly true for the political papers. Each party made an effort to maintain a paper in towns in which the opposing party had a paper. Consequently, a number of towns of less than one thousand population had two papers. Many papers were established just before a political campaign in towns where support was not sufficient to maintain them permanently. After the campaign the presses and equipment would be sold and removed to other locations and, in some cases, they became organs of the opposite party.

Exciting political campaigns caused a large increase in the number of new papers and in the circulation of the papers already established. The agitation over slavery extension after 1847 caused many new papers to be set up. Nearly one-half of the weekly papers in existence in 1851 had been established since 1847. The exciting Know Nothing campaign of 1855 also produced many new papers. By this year the weekly edition of the *Montgomery Advertiser* had reached a circulation of nearly three thousand, which was the largest of any political paper in the state. The larger county newspapers began to reach a circulation of one thousand by this year.

The rapid changes in the fortunes of political newspapers is illustrated by the *Montgomery Atlas*. This paper was begun in 1850. By June, 1851, it had taken the name *Atlas and Secession Banner,* and was claiming a subscription list of three thousand. As the excitement over secession became less, the *Atlas* declined and was succeeded in 1852 by the *True South.*[5]

The dailies of Montgomery and Mobile had efficient news-gathering agencies. In 1855 the *Alabama Journal,* of Montgomery, claimed to have paid correspondents in New York, Philadelphia, Washington, New Orleans, and Mobile. It had regular telegraphic news reports regarding the movements of steamships and

[5] *Alabama Journal,* June 14, 1851;
Blue Papers.

occasional telegraphic intelligence from Washington, which the *Journal* claimed, was very expensive.[6]

Most of the political news regarding national politics, however, was copied by the Alabama papers from papers in other states. The *New Orleans Picayune, Richmond Examiner, Richmond Enquirer, Charleston Mercury, Columbus Times,* and others were frequently quoted. The county weeklies of Alabama usually obtained their news of national politics from the papers of Montgomery or Mobile; they obtained news of state politics from the same sources and from other county papers.

The papers of the fifties devoted more space and emphasis to politics than do those of the present time. The Democratic Party was for the most part better supplied with papers than was the Whig Party, especially in north Alabama and in the white counties of south Alabama. Both parties resorted to the practice of purchasing presses and sending printers with them into the newer counties which had no papers in order to bolster up the fortunes of their party. In this method of propaganda the Democrats were more aggressive and successful than were the Whigs. This gave the Democrats a substantial advantage in political campaigns.

The editors, as a rule, were men of more than average intelligence. Some of them were lawyers and occasionally a preacher was an editor. Among the most notable editors of the state were W. L. Yancey, John Forsyth, J. J. Seibels, J. J. Hooper, W. F. Samford, E. S. Shorter, and J. Withers Clay. All of these men were influential political leaders.

Within the two parties in Alabama from 1850 to 1860 there were various factionalistic and sectionalistic tendencies. Party politics during the decade had many cross-currents and complications. Its history is more complicated than mere party contests between two standardized parties, separated by established traditions and well-defined issues. On no issue, not even on slavery, could either party get concerted effort on the part of its members.

Much of this political factionalism and sectionalism is revealed in the congressional elections in Alabama from 1850 to 1860. As

[6] *Alabama Journal,* March 3, 1855.

the political differences were to a certain extent due to geographical differences, and as each congressional district can be identified with some geographical area, a brief description is given of each district in order to bring out the political variations.

There were seven congressional districts in Alabama in 1850 which were usually designated by the names of the principal town or city within the district. These districts were as follows: first, the Mobile district; second, the Montgomery; third, the Wetumpka, although Selma was the largest town in the district; fourth, the Tuscaloosa; fifth, the Florence; sixth, the Huntsville; seventh, the Talladega. Two of these districts were composed of counties in the Tennessee Valley, one district, of the hill counties of east Alabama; two of them, of Black Belt counties; and two, of the coastal counties, including some of the lower counties of the Black Belt.

The Mobile district was composed of nine counties, situated in the lower basin of the Alabama and Tombigbee rivers in southwest Alabama. Four of these counties were in the Black Belt and the remainder were white coastal counties. This was a cosmopolitan district, the population being equally divided, approximately, among Virginians, North Carolinians, South Carolinians, and Georgians. Mobile, the political center of the district, had a population of over twenty thousand in 1850, including a large number of Northerners and seven thousand foreigners, which complicated the political history of the district. The city had one-third of the entire population of the district which made the district the most urban one in the state.

This district elected congressmen of every political affiliation from 1847 to 1860, making a complete political cycle. In 1847 and 1849, it elected Whigs; in 1851 and 1853, Southern Rights Democrats; in 1855, an American or Know Nothing; and in 1857 and 1859, a Democrat.

The Montgomery district in southeast Alabama was composed of nine counties which extended from Florida to the confluence of the Coosa and Tallapoosa rivers. In this district four important Black Belt counties—Montgomery, Macon, Russell and Barbour—were combined with five white "Cow" counties, which were located in the lower part of the district.

There were two political centers in this district—Montgomery, the political leaders of which were called the "Montgomery Regency," and Eufaula, the leaders of which were called the "Eufaula Regency." The *Montgomery Advertiser* supplied the leadership for the Montgomery group; the Eufaula *Spirit of the South* performed a similar function for the Eufaula group.

This district was the home of the two greatest political leaders of their respective parties—W. L. Yancey, of the Democrats, and H. W. Hilliard, of the Whigs. The wealth of the planters, the ability of the political leaders, and the fact that the capital of the state was in this district, all these, combined to make it the most important district in the state. The contests in it were usually watched with great interest by political leaders in the other districts and even in other states.

The people of the Montgomery district were predominantly Georgians. They read newspapers from their old state and were influenced by political affairs in Georgia. This district elected Whigs to Congress from 1847 through 1853, and Democrats from 1855 through the remainder of the decade. As early as 1850, the political leaders of this district, both Democratic and Whig, were becoming strong advocates for Southern Rights. A redistricting act in 1854 took Montgomery, Macon and Russell counties from the district; Eufaula then became the political center of the district in place of Montgomery and the district became more strongly Democratic than it had previously been.

The Wetumpka district was situated in the center of the state. It was composed of four Black Belt counties, lying in the upper basin of the Alabama River, and four white counties which extended to the foothills of the mountains. South Carolinians predominated in three of these counties; Virginians, in two; and Georgians, in the other three.

S .W. Harris was the political leader in this district until his county, Coosa, was taken from the district in 1854. The district was strongly Democratic in 1847 and in 1849, and elected a strong Southern Rights man in 1851. It was completely broken up by the redistricting act of 1854. Montgomery was placed in the third district by this act and took the place of Wetumpka as the political center of the district.

The Tuscaloosa district was in west Alabama and consisted of six counties, situated in the basins of the Tombigbee and Black Warrior rivers, and extending northward from their confluence. Three of the counties were Black Belt counties and the other two were foothill counties. Virginians predominated in two counties; South Carolinians, in two; and Georgians, in one.

This district resembled the Mobile district in that it was cosmopolitan in population and it changed its political complexion often. It elected a Democrat in 1847 and 1849; a Unionist, in 1851; a Union Democrat in 1853; an American in 1855; and a Democrat in 1857 and 1859. There was a large Whig vote in the district but no Whig was elected to Congress during the decade. The Whigs supported William R. Smith, who was a Union Democrat in 1851 and 1853 and an American in 1855, in order to prevent the election of a Southern Rights Democrat. In no district was the cooperation of the Whigs and Union Democrats more complete than in this district. Smith controlled the district from 1851 through 1857, largely by his personal popularity. Tuscaloosa was the political center of the district.

The Florence district included five counties in the western part of the Tennessee Valley and three hill counties, extending to the headwaters of the Black Warrior River on the south. George S. Houston, of Limestone County, represented this district from 1842 to 1861, except for the session of 1849-50, when he was not a candidate. He was a Union Democrat, when secession became an issue in the early fifties, and was supported by the Whigs who nominated a candidate to oppose him only once from 1847 to 1860. Houston's chief opposition came from the Southern Rights group under the leadership of David Hubbard, of Lawrence County, who opposed Houston in 1847, 1849, 1851, and 1857. Hubbard was elected in 1849, the year that Houston was not a candidate.

The Huntsville district consisted of six counties which were situated in the eastern Tennessee Valley and extended to the Coosa River on the south All of these counties were mountainous. Madison was the most important county in north Alabama and furnished a large number of political leaders, none of whom, however, were elected to Congress during the decade. W. R. W. Cobb, of Jackson County, who was first elected in 1847, was able to defeat every candidate who opposed him up to 1860. Cobb, like Houston, had little opposition from the Whigs, his strongest opposition being from the Southern Rights Democrats. He defeated successively William Acklen, Jeremiah Clemens and C. C. Clay, Jr., three of the strongest leaders in the district. The success of Cobb is notable from the fact that his home county, Jackson, was not the political center of the district. In 1853 he defeated Clay by over two hundred votes in Madison, Clay's home county. Cobb was not educated and his uncouth campaign methods appealed to the voters of his district, which had fewer Whig voters and more illiteracy in it than had any other district in the state. The counties of this district were called the "Avalanche" counties as their Democratic majorties were usually so overwhelming[7]

The political history of the Florence and the Huntsville districts was similar in that both were Democratic from 1847 to 1860. When the Democratic and Whig parties disintegrated in 1851, due to the agitation over slavery extension, both districts elected Union Democrats to Congress, and both returned to the regular Democratic Party when it was reorganized and voted for the National Democratic ticket in the election of 1852.

There were some differences between these two districts, however, which should be pointed out. The Florence district always manifested a tendency to vote more strongly for Unionism than did the Huntsville district. The people of the former were predominantly of Tennessee stock, whereas those of the latter were of Georgia ancestry. There was also an economic difference between the two. The Florence district had many large slave-owners; the Huntsville district, with the exception of Madison County, was composed largely of inhabitants who had few slaves. There were more Whigs in the Florence district, two of whom—Nicholas Davis, of Limestone County, and R. W. Walker, of Lauderdale County,—were nominated by their party as candidates for governor in 1847 and 1853, respectively.

---

[7] Garrett, *Reminiscences of Public Men in Alabama*, pp. 395-97. This sketch of Cobb and his political methods is interesting.

The Talladega district was composed of six counties, situated in the upper valleys of the Coosa and Tallapoosa Rivers. These counties were mountainous and four of them bordered on the state of Georgia. Most of the people in this district were of Georgia ancestry and were influenced by the politics of that state. There were few slaves in the district and illiteracy was high.

This district was Democratic from 1849 to 1860, with the exception of the term, 1849-50, when Alexander White, a Union Whig, was elected. The Southern Rights group was strong in this district during the decade.

In general, the two congressional districts of north Alabama were uniformly Democratic during the fifties; the three districts of central Alabama were Democratic, but less so than those of north Alabama; and the two districts of south Alabama were Whig until 1853, when the party began to disintegrate. The redistricting of the congressional districts in 1854 aided the Democrats in breaking up the Whig control of the two south Alabama districts.*

The control by the Democrats of five of the seven congressional districts in the early part of the decade was out of proportion to the relative voting strength of the two parties. The Whigs in 1850 had about forty-five per cent of the voting population of the state and on the basis of numbers should have had three congressmen instead of only two. The reason the Democrats enjoyed this advantage was that they had put through the legislature, during the forties, two acts which gave them more representatives in the lower house of Congress and in the legislature than they were entitled to, judged by their numbers.

The first of these laws was known as the White Basis act and was passed in 1843. Under this act the congressional districts in

*The party affiliation of the Alabama congressmen from 1847 through 1859 were as follows:

District	1847	1849	1851	1853	1855	1857	1859
First	Whig	Whig	Sou. Rights	Sou. Rights	Amer.	Dem.	Dem.
Second	Whig	Whig	Union	Union Whig	Dem.	Dem.	Dem.
Third	Dem.	Dem.	Seces.	Sou. Rights	Dem.	Dem.	Dem.
Fourth	Dem.	Dem.	Union	Union Dem.	Amer.	Dem.	Dem.
Fifth	Dem.	Dem.	Union	Union Dem.	Dem.	Dem.	Dem.
Sixth	Dem.	Dem.	Union	Union Dem.	Dem.	Dem.	Dem.
Seventh	Dem.	Dem.	Union	Sou. Rights	Dem.	Dem.	Dem.

Alabama were formed on the basis of white population alone, slaves not being counted. Under this principle it required a larger number of Black Belt counties, where the Whigs were strong, to form a congrssional district than would have been required if the slaves had been counted. The Whigs opposed this principle. They claimed that it was a violation, in spirit at least, of the clause in the Federal Constitution which provided that Congress should count slaves as three-fifths of the white population in determining the number of representatives which each state should have in the lower house of Congress.

The second act which the Democrats passed for party advantage was a gerrymander. This consolidated as many Whig counties as possible into two congressional districts and distributed the remaining Whig counties among the other five districts in such a way as to give the Democrats a majority in all of these five districts. In the five districts which were Democratic in 1850, there were thirty-three counties, whereas, in the two Whig districts, there were eighteen counties. In the three strongly Democratic districts of north Alabama, there were nineteen counties—only one more than the two Whig districts of south Alabama embraced.

The legislature of 1853-54 made some changes in the congressional districts to give further advantages to the Democrats.

This completes the survey of Alabama as it was in 1850. An attempt has been made to show some relationship between the geographical areas and the political parties at the beginning of the decade. Geographical differences caused sectionalism which caused political differences. It must be remembered, however, that there is always the danger of overemphasizing the influence which geographical factors have exercised upon historical events and movements. This is particularly true in the history of political parties where leadership is such a potent factor. Personalities counted for much in politics in Alabama during the fifties and strong political leadership often caused a different political complexion in counties of similar geographical features.

CHAPTER II.

PRELIMINARY SURVEY OF POLITICAL PARTIES, 1847-49

The Democratic Party in Alabama in 1847 was divided into two wings, the States Rights group which was under the leadership of W. L. Yancey and Senator Dixon H. Lewis, and the Union group whose principal leader was William R. King. The agitation in Congress over the Wilmot Proviso, the purpose of which was the exclusion of slavery from the territory which was to be acquired from Mexico, strengthened the States Rights group. Even in north Alabama, which was conservative regarding slavery extension, there was developing a feeling that the Northern abolitionists were becoming a menace to the rights of the South in slave property. In this section, where John C. Calhoun had never been a leader of political thought, due to his advocacy of nullification in the early thirties, there began to develop a better feeling towards the great South Carolinian and his attitude for the rights of the South.

Opposed to this divided Democratic Party was the minority Whig Party whose strength, as we have seen, was principally in the Black Belt counties but which had considerable strength in the western counties of the Tennessee Valley and in some of the counties which bordered on the Black Belt.

In May, 1847, the Democratic state convention met at Montgomery and, under the control of the States Rights leaders, nominated Reuben Chapman, of Madison County, the candidate for governor. With respect to slavery extension, the convention adopted resolutions, introduced by Yancey, which were practically the same as Yancey's famous "Alabama Platform" which was defeated in the Charleston convention the following year. The important principles in this platform were that neither Congress nor a territorial legislature had any right to prohibit the extension of slavery into the territories, and that the Alabama delegates would not support any man for president who did not take this attitude.

Captain Nicholas Davis, of Limestone County, was the Whig candidate for governor.

In the election in August, the two groups of Democrats united in support of Chapman and defeated the Whigs by a vote of over 34,000 to 28,000, a majority of more than six thousand out of a total vote of nearly 53,000.

In the congressional elections the Democrats carried the five districts in north and middle Alabama, and the Whigs carried the Montgomery and Mobile districts of south Alabama. The Democrats carried the state senate by a majority of one, and the lower house by a majority of thirty. The control of the legislature was important because a United States senator was to be elected during the session of 1847-48.

The legislature convened in November, 1847, and party strength came to a test soon thereafter in the balloting for a United States senator. Dixon H. Lewis, a leader of the States Rights Democrats, William R. King, leader of the Union Democrats, and Arthur F. Hopkins, a Whig, were the candidates. Eighteen ballots were taken with no candidate receiving a majority. The strength of Lewis and King was practically equal; the Whigs, holding the votes necessary to elect, continued to support Hopkins. The intense feelings in this election is indicated in a letter written by T. B. Cooper, a Whig member of the legislature from Cherokee County, to his wife.

> The King men stand at 25 to 27 in number and will not yield, the Whigs vote for Hopkins, and while this state of things goes on an election will never be made, both parties want the Whig votes, the King men bid high for it, one proposition was to elect Hopkins if the Whigs would help elect Bagby—and let King withdraw—that trade could not be effected, some of the Whigs would not be sold and some of the Democrats would not vote for Hopkins, McClung is figuring to be made Senator in Bagbys place and holds to the Lewis party, the feeling is getting pretty high, every other election is lost sight of, and somebody is going to be sacrificed in this race, it may be me, God only knows, the friends of King bid high for help—but the Chivalry is the strongest party here, Lewis and King are both here, the wires are continually

moving * * * * if the Whigs and Hunkers unite, I do not know what will be the result.[1]

Lewis finally secured the support of enough of the Union Democrats of north Alabama to win the election. Judge John A. Campbell, of Mobile, who later became an associate justice of the United States Supreme Court explained the victory of Lewis as a rebuke to King, due to King being too closely affiliated with the Northern wing of the Democratic Party. Campbell wrote to John C. Calhoun as follows:

Col. King was bound up with the Northern Democrats of a very doubtful order, and as he was a candidate of the Hunkers here, this was a work very well done. Mr. Lewis I fear, has made pledges which will greatly embarrass him and estrange his friends in this section. He pledged himself, I learn, to abide a National Convention for the selection of a candidate *preferring* a northern man. He pledged himself to sustain Mr. Poly further than his message calls for support.[2]

Lewis' pledge to the Union Democrats caused him to lose some support among the States Rights group of central Alabama. It influenced his Southern Rights supporters in the Charleston convention in 1848 to accept the platform and the candidate of the convention, and to refuse to follow Mr. Yancey when he withdrew from the convention after the defeat of his "Alabama Platform."

The Democratic Party in Alabama was threatened with a serious split as the presidential election of 1848 approached. Most of the Democrats of north Alabama were advocating the nomination of a Union Democrat. The States Rights men were threatening to refuse to support the nominee if he should be of the "Hunker" type. With conditions thus confused, the Democratic state convention met in Montgomery in February, 1848, to make plans for the national convention.

---

[1] This letter was dated at Montgomery, December 13, 1847, in Alaba.na Archives and History Department. The Whigs called the States Rights Democrats the "Chivalry"; they called the Union Democrats "Hunkers."

[2] Letter dated at Mobile, December 20, 1847, in *Amer. His. Asso. Report* (1900), "Correspondence of John C. Calhoun," pp. 1152-55. Cited henceforth as Calhoun Correspondence.

Yancey controlled the convention and was able to get his resolutions which embodied the "Alabama Platform" adopted without a dissenting vote. This attitude of the convention won back to the party such Democrats as Judge Campbell, who had declared that he would support General Taylor for president in preference to a Northern Democrat of the "Hunker" type, such as Buchanan. Campbell gave a good analysis of the political situation in a letter to Calhoun as follows:

> It was a profound conviction of our inability to meet those men ("Hunkers") successfully with any Democrat I could name that induced me (of course there were other reasons) to favor the Taylor movement. They at once spoke of Woodbury to hush our mouths on the subject of Taylor. The plain reason of this is, that the Mountain democracy command the State and our politicians defer to their wishes. The whole of the talent of the democratic party in this State is with us but, the county leaders are not. And our leaders are unwilling to combat. They succumb continually to these mountaineers.

> The whole strength of the Hunkers of this State will be given to Buchanan. He is the administration candidate in the South. He expects the South to aid him against a Wilmot Proviso Northern man. How can we get rid of him? There is but one mode. It is for some public men to take bold decided ground against him. I will not vote for him myself.****[3]

By the summer of 1848, Yancey felt that he had Alabama definitely lined up for the Southern Rights position. On June 21, 1848, he wrote to Calhoun from Montgomery:

> We have at last started. We have consulted sufficiently to effect a start. Taylor's position in the late Whig convention has thrown into our arms all those Democrats who were for him heretofore. Belser resigns his place on the Taylor electoral ticket. Campbell of Mobile quits his Taylor ground and is with us. Here, Goldthwaite, Elmore, Mayo, Semple, Harris, Belser, and kindred spirits are with us. We are raising funds to establish a press here. In that we need aid; but *we will* publish it at all hazards. We will address the people in a manifesto very soon this week. We will call a mass convention here on the 12 July. At that convention we will nominate the ablest and purest electoral ticket every put into the field in this State. But upon whom shall we rally for President?

---

[3] Calhoun Correspondence, pp. 1152-55.

Tazewell and Jeff Davis are suggested here. Will they do? Will you write to Tazewell for us? and write me frankly your opinions? The skies are brightening. I was despondent a week ago, I am now hopeful. We are all so. We will move in force and effectively.[4]

Yancey was greatly disappointed at the refusal of the Democratic national convention to accept the "Alabama Platform" and also at the refusal of the Alabama delegation to follow him when he withdrew from the convention hall. He made only two speeches during the presidential campaign. At Camden, Wilcox County, he made a bitter attack on the Democratic Party for its nomination and support of Cass. Seldom had any Whig, according to DuBose, Yancey's biographer, ever attacked the Democrats with such bitterness.[5] After Yancey ceased his efforts the campaign became listless and devoid of much enthusiasm on either side.

Cass carried the state by a majority of less than one thousand out of a total of 61,000. He carried only five counties south of the moutains; this defection of the Democrats in central and south Alabama came near causing the Democrats to lose the state. Cass carried fewer counties than did Taylor but his majorities in the "Avalanche" counties of north Alabama were larger. The influence of Yancey and his group and their lack of support of Cass came near causing the Democrats to lose the state.

Soon after the presidential election, a caucus of Southern congressmen met in Washington, January 22, 1849, and adopted Calhoun's "Southern Address," which was a strong demand for the rights of the South respecting slavery extension. The "Address" was practically a party issue as only two Whig congressmen had favored it and only four Democratic congressmen had opposed it. One of the Democrats who refused to sign it was George S. Houston of the Florence district. Houston returned to his district and began a contest to get the leadership of the Democratic Party by making Calhoun's "Address" an issue in the state election in the fall. He planned to get control of the legislature by the election of Unionists to that body and then to secure his own election to the

---

[4] Calhoun Correspondence, p. 1177.
[5] DuBose, Life of Yancey, pp. 225-26.

United States Senate. The opportunity seemed particularly promising as there were two senators to be elected by the legislature.

During the spring Houston was in close communication with Howell Cobb, who was the great leader of the Union Democrats of Georgia and one of the non-signers of Calhoun's "Address." Houston attended the different circuit courts in his district and made efforts to induce mass meetings to pass resolutions condemning the "Address." He learned, however, that the sentiment in favor of Calhoun's position was strong, even among the north Alabama Democrats, and that there was discontent among his friends because he had refused to sign the "Address."[6]

While Houston was getting instructions from Cobb, the States Rights Democrats of Alabama were in communication with Calhoun at his home at Fort Hill, South Carolina. Hilliard M. Judge wrote to Calhoun from Eutaw, Greene County, on April 9, 1849, that

> almost all counties of South Alabama have responded most emphatically to the Southern Address without distinction of party. North Alabama is much less interested and will be slow in her action, yet I think she will follow the lead of the Southern portion of the State. A favorable omen of public opinion there, is furnished by Houston's refusal to be a candidate for reelection. Hilliard will be beaten in his District, by a Whig or Democrat who is sound, as may seem best calculated to accomplish this result.[7]

Mr. Judge further stated that Houston was being forced to defend himself in north Alabama for having refused to sign the "Address," which Houston was doing by claiming that the slavery question was being agitated for party purpose and advantage alone. In evidence of this, Houston was claiming that Calhoun had told Senator Douglas, of Illinois, during the discussion of the California bill, that "it would never do to settle this question of slavery—that its agitation was necessary to the success of the Democratic Party in the South." Mr. Judge ended his letter with these words:

---

[6] Letter from Houston to Cobb, March, 1849, in *Amer. Hist. Asso. Report* (1911), II. 158, 159, "Correspondence of Toombs, Stephens, and Cobb." Cited henceforth as Correspondence of Cobb.

[7] Calhoun Correspondence, pp. 1195-97.

Let South Carolina hold back—a little, until her more slothful Sisters can be equally instructed in their rights and duty under the present emergency, the whole South will then present an unbroken front, and thus accomplish peaceably what we desire! This delay is not so necessary for Alabama as for the more Western States, for next to South Carolina, Alabama is better prepared for resistance than any other Southern State.[8]

H. W. Conner wrote Calhoun from Charleston, South Carolina, in January, a summary of the political situation in Georgia and in Alabama. He stated that the leaders of east Alabama were sound, and that the leaders, such as, Yancey, Elmore, Belser, and Goldthwaite were ready to act. His knowledge of north and west Alabama, he stated, was based on hearsay. North Alabama was governed a good deal by party affiliation; west Alabama was in sympathy with Calhoun's position; south Alabama was also favorable to Calhoun, except at Mobile, where the Northern population were opposed to him. The people of Alabama as a whole, concluded Conner, were sound in everything, but there was a difficulty in getting the politicians lined up for State Rights.[9]

As the August election approached, the elements of discord within the Democratic ranks became more pronounced. It was a Democratic custom to give a governor the nomination for a second term without the formality of calling a state convention, but, due to the opposition which had developed in north Alabama against him, Governor Chapman asked that a convention be called to make the nomination.[10] The opposition to Chapman was due to the fact that he had allied himself with the States Rights wing of the Democratic Party. Senator Lewis had died in 1848 and Chapman had oppointed ex-Governor Benjamin Fitzpatrick, of the Lewis-Yancey group, to fill the vacancy. The governor was also in close alliance with C. C. Clay, Jr., who was becoming one of the most influential and able States Rights leaders in north Alabama.[11]

With the situation thus confused, the Democratic state convention assembled in Montgomery in June, 1849, under the domina-

---

[8] *Ibid.*
[9] Calhoun Correspondence, pp. 1188-89, Jan. 12, 1849.
[10] Garrett, *Reminiscences of Public Men in Alabama*, p. 512.
[11] Letter from Houston to Cobb, June 26, 1849, Correspondence of Cobb, pp. 166-67.

tion of the States Rights group. Many of the leaders of this group, among whom were Yancey, John Cochran and Eli S. Shorter, of Barbour, C. W. Lee and W. M. Brooks, of Perry, and James E. Saunders, of Mobile, attended with the purpose of getting the convention to nominate Chapman. These leaders soon saw the necessity of sacrificing Chapman in order to secure the assurance of success for the party in the August election, and they accepted Judge Henry W. Collier, of Tuscaloosa, as a compromise candidate.[12]

The compromise which resulted in the nomination of Collier was described in a letter from Houston to Cobb. Under this compromise, according to Houston, ex-Senator King, who was a Unionist, was to be elected to Lewis' seat when the legislature should assemble in November.[13]

The mountain democracy in this convention had forced the south Alabama leaders to accept Collier and King, both conservatives, but the leadership of the party remained in the hands of the States Rights men. It was a clever move on the part of the two Democratic wings to make this compromise, even though it caused the defection of Yancey. It united the party in support of Collier and brought King into cooperation with the strong States Rights leaders of Montgomery, the "Montgomery Regency" group, who were to exercise such an important leadership during the early fifties. Senator King remained in cooperation with this group until his death in April, 1853.

The completeness of the victory achieved by the States Rights group in this convention is attested by Houston. He wrote Cobb in June that Alabama is gone "hook and line" into the Calhoun camp unless the Whigs can get it, which, he thought, was improbable. "My district," he wrote, "is lost and a rabid Calhoun man, an old nullifier and an enemy of mine, will be elected." Houston's explanation of this situation was that his Union friends were afraid of the slavery question.[14]

During the spring the Whig leaders made an effort to bring out a candidate for governor. J. J. Hooper, editor of the *Chambers*

---

[12] Garrett, *op. cit.*, p. 513.
[13] Houston to Cobb, July 28, 1849, Correspondence of Cobb.
[14] Correspondence of Cobb, letter dated June 26, 1849. The "rabid Calhoun man" to whom Houston referred was David Hubbard, of Lawrence County, a strong Southern Rights man.

Tribune, the leading Whig paper in east Alabama, suggested James E. Belser, of Montgomery.[15] But the Whigs were not able to agree upon a candidate and Collier was elected without opposition. The management of the campaign showed shrewd leadership by the "Montgomery Regency."

The difficult position of the Alabama Whigs at this time was due to the attitude of the national Whig Party towards slavery extension. Soon after his inauguration, President Taylor came under the influence of W. H. Seward, his secretary of state, and the anti-slavery groups of Whigs in Congress. This attitude of the administration caused a breach between the Southern and Northern Whigs.

The state election in August, 1849, did not reveal any radical changes from the election results of 1847. The Democrats again carried all of the congressional districts except the Mobile and Montgomery districts. The results showed a strong tendency of the people to support the States Rights principle and to vote for the men who had signed Calhoun's "Address."

In the Mobile district the record of the Taylor administration towards slavery extension was made the leading issue. Judge W. J. Alston defeated his Democratic opponent, C. C. Sellers, by a majority of about three hundred. This majority was about one thousand less than the majority given Taylor for president in this district the preceding year.[16]

A significant political development took place in the Montgomery district in this election. In 1847 the Whigs had elected H. W. Hilliard to Congress without opposition, and in 1848 they had given Taylor a majority of more than 2,500 for president. In 1849 one Whig opposed another one in a campaign which became famous as the "War of the Roses." James L. Pugh, of Barbour County, was an independent Whig candidate against Hilliard and was supported by the Democrats. Yancey was induced to return from South Carolina, where he was on a visit, and to take the stump for Pugh. The regular Whigs attempted to discredit Yancey by associating his name with Calhoun and the secession movement

---

[15] *Alabama Journal,* June 26, 1849.
[16] *Mobile Register and Journal.* Aug. 11, 1849.

in South Carolina. J. J. Hooper claimed that Yancey, the "Chunky Statesman," had probably brought back to Alabama "the latest order from headquarters at Fort Hill."[17]

Pugh swept the "Cow" counties in the lower part of the district and Hilliard won only by getting large majorities in the Black Belt counties in the upper part of the district.

After this split in the Whig Party, Pugh and other Whigs remained in the Democratic camp. He and other leaders of Barbour County, principally lawyers of Eufaula, made up a strong Southern Rights group. Other members of the group were Eli S. Shorter, elected to Congress in 1855 and 1857; John Gill Shorter, elected governor in 1861; John Cochran, candidate for congressman in 1851; Jefferson Buford, Alpheus Baker, E. C. Bullock, L. L. Cato, Sterling G. Cato, Jere N. Williams, and Henry D. Clayton. This group was usually referred to by the newspapers as the "Eufaula Regency." These men were the most consistent secessionists in the state during the fifties. They refused to make any concessions to preserve the Union, maintaining their position, even after Yancey ceased his efforts for secession.

This breach in the Whig Party was the beginning of the disintegration of the Whig Party in the eastern counties of the Black Belt, and culminated in strong support for Breckenridge in 1860 and for secession in 1861.

In the three congressional districts of middle Alabama—the Wetumpka, the Tuscaloosa, and the Talladega—the Democratic incumbents were reelected without great opposition.

Houston was not a candidate for reelection in the Florence district as he hoped to secure his election to the United States Senate by the legislature which was chosen in this election, and David Hubbard, a strong Southern Rights man, was elected by a minority vote over a Whig and another Democrat.

W. R. W. Cobb was elected in the Huntsville district and contiued to represent this district up to secession. In this election Cobb defeated Jeremiah Clemens, who later in 1849 was elected to

---

[17] Letter in *Alabama Journal*, Aug. 11, 1849. Hooper was probably the most able of the Whig editors. He combined wit and force in his writings and his attacks on the Democrats were highly effective.

the United States Senate, and in 1853 he defeated C. C. Clay, Jr., who was also elected senator later in the year of his defeat.

Cobb was an uneducated man but was a whole-souled fellow, both of which explain his popularity in his district. His ability to use a situation for his advantage is illustrated by a story which was told about him when he was a member of the lower house of the legislature. A member from a south Alabama county, in order to discredit Cobb and his lack of culture and education, alluded to the fact that Cobb had once peddled clocks in south Alabama. "Yes," replied Cobb, "it is true I once let some clocks go among the gentleman's constitutents and they've been going on *tick* ever since. As long as the gentleman has brought up the business, I wish he'd foot the bills."[18]

The Whigs gained fifteen members in the lower house and the Democrats gained seven, a net gain of eight members for the Whigs in the house. The Whigs gained control of the senate by a majority of one, by electing their candidate in the Bibb-Shelby district. Garrett explained the Whig gains by saying that they brought forward as candidates their best and most talented young men.[19]

The Whig gains were made in the white counties, both of north and south Alabama; the Democratic gains were made in the Black Belt counties. The results indicated that north Alabama was becoming more unified for conservatism and that south Alabama was becoming more unified against Northern aggressions; these tendencies continued through the exciting controversy over slavery extension in 1850 and 1851.[20]

The legislature convened November 12, 1849. Governor Chapman sent to the house a message of thirty-two pages, the last seven of which were devoted to the question of slavery in the territories and the action of Congress on this question. The governor took strong ground for Southern Rights in this message, recommending that the legislature make provision at once for the calling of a state convention upon the passage by Congress of the Wilmot Proviso, or any other measure having a tendency to exclude slavery from

---

[18] *Alabama Journal,* March 5, 1849. This story was told by J. J. Hooper.
[19] Garrett, *op. cit.,* p. 513.
[20] *Mobile Register and Journal,* Aug. 24, 1849.

any of the territories, and suggesting that the sister Southern states be invited to unite with Alabama in a convention to consult upon the general state of the Union, and as to the best means of preserving their common rights. The governor felt that a more important subject "never presented itself to the consideration of a people; for it concerns not merely our property, but is a question of State and individual honor—of self-preservation."[21]

This message was written and issued under the influence of Calhoun. In October, preceding the meeting of the legislature, Chapman, saying that he was availing himself of his long friendship for Calhoun, had asked Calhoun's views on the question of slavery extension and his opinion on the advisability of including in his message the suggestion for a state convention. Chapman wrote that since his message was to be the first to be sent to a legislature in any Southern state since the adjournment of Congress, he was "solicitous as it is certainly important for the interests of the South, that the question now at issue between the Southern and Northern portions of the Confederacy shall be presented as strongly as the nature of the message will allow."[22]

In December, Governor Collier, who had succeeded Chapman as governor in November, after the latter had delivered his message to the legislature, sent to the legislature a letter which he had just received from Senator Fitzpatrick and six of the seven Alabama congressmen from Washington. It was stated in this letter that for three weeks the House of Representatives had been unable to elect a speaker, due to the agitation caused by the abolitionists opposing slavery extension, and that the Federal Government had become inoperative and was threatened with immediate dissolution. Collier recommended that the legislature state the position of Alabama on the question of slavery extension. The senate quickly passed a resolution stating that

we are well acquainted with the spirit of the people of Alabama and we assert that it is their fixed purpose never to submit to the threatened encroachment of their rights, that they will

---

[21] Garrett, *op. cit.*, p. 514.

[22] Chapman to Calhoun, Oct. 19, 1849, Calhoun Correspondence; *Macon Republican,* Nov. 22, 1849.

never submit to any act of the Government of the United States which excludes the South from a fair and just enjoyment of the territory acquired from Mexico, and which is the property of the states of this Union.[23]

In the event of the passage of any act similar to the Wilmot Proviso, the senate called upon the people of the slave states to meet in convention and to take such action as the defense of their common rights might demand.

The house also passed resolutions on this subject but no one set of resolutions was passed by both houses.[24]

While the legislature was in this aggressive state of mind it was called upon to elect two United States senators. The vacancies had been caused by the resignation of Senator Bagby in 1848 to become minister to Russia, and by the death of Senator Lewis the same year. These elections were the signals for party and factional contests in the legislature.

Ex-Governor Chapman, W. R. King, and Arthur F. Hopkins, an old Whig "war horse," were the candidates balloted upon for the seat of Bagby. Chapman, as already mentioned, had lost the support of the conservative Democrats of north Alabama, his home section, by his appointment of Fitzpatrick to the Senate in 1848. The objection of the conservatives to Fitzpatrick was that he was too aggressive for Southern Rights and that he was too closely affiliated with the "Montgomery Regency."

King had been defeated by Lewis in 1847. Later King had acted with the leaders of the "Montgomery Regency" whose support, together with that of the north Alabama Democrats now elected him to the seat of Bagby.[25]

---

[23] *Macon Republican*, Dec. 27, 1849; DuBose, *op. cit.*, p. 241.

[24] *Montgomery Advertiser*, Jan. 9, 1850.

[25] *Macon Republican*, Dec. 6, 1849; Garrett, *op. cit.*, p. 523. Three ballots were taken; the first and third were as follows: King, 57; Chapman, 15; Hopkins, 59; King, 71; Chapman, withdrawn; Hopkins, 58.

An insight into political methods is given in a letter written by T. B. Cooper, of Cherokee County, to his wife a few days after this election, regarding the hospitality of King. "I am not in a very good fix for writing this morning," Cooper wrote. "I was at a party given by Col Wm R King at the Exchange last night and wine passed pretty freely, so I have some head ache would not be surprised if I get sick." From manuscript letter in Alabama Archives and History Department.

Senator King was regarded as a Southern Rights man at this time but his position was rather that of a moderate. He stated his view of the political situation in a letter, written a short time after his election to the Senate. This letter shows the difficult position in which the Southern congressmen were placed by the slavery extension agitation.

I am again in the Senate,—and*** assiduously engaged in making efforts so to better this alarming question as to protect the rights of the South, and save the Union—whether these efforts will prove successful is I fear exceedingly doubtful. Had the South presented an undivided front, there would I think have been little or no difficulty, but such I am sorry to say has not been the case.

King, like many other leaders before and after this time, blamed the Southern people themselves for their failure to secure their rights, guaranteed under the constitution. Like Yancey, King attributed this failure to the inclination of the people to support parties rather than principles. Regarding parties he wrote:

The baneful spirit of party has divided and distracted our people and those unfortunate divisions have encouraged the North to persevere in their course of aggressions. Union among ourselves alone was wanting to insure success, for so long as it was believed that there would be united action on the part of the South, meetings were called, numerously attended; the abolitionists denounced in no measured terms and their Representatives were called on to inspect the constitutional rights of the Slave holding States.

Senator King ended his letter with a gloomy picture of the future of the South:

I sincerely hope that we may yet succeed, but am forced to say things look gloomy. The death of Mr. Calhoun is a severe blow to the South, for there was no man more devoted to its interests than was he. The Administration after having violated its every pledge to place in office its unscrupulous adherents, has become and justly too, the most unpopular ever known in the country. Even the Whigs have lost all confidence in it, and it is destined to go out of office, despised by every upright and honorable man in the nation.[26]

The contestants for the other senatorial seat were ex-Governor Fitzpatrick, Jeremiah Clemens, a north Alabama conservative Democrat, and Arthur F. Hopkins. On the first ballot Fitzpatrick received fifty-eight Democratic votes for fifteen for Clemens, and on the fifth ballot he lacked only one vote of having the necessary majority for election, when an adjournment was taken. During the night the Whigs held a caucus; the next day they withdrew their candidate, Hopkins, and voted with the north Alabama Democrats for Clemens, who was elected on the sixth ballot.[27]

The Democrats of the "Montgomery Regency" were deeply chagrined at the defeat of Fitzpatrick. Clemens was not a good party man and was not sufficiently aggressive for the rights of slavery to satisfy the party leaders. Charges were made that a bargain had been made between the Whigs and Clemens, whereby the Whigs had withdrawn Hopkins and voted for Clemens in return for which he was to support the President and the Whig administration. This charge of a bargain was brought forward by the anti-Clemens press when he asked for reelection before the legislature in 1851.

The Whigs received more comfort from the defeat of Fitzpatrick than from the election of Clemens. The *Macon Republican* stated that it liked Clemens because he lived in north Alabama and because it wanted to defeat the Democratic leaders of middle Alabama. It said that the Whigs supported Clemens as the lesser of two evils. It admitted that there were two objections to Clemens,

---

[26] King to M. P. Blue, dated Washington, Apr. 11, 1850, in Blue Papers.

[27] *Macon Republican*, Dec. 6, 1849. The vote on the first ballot was as follows: Fitzpatrick, 60 (58 Democrats and 2 Whigs); Clemens, 21 (15 Democrats and 6 Whigs); Hopkins, 50 (all Whigs). The sixth ballot was: Fitzpatrick, 58 (54 Democrats and 4 Whigs); Clemens, 66 (17 Democrats and 49 Whigs); Hopkins, withdrawn.

The Democrats who voted for Clemens were from Benton, Blount, DeKalb, Jackson, Lauderdale, Madison, Marshall, and St. Clair. All of these were North Alabama counties.

namely, he was a Democrat, and he colored his water a little too deeply.[28]

This defeat of Fitzpatrick and the Southern Rights Democrats was significant. It showed that there could not be party success without the cooperation of the two wings of the party, and that the more aggressive wing could not advance too rapidly without danger of losing the support of the conservative mountain group.

A summary of the period from 1847 through 1849 shows that the Democratic Party maintained a supremacy during these years, despite the division of the party into two groups. The States Rights group, with Yancey as the most important leader, furnished the leadership for the party, although this group was forced to make concessions to the Union Democrats by agreeing to the selection of conservatives for office.

The belief that Cass was not sufficiently committed to slavery extension and the feeling that Taylor would be more sympathetic towards slavery interests, caused many of the Southern Rights Democrats in the Black Belt counties to support Taylor in the presidential election in 1848 and came near causing the Whigs to carry the state.

The Southern Rights leaders made concessions to the Union Democrats in 1849, but, even then, the Whigs obtained a majority in the state senate and secured the election of a Union Democrat to the United States Senate by a fusion with the Democrats of north Alabama.

The year 1849 closed with the Whigs stronger than they had been since 1847. They held the balance of power between the two Democratic groups, but were not strong enough to elect their candidates to the United States Senate, which was the test of party supremacy. The year closed with the future of each party clouded in uncertainty.

---

[28] *Macon Republican*, Dec. 6, 1849.

CHAPTER III.

THE SECESSION MOVEMENT AND THE DISINTEGRATION
OF THE OLD PARTIES, 1850-51

The debates in Congress on the question of the extension of slavery into the territories acquired from Mexico and the effort of Calhoun to unite the South through a Southern convention for the protection of Southern Rights were the two political questions that the people of Alabama were most interested in when the year 1850 opened.

The first step to achieve Calhoun's purpose was taken in October, 1849, when Mississippi, in conformity to Calhoun's wishes, held a state convention and issued an invitation to the other Southern states to send delegates to a Southern convention which was to be held in 1850.

The Alabama legislature responded to this invitation by assembling in an informal caucus on February 6, 1850, and selecting thirty-six delegates to attend the Southern convention which was to meet in Nashville in June. The delegates were divided equally between the Whigs and the conservative Democrats.[1]

During the spring, meetings were held in Alabama to discuss the proposed convention. The Southern Rights group were aggressive in an effort to influence the delegates to take strong grounds for the protection of slavery. Their leaders were getting encouragement from the South Carolina leaders. Calhoun wrote to Hilliard M. Judge, one of his supporters in Alabama, as follows:

Your suggestion as to the necessity of a convention of the Southern States is perfectly obvious. We can not get along any other way—the North will not be deterred from her course of wanton aggression by resolutions of the States legislatures, but let the legislatures first declare the principles and the people of the States can give them force and effect in convention.[2]

---

[1] *Alabama Journal*, Feb. 12, 1850;
Hodgson, *Cradle of the Confederacy*, p. 278.
[2] Calhoun Correspondence, p. 207, March 15, 1850.

The Southern Rights men circulated a pamphlet which had been printed at Columbia, South Carolina, which gave reasons why a conflict between the North and the South was inevitable. A number of mass meetings in Alabama passed resolutions advocating secession.[3]

The Whig leaders and press became alarmed at the aggressive attitude of the States Rights Democrats. They began to criticize the plan of a Southern convention by saying that the people should have been given the right to elect the delegates instead of their appointment by the legislature. Mr. Hilliard, one of the most prominent of the Whigs, wrote the following regarding a convention:

As to the Nashville Convention, my opinion as things now stand, is against it. I adhere to the position taken by me last summer—that no convention ought to be be held in *advance* of some act of aggression on the part of the government. The most the legislature should have done, was to agree upon some clear, sensible firm resolution upon the subject, and empower the government, in the event of an aggression, to call a convention of the *people* to consider the question in all its bearings; the wrong, the remedy.[4]

Hilliard denied that the legislature had any authority to appoint delegates and he advised all Whigs to remain aloof from this movement. Hilliard, at this time, believed that the territory acquired from Mexico would be organized into governments without the Wilmot Proviso applying to any portion of it.

Only twenty-one of the thirty-six delegates appointed to represent Alabama at the Nashville convention attended. Of these fourteen were Democrats and seven were Whigs. Six of the delegates were from north Alabama, twelve were from the Black Belt, and three were from Mobile. Twelve of them were lawyers, six were planters, and the remainder were merchants or physicians. These delegates represented the conservative sentiment in Alabama. Mr.

---

[3] *Alabama Journal,* April 23, 1850.

[4] *Republican Banner and Nashville Whig,* April 23, 1850, quoted in *Ala. Hist. So. Proceeds.,* V. 213.

Yancey and the radical States Rights men refused to participate in the convention.[5]

The resolutions passed by the Nashville convention were conservative in sentiment. The most important one was a demand for the extension of the Missouri Compromise line to the Pacific Ocean and the right to carry slaves into the territories south of this line.[6]

After the return of the Alabama delegates from the Nashville convention, mass meetings were called to discuss the resolutions of the convention. Some of these meetings approved and others disapproved the resolutions; party affiliation apparently was not a deciding factor which determined the attitudes which were taken. A large group of merchants and planters assembled in Montgomery, July 13, 1850, to receive a report from some of the delegates to Nashville. A majority report favoring the resolutions of the Nashville convention and a minority report opposing them were presented and debated. Yancey, who had not been a delegate to the convention, opposed the majority report in a powerful speech. He stated that it was his belief the North would not do justice to the South and that it was time to set our house in order and to sustain Texas, if need be, with military support.[7]

The Whigs had held aloof to a large extent from participation in the Nashville convention, as they feared it, due to its initiation by Calhoun, but, after the return of the delegates, they, as a rule, accepted the resolutions of the convention. The *Alabama Journal* advised the Whigs to accept them and not to attack the compromise measures while they were being debated in Congress.[8]

In north Alabama meetings were held which accepted the resolutions of the Nashville convention and approved the later compromise measures of Congress. Many meetings in the Black Belt also approved the compromise. Two such meetings in the important counties of Montgomery and Marengo had an influence in deterring

---

[5] These figures were compiled from biographical sketches of the delegates as given in Garrett, *Reminiscences of Public Men in Alabama,* and Brewer, *Alabama.*

[6] DuBose, *op. cit.,* p. 247.

[7] DuBose, *op. cit.,* pp. 247-49.

[8] *Alabama Journal,* June 25, 1850.

the secessionists from urging the governor to call a special session of the legislature to consider steps for secession.[9]

Late in the summer, Congress passed the compromise measures which were intended to settle the question of the extension of slavery in the territories. Yancey immediately began an attack upon them. In reply to an invitation to address a meeting in Lowndes County, which he was forced to decline on account of a business trip to Butler County, he stated fully his opinion of the situation as follows:

> Congress has proceeded as calmly and deliberately to consummate this great fraud upon the South as if the people had never remonstrated against the wrong—in fact, as if it was in full accord with our wishes.

> Congress has boldly tendered it—submission or secession. I have no doubt but that it will be as boldly met by the people; and that being denied equality in the Union, they will maintain independence out of it. But we can do nothing save through a convention of the people of the States.****

Yancey concluded his letter by calling upon the people for action.

> I am for action, gentlemen, and not talking. At this time, action is eloquence. Our most efficient means of action will be found in the organization of the people in Southern Rights Clubs.[10]

The *Montgomery Advertiser* joined Yancey in opposition to compromise and in his advocacy of the formation of a Southern Rights party for the protection of the South. J. J. Seibels, editor of the *Advertiser*, wrote that "submission or resistance are now the only alternatives**** We shall not hesitate to choose the latter."[11]

The Democratic *Dallas Gazette* in an editorial said: "We believe in the right of secession. We believe the late compromise measures

[9] DuBose, *op. cit.*, pp. 251-52.
[10] *Huntsville Democrat*, Oct. 17, 1850.
[11] *Montgomery Advertiser*, quoted in *Washington Republican*, Oct. 7, 1850.

will warrant the secession of any slaveholding state from the Union. **** We believe it the duty of every Southern State, collectively or *alone* to secede from the Union as soon as possible."[12]

The most advanced step looking towards secession came from the "fire-eaters" of southeast Alabama under the leadership of the "Eufaula Regency." A group of prominent business men, planters and lawyers met at Eufaula on October 22, 1850, and drew up a petition to Governor Collier in which it was stated that the crisis demanded that the legislature be called into a special session to take steps to protect Alabama from the aggressions of acts of Congress.[13]

A great deal of the secession sentiment in Alabama at this time was inspired by influences from South Carolina. In June, John T. Seibels, of Columbia, South Carolina, wrote to his son, J. J. Seibels, editor of the *Montgomery Advertiser,* pleading that the *Advertiser* take high grounds for Southern Rights. He urged his son to advise the people and the press of the South to discontinue subscribing or exchanging for the *National Intelligencer,* which Seibels called a vile paper with a pernicious influence. The influence of Calhoun, even though he was dead, was still evident, for the older Seibels, in mentioning the death of a relative of his named Elmore, stated that he was proud of the fact that Elmore was buried in a casket of the same material as that in which Calhoun had been buried.[14]

In October, Seibels wrote to his son as follows:

> I think the best argument, or rather political weapons you can use in advocacy of the rights of the South, would be to publish the proceedings of meetings to be held in Pittsburgh, Pa., Rochester, N. Y., Lowell and Boston, and you will see an article in the "Journal of Commerce" of the 20 Sept. which out Herods Herod, in relation to the Fugitive slaves, the slave Bill, etc. samples of which I herein enclose.   It is a complete *knock down argument* to anything that the submittionists or Tories can advance, that the slavery in Congress has received its *quietus* by the

---

[12] *Dallas Gazette,* quoted in *Mobile Advertiser,* June 4, 1851.
[13] *Spirit of the South,* Nov. 5, 1850. "Fire-eater" was the name given to the secessionists in 1850. Garrett, p. 545, says that this term was originated by Colonel Howell Rose, of Coosa County, an inveterate supporter of the Union Party.
[14] Letter in possession of Emmett Seibels, Montgomery, Alabama.

passage of the late fugitive slave bill. A mere *test* thrown overboard to amuse the whale. I sincerely wish that the Georgians would souse Toombs and Stephens, the renegrades, in a hogshead of Tar & then give them a coating of a feather bed.[15]

Editor Seibels was in communication also with Governor Hammond of South Carolina. In September, 1850, Seibels asked Hammond what South Carolina would do with respect to secession if Georgia "backed out." This was at the time that defeat of secession in Georgia was apparent. Seibels told Hammond that Georgia's decision "would at once determine the course of Alabama, Mississippi, and Florida."[16]

The *Macon Republican* warned its readers that there was danger of secession and began to fill its columns with arguments for compromise. It apologized to its women readers for reducing the space which it had been devoting to news of interest to women by saying that the Union was in danger and women must learn to read politics.[17]

The Alabama senators, Clemens and King, both of whom had voted for the compromise measures, returned to the state and urged the people to accept the compromise.[18] Senator King declined an invitation to speak at Tuscaloosa, saying that in the excited state of the public mind, nothing should be done which could by any possibility add to the excitement, or have the appearance of arraying one portion of the people of the state against the other.[19]

The political result in Alabama of the agitation over the Nashville convention and the debates on the compromise measures was that the Union Democrats began to affiliate and form a new political party, based upon an acceptance of the Compromise of 1850 as a finality. This party realignment forced the Southern Rights men, led by Yancey and the *Montgomery Advertiser,* to the organization of a Southern Rights Party. Both of these party transitions were taking place as early as the summer of 1850. This party realignment continued until by the end of the year there were

---

[15] Seibels Papers.
[16] Shryock, *Georgia and the Union in* 1850, p. 302.
[17] *Macon Republican,* July 25, 1850.
[18] *Huntsville Democrat,* Nov. 7, 14, 1850.
[19] *Ibid.,* Nov. 28, 1850.

two loosely organized parties, lacking only leadership and closer organization to be real political parties.

The formal organization of the Union Party took place at Montgomery on January 19, 1851, in a state convention which had been called by a caucus of the Union members of the legislature. A majority of the members of the convention were from the Black Belt counties. The convention passed resolutions favoring the Compromise of 1850 and denying the right of secession, but, in order to defend itself against the charge of being too submissive to compromise, it passed resolutions maintaining the right of revolution, claiming it "a paramount right which belongs to every free people to overthrow their government when it fails to answer the ends for which it was established."[20]

The challenge of the Unionists was answered by the opponents of compromise who met in Montgomery on February 10, 1851, and organized a Southern Rights Party. Almost all of the ninety-seven delegates to the convention were Democrats from the Black Belt counties. The convention was dominated by Yancey, Seibels, John A. Elmore, S. F. Rice, A. P. Bagby, George Goldthwaite, and Thomas Williams. All of these men lived in or near Montgomery and most of them were of South Carolina ancestry. Colonel Williams was made chairman of the convention. In his remarks accepting this position he exhorted the convention to act promptly and to show to the world that they were willing to meet the present crisis like men.[21]

The convention passed a resolution that "a tame submission to **** this hostile legislation (the Compromise of 1850) would not in our opinion be conducive to the peace, happiness, prosperity and honor of the Southern States." An additional resolution demanded the suspension of old parties and the formation of a new Southern party, and requested the governor to call the legislature into a special session to enable the people to elect delegates to a Southern convention which should decide whether the Southern states should secede.[22]

---

[20] *Spirit of the South*, Feb. 18, 1851.
[21] *Spirit of the South*, Feb. 18, 1851.
[22] Hodgson, *op. cit.*, p. 290.

The convention did not favor immediate and separate states secession. Its position was expressed in the following resolution: "We would not now declare that Alabama should secede at any particular time, but simply that it is her duty to prepare for secession; and that if any other Southern state secedes, good faith to such State requires that we should sustain her by all means within our power, and should likewise secede." The *Huntsville Democrat* in quoting this resolution stated that Mr. Yancey wrote it.[23]

Mr. Hodgson, in his description of the convention, states that Mr. Yancey was opposed to the half-aggressive policy of these resolutions. He favored separate and unconditional secession. He made a speech in which he said that he had private advices that South Carolina had collected one hundred pieces of artillery, more than 20,000 small arms, ,and a large quantity of military stores, and that South Carolina would secede in the spring. Yancey closed this speech by saying that the issue was secession or submission, and that he was "decidedly in favor of preparing the State by all proper means for exerting the right of secession."[24]

On the contrary, Mr. Seibels, according to Hodgson, favored secesson only by cooperation with the other Southern states. He soon saw that the Montgomery platform was regarded as a step towards secession and he began to tone down his editorials in the *Advertiser.* He saw that a majority of the people were opposed to secession and that T. H. Watts and the other leading Whigs were leaning strongly towards submission in order to provoke the Southern Rights group to take a stronger stand for secession. And, according to Hodgson, Seibels refused to be lead into this "trap."[25]

Many of the Democrats, particularly those in the mountain and southern counties, refused to join the Southern Rights movement. The *Mobile Register,* the leading Democratic paper of south Alabama, claimed that the Montgomery platform would be condemned by three-fourths of the people of the state, and that there was not a county in which a majority of the people were in favor of secession. This paper claimed that Dallas, Lowndes and Montgomery were the only counties in which there was any great disaffection, and

---

[23] *Huntsville Democrat,* Apr. 10, 1851.
[24] Hodgson, *op. cit.,* p. 305.
[25] Hodgson, *op. cit.,* p. 291.

stated that only eleven counties had been induced to send delegates to the Montgomery convention.[26]

The old Whig press attacked Yancey and the Montgomery platform. The *Alabama Journal* and the *Macon Republican* claimed that a majority of both Democrats and Whigs opposed the proposed new party. The *Southern Advocate,* of Huntsville, the leading Whig paper of north Alabama, attempted to discredit the movement by reporting that Yancey was said to be connected with the *Montgomery Atlas,* a paper which had unfurled the banner of secession. The *Advocate* gave the following words of advice to "Yancey, the Atlas, and Company :"

> If you happen to get Alabama out of the Union, North Alabama will secede from the new kingdom and petition to be admitted again into the Union attached to Georgia or Tennessee. It will be decidedly unpleasant for us to have to pay for *exporting* our cotton to *our* markets.[27]

The campaign of 1851 began early in the spring with indications that the elections would be bitterly contested. Three old Whig papers—the *Alabama Journal, Macon Republican,* and *Southern Advocate*—attempted to bring out an old Whig to oppose the reelection of Governor Collier, but by the beginning of summer most of the old Whig papers were supporting him.

The extreme advocates of Unionism attempted to defeat Collier by bringing out B. G. Shields, of Marengo County, as a candidate on the principle of unconditional submission to the Compromise of 1850. Shields took the stump and attacked Collier for Collier's refusal to promise that he would send troops to suppress South Carolina in case of the secession of that state.[28]

Collier did not take a decided attitude on any issue. In a letter to the *Tuscaloosa Observer* he stated his position as follows:

1. Disapproval of the Montgomery platform of 1851.
2. Neither approval nor disapproval of the Compromise of 1850.
3. Opposition to a Southern convention until the Southern people demanded it.

---

[26] *Mobile Register,* cited in *Macon Republican,* Mar. 6, 1851.
[27] *Southern Advocate,* May 14, 1851.
[28] DuBose, *op. cit.,* p. 261.

4. Modification of some of the compromise measures, but opposition to secession for anything which had occurred up to this time.[29]

In the spring, the Southern Rights group had opposed Collier, due to his refusal to call a special session of the legislature to take steps for the secession of the state, but by the summer the leaders of this group, such as Fitzpatrick and Seibels, were supporting him.

In the August election, Collier received over 37,000 votes to less than 6,000 for Shields. The total vote in this election was about 19,000 less than the vote in the gubernatorial election of 1847. Mr. Yancey, although not a candidate, received four hundred and eleven votes.

In the early part of the campaign, both Unionists and Southern Rights men attacked Collier as a weakling who straddled on every political issue.[30] His election in August by the votes of both groups indicated that the people had accepted the compromise measures as a finalty.[31]

Governor Collier's address at his inauguration was, as had been expected, in favor of compromise. It satisfied both the Southern Rights men, who said that it was a sufficient defense of the South, and the Unionists, who claimed that it was favorable to Unionism. The *Alabama Journal* in commenting on it said that the address was "Collierish.."[33]

The political significance of Collier's election came out during the ensuing session of the legislature which met in November. He was one of the first of the leaders to undertake the reorganization of the Democratic Party in 1851-52. The Whigs by helping to elect him governor contributed to the dissolution of the Whig Party through which they had hoped to defeat the Democrats. It was a good display of political management which Collier exhibited in getting his reelection by support from both political groups.

During the spring and summer of 1851 both Union and Southern Rights parties held county conventions to make nominations of candidates for the legislature. Each party worked to get the most

---

[29] *Huntsville Democrat,* Aug. 7, 1851.
[30] *Southern Advocate,* April 30, 1851.
[31] *Macon Republican,* Aug. 21, 1851.
[32] *Alabama Journal,* Dec. 20, 1851.

strength possible by nominating a fusion ticket, composed of members of both the old parties. The Southern Rights Party had as leaders men of such diverse attitudes as Yancey and Judge S. F. Rice, both secessionists, and ex-Governor Fitzpatrick and Senator King, both moderates and opponents of secession. The Union Party had a combination of personalities just as strange.

The breaking of old party lines and the problems of political realignments made the work of the leaders very difficult in this campaign. The best leaders of the Southern Rights Party were the old members of the "Montgomery Regency" Their problem was to hold the north Alabama Democrats in alliance with the secession Democrats of south Alabama who were under the leadership of Yancey. Yancey was a difficult problem for the more conservative leaders. He had lost his leadership of the Democratic Party by 1849, but his influence with a minority of the party was still so great that he could not be ignored. The following letter written by Crawford M. Jackson to Bolling Hall shows something of the difficulties of the Montgomery group of leaders during the campaign:

> In an interview today with our trustworthy friends Govr. Fitzpatrick & Maj. Elmore, we conversed fully and freely upon our prospects & conditions in the present confused state of our county affairs. I am free to say to you that developments are dangerous to our success, unless we exercise prudence, caution & firmess. The Govr., as I then thought, could not converse fully with us on last evening. His views & those of Maj. Elmore are I think of great importance, & especially to you. I think it absolutely necessary that you should be advised touching certain matters, at the earliest possible moment. No time is to be lost—go up in the morning early & see the Govr. & Maj. E—go to breakfast, so that you may be certain to see them I would not trouble you if I did not deem it important.[33]

Hall was elected to the legislature from Autauga County and the Southern Rights Party elected its candidate to Congress from this district but they were not so successful in the election of members to the state legislature and in the elections in the other congressional elections.

---

[33] Bolling Hall Papers. This letter was dated at Auburn Hill, May 26, 1851.

The election of members of the legislature resulted in majorities for the Unionists in both houses. Twenty of the thirty-three senatorial districts of the state elected senators. Of these, thirteen elected Unionists and seven elected Southern Rights men. Of the thirteen senators who were elected in 1849 and whose terms extended through 1851, nine changed to Unionists and four become Southern Rights.

Thus the senate, which in 1849 had been composed of seventeen Whigs and sixteen Democrats, was in 1851 composed of twenty-two Unionists and eleven Southern Rights men. Fifteen of the seventeen Whig senators of 1849 became Unionists in 1851 and two became Southern Rights; seven of the sixteen Democratic senators of 1849 became Unionists in 1851 and nine become Southern Rights.

The two Whig districts which became Southern Rights were Barbour and Mobile. The nine Democratic districts which became Southern Rights were in east and southeast Alabama and in the Black Belt. The seven Democratic districts which were represented by Unionists in 1851 were in the Tennessee Valley and in the hill counties of north Alabama.*

The house of representatives changed from a composition of fifty-seven Democrats and forty-three Whigs in 1849 to one of thirty-eight Southern Rights and sixty-two Unionists members in 1851. Eleven Democratic counties, situated on the border of the Black Belt, became Southern Rights and twelve Democratic counties, eight of which were in north Alabama, became Unionists. Six Whig counties, situated in the Black Belt, became Unionists; and only four Whig counties became Southern Rights. Ten counties which had a mixed delegation of Whigs and Democrats in 1849 became solidly Unionist in 1851.

In this election the Whigs and Democrats of north Alabama united with the Whigs of the Black Belt to form the Union Party

---

*The Democratic districts which became Southern Rights included the following counties: Autauga, Coosa, Calhoun, Cherokee, DeKalb, Clarke, Baldwin, Washington, Dale, Henry, Pickens, Randolph, Tallapoosa, St. Clair, Jefferson and Sumter.

The following old Democratic counties changed to Unionism: Blount, Marshall, Fayette, Marion, Franklin, Lauderdale, Limestone, Morgan, Jackson, and Madison.

and to elect Unionists—many of whom were old Democrats—to the legislature. The Democrats in the Black Belt counties and in some of the counties which bordered on it united with the Whigs in the same counties to form the Southern Rights Party.

The Unionists had a majority of almost two to one in each house, but their success in the future was not entirely assured because sixty-six members of the house were former Democrats and only thirty-three were old Whigs. The future of the Union Party depended upon its getting some issue upon which it could maintain its ranks undivided.

The Georgia Platform was generally accepted by both parties as the issue in the congressional elections in Alabama in 1851. This platform had been adopted by a convention in Georgia in December, 1850, and it embodied the ultimatum of the Southern pro-slavery Unionists to the North. It declared that, although the state did not entirely approve of the Compromise of 1850, it would accept it as a final adjustment, but that it would resist, "even to a disruption of the Union," any future act prohibiting slavery in the territories, any refusal to admit a slave state, or any modification of the fugitive slave law. The action of this convention had great influence in developing sentiment in Alabama for conservatism. The secession of Alabama was practically impossible after Georgia took this attitude.[34]

Nine of the candidates in Alabama for Congress were in favor of the Georgia Platform, or some similar form of compromise; four were secessionists or Southern Rights men, and only one favored unconditional Unionism.

In the Mobile district Judge John Bragg, a Southern Rights Democrat, who favored the Georgia Platform, defeated C. C. Langdon, who ran as an unconditional Union candidate. Langdon was of Northern birth and was editor of the *Mobile Adertiser,* an old Whig paper. The campaign was mde bitter by Langdon's personal history being made an issue.

The Montgomery district witnessed the most intense and bitter campaign of the entire state. Both Hilliard and Yancey, leaders respectively in the old Whig and Democratic parties, refused nomi-

---

[34] Shryock, *op. cit.,* pp. 331-32.

nations, but both took the stump—Hilliard for James Abercrombie, who favored the Georgia Platform, and Yancey for John Cochran, who claimed to be a secessionist. While Abercrombie and Cochran were speaking in the lower counties of the district, Hilliard and Yancey were engaged in joint debates at Union Springs, Enon, and Glennville, in the upper part of the district. Large crowds gathered to hear these speakers, some coming even from Georgia and Florida. The feelings became so strong that the final debate at Eufaula was called off.[35]

In his speeches Yancey claimed that the South had lost everything by the Comprosise of 1850 and that secession was the only resort.[34] He attacked Hilliard for having made speeches to "abolitionists and negro thieves" in the North from the same platform with Webster. It was claimed that Hilliard was working for his party only to get an appointment as ambassador to Russia from Fillmore, the "free-soil president."[37]

At various meetings during the campaign the secessionist speakers induced their audiences to adopt resolutions pledging the people not to employ any lawyer, physician, or clergyman who did not favor the Southern Rights position.[38]

Hilliard and Abercrombie, in their speeches, claimed that the right of revolution rather than that of secession was the principle upon which the South must oppose the aggressions of the North. They pointed out the dangers of secession. Abercrombie's conservatism is indicated in the following declaration made in one of his speeches:

> If this Union, and the South, too, is broken into fragments by the secession of any one, two or three of the Southern States, I could but view it as the greatest possible calamity to human liberty. It would, in my humble opinion, hasten beyond any possible contingency, the destruction of that peculiar property, the preservation of which is the interest of all of us; a destruction which can never occur so long as the South remains united —united too as a component part of the whole country.[39]

[35] *Macon Republican,* Aug. 21, 1851.
[36] *Spirit of the South,* July 16, 1851.
[37] *Ibid.,* July 22, 1851.
[38] *Macon Republican,* Aug. 21, 1851.
[39] *Spirit of the South,* June 17, 1851.

Cochran's position for disunionism was attacked by the Unionists. A letter was published which Cochran had written to Thomas Ritchie, editor of the *Washington Union,* in September, 1850, in which he said that he prayed for the South to tear herself away from the Union, and made a plea for the Southern people to stop buying Northern goods or reading Northern papers. Cochran ordered Ritchie to discontinue his subscription to the *Union,* because Ritchie as editor was the enemy of the South and was giving aid and comfort to its destroyers.[40]

Political songs gave color to this campaign. One of these songs shows the influence of South Carolina upon Cochran and the other political leaders of east Alabama. The first two stanzas of this song were as follows:

> Now turn out for your native land
>   And raise the standard high,
> For Cochran leads a gallant band
>   To glorious victory.
> The South he'll give those peaceful joys
>   Our Fathers thought were meet;
> "Southern Rights" forever, boys,
>   For Cochran can't be beat.
>
>> Oh, John Cochran,
>> You're the man for me;
>> You'll maul that old "Sub" Captain
>> You're the People's nominee.
>
> We live in Alabama
>   'Mongst the noble and the free,
> We'll go to Carolina
>   To meet the enemy.
> It may be we shall die there,
>   But happy it will be,
> To spend our latest efforts
>   In the cause of Liberty.
>
>> Oh, Carolina,
>> That's the land for me:
>> Of all the lands in Sunny South
>> Carolina, still for me.

[40] *Alabama Journal,* July 12, 1851.

The song then described the bringing of "Parson" Hilliard into the district to make speeches for the "Sub" candidate, Abercrombie, and ended with the boast that "We'll beat the "Parson's" Captain, with the People's nominee."[41]

Abercrombie won by a majority of sixteen hundred. This election was of particular significance as the issue between the Secessionists and the Unionists was fairly well drawn and the latter won by a decisive majority. It was a victory for planter conservatism, represented by Abercrombie, who was a large planter, against the aggressive lawyer group, represented by Cochran, who was a lawyer of Eufaula. There could be no doubt of the desire of the people of this district, the home of Yancey and the other important political leaders of Montgomery and Eufaula, to accept the compromise position.

S. W. Harris, an old Democrat and a strong Southern Rights man defeated the Unionist, Judge W. S. Mudd, who had been a Whig, in the Wetumpka district.

In the Tuscaloosa district John Erwin, a large planter of Greene County, was defeated by a majority of fifty-nine by Judge William R. Smith. Both of these men had been Whigs, but both had become Democrats. Smith was a Unionist and Erwin was a Southern Rights man.

In the Florence district, George S. Houston, who had represented the district continuously from 1841, except for the term from 1849 to 1851, won over David Hubbard, of Kinlock, Lawrence County. Hubbard was a strong Southern Rights man and was defeated by a combination of Whigs and conservative Democrats supporting Houston. Both Houston and Hubbard were Democrats.

W. R. W. Cobb was opposed in the Huntsville district by Robert Murphy, who was supported by the *Huntsville Democrat* and the Southern Rights advocates.

Cobb made a demagogical campaign, posing as the friend of the poor against the rich. In his speeches he resorted to all sorts of

---

[41] Some of the lines of this song were remembered and sung to the writer by Jerry Norton, an ex-slave, in Clayton, Alabama, in the summer of 1928. Jerry had a clear recollection of the campaign with its excitement. His master, James Norton, supported Cochran. Later the song was found in the issue of the *Spirit of the South* of July 29, 1851.

tricks, such as the rattling of tinware and crockery, to keep the attention of his audiences. He had introduced bills in Congress to secure indigent people from seizure for debts; in the bills he had minutely named all of the articles which were to be exempt, not omitting the most insignificant articles of the kitchen. He sang homely songs which he had composed for his stump speeches, one of which had a score of verses. One of his songs began with these words, "Uncle Sam is rich enough to give us all a farm." As Mr. Cobb sang, he winked, first at one and then at another of his admiring listeners, punctuating his phrases by chewing with great gusto a piece of onion and the coarsest "pone" bread. His political methods made him one of the best vote-getters in Alabama, particularly among the less educated people. He was reelected in this district.[42]

The Talladega district, the "bloody seventh," witnessed a bitter contest between S. F. Rice, a secessionist, and Alexander White, a Union Whig. Rice was a graduate of South Carolina College, at Columbia, and had had an erratic political career. He had been defeated for Congress as a Democrat in 1845, had become a Whig in 1848, and was a secessionist on the Southern Rights ticket in 1851.[43] Rice's political instability caused a defection of a number of Democrats and he was defeated.

A good analysis of the defeat of Rice was given in a letter to Marion A. Baldwin at Montgomery, written by Thomas A. Walker, of Cherokee County. This letter was as follows:

> You will see 224 democrats in this county would not vote for Rice. If Rise is elected, Benton (later Calhoun County) has done it. We think he is elected, but we are no means certain of it. He is the deadest weight to carry in this end of the district we ever had. We are fearful he is beat in Cherokee. The floating news is unfavorable. I hope Cochran is elected.[44]

The Unionists won five of the seven congressional districts. They lost the Mobile district, in which their candidate was for un-

---

[42] Mrs. Virginia Clay-Clopton, *A Belle of the Fifties*, p. 21. Cobb defeated C. C. Clay, husband of Mrs. Clay-Clopton, for Congress in 1853. She stated that in ability her husband was to Cobb "as a Damascus blade was to a meat-axe."

[43] Garrett, *op. cit.*, pp. 194-95. Rice became a Know Nothing in 1855, a secssionist again in 1861, and a Republican in 1870.

[44] Manuscript letter in Alabama Archives and History Department. Letter dated August 6, 1851.

conditional union, and the Wetumpka district, which was a Democratic stronghold.

The Southern Rights candidate received an aggregate majority of 359 in the four districts of south Alabama, but lost the two districts in north Alabama, in which they had opposition from the Unionists, by an aggregate majority of 4,566. The Southern Rights candidate was defeated in the east Alabama district by 373 majority.

The congressional results indicate, with respect to secession, that a majority of the people of Alabama were opposed to this policy in 1851, and they indicate, with respect to party politics, a strong tendency of the people to vote according to their old party affiliations. Out of a total vote of about 75,000, the aggregate majority of the Unionists was less than five thousand.[45]

The successful Unionists in north Alabama were Democrats who had become Unionists, hence the Whigs could get little encouragement from the election unless they could prevent these Democrats from returning to their old party. Only two successful candidates, Abercrombie and White, had been Whigs. This was the same number of seats held in Congress by the Whigs up to 1851.

The Unionist papers interpreted the election of 1851 as an indication that the people of Alabama would abide by the Compromise of 1850.[46] The secessionist papers, of which there were six in 1851, interpreted the results as a total surrender of the rights of the South. The *Hayneville Chronicle* said that "the proposition then amounts to a total surrender of ourselves and all we have, into the hands of an Abolition party."[47] The *Spirit of the South* said that the Southern Rights Party in Alabama seemed scattered to the four winds of Heaven. "Office, power, patronage, spoils, are magnets of greater power, than truth, justice, principle, consistency."[48]

J. J. Hooper, editor of the *Chambers Tribune,* gave the best interpretation of the effect this election would have on the political parties.

---

[45] *Spirit of the South,* August 26, 1851, claimed that the Unionist majority was only 2,229 for the entire state; the *Southern Advocate,* November 12, 1851, gave their majority as 6,200. Both estimates were based on unofficial returns. In the congressional elections in 1849, the Democrats had carried the three north Alabama districts by about 12,000 majority.

[46] *Macon Republican,* Aug. 21, 1851.

[47] *Ibid.,* Oct. 23, 1851.

[48] *Ibid.,* Oct. 23, 1851.

He stated that this election had killed the Whig Party "as dead as a mackerel," and that by the time of the election of a president in 1852, it would be difficult to find a "specimen of the Whig family." The reason for this extinction, according to Hooper, was that the rule of the Northern Whigs was abolitionward, consequently the Southern Whigs could not cooperate with them. The South had never had any interest in the protective system, but acting in good faith, it had tied itself to a popular issue and had fallen with it. The Union Whigs in several Southern states were preparing to support the Democratic ticket in 1852 as they believed that the Democratic nominee would be true to the South and the Union. The Northern Democrats, concluded Hooper, were as a rule sounder on the slavery issue than were the Whigs.[49]

The *Mobile Register* agreed with Hooper that the election had killed the Whig Party in Alabama. It stated that the late coalition of Fillmore and Seward had effectively destroyed this party in the South.[50]

The *Alabama Beacon,* a Democratic paper of Greensboro, commented on the success of the Union Party in electing a majority of the members of the legislature as follows:

> With this result we are not disappointed—nor can we say that we much regret it—notwithstanding that our sympathies are decidedly with the Southern Rights party. When Mr. Yancey, and others, hoisted the banner of Secession, we foresaw and predicted that, the *Cause of the South* would thereby be injured in the State. The result of the recent elections, will prove that we were not mistaken. *Ultraism* on one side, rarely fails to beget *Ultraism* on the other side. And the ultra doctrines of Yancey, Campbell, Cochran, and others have tended not only to paralyze the efforts of the friends of the South who occupied conservative ground, but to cause many of the Union men to take stronger grounds in favor of the Union, than they otherwise would have done. But for this ultraism, but few persons could have been found in the limits of Alabama, subscribing to, or countenancing the ultra, as we think, most dangerous doctrines promulgated by Mr. Shields, who was urged to run—

---

[49] Letter in *Alabama Journal,* Sept. 3, 1851.
[50] *Mobile Register,* cited in *Alabama Journal,* Sept. 13, 1851.

and finally, though against his wish, supported—as the Union candidate for Governor.[51]

The *Beacon's* analysis of the political thinking of the people in 1851 was an excellent one. A few people in the state favored secession and a few, on the contrary, stood for unconditional submission to the efforts of the North to restrict slavery extension. Between these groups were the great mass of the people who stood strongly against Northern aggressions, although they were divided as to the best method of defending Southern Rights into the Unionists and Southern Rights parties.

Some writers have believed that the South came near to secession in 1850-51. James Ford Rhodes concluded that secession might have occurred but for the passage of the compromise acts. Professor A. C. Cole, a careful student of party politics of this period, concluded that the danger did not cease in Alabama until after the election in August, 1851. His conclusion was based largely on sentiments expressed by the more radical papers and political speakers and these represented only a small proportion of the people of the state.[52]

Most of what was written or spoken regarding secession considered it as an abstract principle, rather than a policy to be put into practice. The *Mobile Register* gave a good exposition of the situation, saying that the Southern Rights men in the election of 1851 were contending only for the principle of secession as a super-constitutional remedy and not for the exercise of it for the then existing causes. It stated that the Union men were pledged to resist further Northern aggressions, even to a disruption of the Union, and that this position was not greatly different from that of the Southern Rights men.[53]

The newspapers in Alabama did not favor secession in 1851. According to the *East Alabamian,* of Crawford, Russell County, the attitudes of the papers in November, 1851, were as follows: for secession, six; opposed to the Compromise, nineteen; for Unionism, twenty-two; neutral in politics, three; religious, two.[54]

---

[51] *Alabama Beacon,* Aug. 16, 1851.
[52] Cole, "The South and the Right of Secession in the Early Fifties," in *Miss. Valley Hist. Rev.* (1914, I. 376-99.)
[53] *Mobile Register,* in *Alabama Journal,* Aug. 20, 1851.
[54] Cited in *Macon Republican,* Nov. 20, 1851.

On January 1, 1852, the *Macon Republican* printed the names of the forty-five papers which it received as exchanges, together with the places of publication, dates of their establishment, and their political attitudes. Twenty of these papers were for Unionism as follows:

Alabama Journal, of Montgomery; Huntsville Advocate; North Alabamian, of Tuscumbia; Mobile Advertiser; Selma Reporter; Tuscaloosa Monitor; Eutaw Whig; Eufaula Shield; Sumter County Whig, of Livingston; Macon Republican; Talladega Reporter; Chambers Tribune, of LaFayette; Alabama Argus, of Demopolis; Camden Phenix; Auburn Herald; State Register, of Montgomery; Girard Independent; Hayneville Watchman; Troy Palladium; and the East Alabamian.

Three papers were for secession as follows:

Hayneville Chronicle; Spirit of the South, of Eufaula; and the Dallas Gazette.

Nineteen papers were advocating a reorganization of the Democratic Party. They were:

Florence Gazette; Mobile Register; Huntsville Democrat; Advertiser and Gazette, of Montgomery; Jacksonville Republican; Talladega Watchman, Herald and Tribune, of Mobile; Tuscaloosa Observer; Wetumpka Guard; South Alabamian, of Greenville; West Alabamian, of Carrollton; Grove Hill Herald; Eutaw Democrat; Camden Republic; Abbeville Banner; Marion Commonwealth; Sunny South, of Jacksonville; Alabama Standard, of Montgomery; and the Sumter Democrat, of Livingston.

One paper was neutral in politics and two were denominational.

Economic conditions in Alabama were not conducive to secession. The economic situation was well described in an editorial in the *Spirit of the South* in October, 1850, as follows:

The present apparent prosperity of the South is one of the causes of whatever there may be of reluctance among her people to advocate resistance, because there is plenty to live on, because we are out of debt, and cotton brings a good price, many are in so good a humor and so well satisfied with themselves and things around them as to shut their eyes to the future in the consoling reflection that the future cannot hurt them.[55]

The *Alabama Journal* expressed the same idea in quoting an intelligent planters:

> Disunion will not give us a better price for cotton—will not increase the value of slave property—will not render them more secure—will not diminish taxation—but will be likely under the best imaginable state of affairs, to double taxation, diminish the price of our staples, and reduce the value of negroes and land, fifty per cent. I am willing to die in the last ditch for my just rights, if it becomes necessary, but have no desire to involve my own interests and those of my section in irretrievable ruin, merely for the benefit of those who have nothing to lose but everything to gain by revaluation; and who hope to ride the storm to place and power.[56]

The *Journal* added that there were many valuable citizens who agreed with the sentiments of this planter, and these men are getting tired of the system of meetings and the passing of resolutions which amount to nothing.

Just as economic conditions were operating against secession in 1850, so political factors were operating against it. Secession was impossible so long as there were two political parties with almost equal numbers, each of which had leaders whose ideas on secession were not uniform. Within both parties in 1850 were men who were divided over the degree to which, and the method by which, the rights of the South should be protected. Secession could come only with the disintegration of one of the parties, as occurred in 1860.

There were too many groups in Alabama in 1850-51, with too varied interests, and too much sectionalism, due to a lack of transportation and other factors, for one political group to get enough unanimity to carry the state out of the Union. Judge A. B. Moore, who became governor of the state in 1859, was probably not far from the truth when he wrote to Bolling Hall in November, 1850, that 99 per cent of the people of Alabama favored some kind of resistance to the North, but that few would go so far as to advocate secession as a remedy.[57]

---

[55] *Spirit of the South,* Oct. 22, 1850.
[56] *Alabama Journal,* July 23, 1850.
[57] Letter from A. B. Moore to Bolling Hall, Nov. 20, 1850, in Bolling Hall Papers.

CHAPTER IV.

THE REORGANIZATION OF PARTIES, 1851-52

The Democratic leaders began a process of reorganization soon after the election of 1851 with the purpose of recovering the political supremacy which they had lost by going into the Southern Rights movement. The *Southern Advocate,* an old Whig paper, stated that J. J. Seibels, who had been "rusticating in the Chivalry State" of South Carolina, had initiated this reorganization in a letter which he had written in September from Columbia, "the headquarters of secession," to the *Montgomery Advertiser.* This reorganization, according to the *Advocate,* simply meant "putting the state back under the "Montgomery Regency.""[1] Other prominent leaders in this reorganization were Governor Collier, Fitzpatrick, King, F. S. Lyon, and William Garrett.[2]

In an editorial in the *Advertiser,* Seibels admitted that the defeat of the Southern Rights Party in August was an indication that the "Southern people seemed determined to submit and we are determined to offer no further opposition to it."[3] The *Tuscaloosa Monitor* stated that the *Advertiser* was one of the first "lame duck" papers to get to shelter after the election.[4]

The *Advertiser* announced its support for Senator King as the Democratic nominee for the presidency in 1852. It admitted that it had not always agreed with the politics of King, but that it was willing to put aside past differences in order to get harmony in the Democratic Party.[5] King had never been an extreme States rights man and had voted for the compromise measures in 1850.

In November the Democratic leaders issued an appeal to the Democrats of Alabama to reorganize the party. This appeal stated that

----

[1] *Southern Advocate,* Sept. 17, 1851.
[2] In 1853 after the Democratic Party returned to power, the press discussed at some length the leaders to whom credit was due for the successful reorganization.
[3] *Montgomery Advertiser,* Oct. 16, 1851.
[4] *Tuscaloosa Monitor,* Nov. 6, 1851.
[5] *Montgomery Advertiser,* Sept. 27, 1851.

the cause that recently threatened the integrity and unity of the Democratic party in Alabama no longer exists. Southern people have acquiesced in the Compromise measures. Therefore Democrats must cease opposition to these measures.[6]

This appeal ended by asking the Democrats of every county to appoint delegates to a convention which was to convene in Montgomery on January 8, 1852, to select delegates to the Democratic national convention.

The Democrats had two objectives to accomplish by this reorganization—they were taking steps to get control of the legislature which was to meet in November and elect a United States senator, and they were organizing their forces to carry the state for the Democratic national ticket in 1852. Control of the legislature would be accomplished if the Union Democrats could be induced to break away from the Union Party as sixty-six of the one hundred members of the house and sixteen of the thirty-three senators were old Democrats.

Conditions were very favorable for the Democrats to reorganize their old party as they had better national leadership than had the Whigs. Influential Southern Whigs were breaking with their national party, due to a growing feeling among them that the Northern Whigs were fast becoming abolitionists. J. J. Hooper, a leading Whig, stated that, as a rule, the Northern Democracy was sounder on slavery than was the Whig Party. He said that it must be confessed that the interpretation of the Constitution by the Democrats was more favorable to the South than that of the Whigs, and candor compelled this admission although it was a bitter confession to his Whig pride to do so.[8]

The attempt of the Democrats met with opposition from both the Union Democrats and the extreme Southern Rights men. Many of the Southern Rights group were still advocating secession. The attitude of this group was expressed by the *Spirit of the South* which favored maintaining a disunion organization. This paper was not discouraged over the failure of secession but felt that the issue had

---

[6] *Alabama Journal,* Dec. 6, 1851.
[7] *Montgomery Advertiser,* Nov. 27, 1851.
[8] *Chambers Tribune,* cited in *Alabama Journal,* Sept. 6, 1851.

only been precipitated a little too early for success. In an editorial entitled "What is Our Duty" it said:

> To fold our arms in a fit of ill humor and leave our country in the currents of the maelstrom which is driving her to destruction? No in the name of God and our liberties, *No!* It is our duty to redouble our exertions; to enlighten the uninformed; to arouse the indifferent; to dispel clouds from the minds of the prejudiced; but above all, to keep up our organization, and save our people from the fatal fanaticism of old party politicians.

This paper thought that a policy of patient waiting and of gradual education would ultimately bring success to its cause.

> Time will do wonders for us. It will develop the designs of abolition, and the fatal effects of submission. Our people will become familiar with the idea of disunion; they will lose their respect for a government which fails to protect them in their rights. They will understand their rights and the principles upon which our system of government is built. And when *the fullness of time is come,* they will strike for independence and establish a Southern Confederacy, 'and the gates of hell shall not prevail against it.' ****
>
> If on the other hand we disband and squabble for the spoils of party as heretofore, all is lost—life, liberty, lands, negroes, country, all is lost—overwhelmed on the torrent of anarchy which abolition will pour upon our glorious land.[9]

Such expressions by the disunion papers embarrassed the papers which were working for reorganization of the party. The *Montgomery Advertiser* was the particular target for the attacks of the disunion papers as the *Advertiser* had been the leader for secession in 1850, and had then been the first paper to change its policy after the defeat of secession in 1851. The *Dallas Gazette* pictured the *Advertiser* in company with the Northern abolitionists who would be in the Democratic national convention which was to assemble at Baltimore.[10]

The Whigs, who were in a majority in the Union Party, were opposed to a return to the old parties as the Whig Party had been a

---

[9] *Spirit of the South,* quoted in *Macon Republican,* Oct. 16, 1851.
[10] *Dallas Gazette,* in *Montgomery Advertiser,* Mar. 16, 1852.

minority party and they realized that they could retain the advantage they had won in the election in 1851 only by maintaining the Union Party. The Unionists had a majority in the legislature which was to elect a successor to Senator Clemens, the leading Unionist of north Alabama, during the approaching session. Their only hope of reelecting Clemens was to maintain the Union Party.[11]

The chief spokesmen in opposition to party reorganization were the two old Whig papers—the *Alabama Journal* and the *Macon Republican*. The *Journal* pointed out that the Democratic leaders had been secessionists, and that some of the Democratic papers were continuing to advocate secession. The Union Party, it stated, still existed in Georgia and in Mississippi and it should not be broken up in Alabama.[12]

The *Journal* was trying to keep the Union Democrats in alliance with the Whigs. It criticized the efforts of certain Whigs who were reviling the Union Party and the Union Democrats. It claimed that the issue was not which of the Northern parties had been more conservative, but which would stand up more zealously for the preservation of the Compromise as the final settlement of the slavery agitation. In order to maintain the Compromise, the *Journal* declared that it was willing to avoid all mention in the future of the names of both the old parties.[13]

The *Macon Republican* claimed that Northern Democracy was no sounder on slavery than was Northern Whiggery.[14] It stated that the Democrats would find it difficult to reorganize their party as a majority of the members of the legislature had been elected as Unionists and were honor bound to stand for the issues on which they had been elected.[15]

A writer in the *Alabama Journal* depicted the crisis which the Whigs faced. He claimed that the Democrats were "playing a game" in bringing Senator King forward as a candidate for vice-president, for through him they could urge the Alabama Democrats to support the Democratic national ticket with the favorite son plea. He

---

[11] *Alabama Journal,* Sept. 27, 1851.
[12] *Alabama Journal,* Nov. 4, 1851.
[13] *Ibid.,* Sept. 6, 1851.
[14] *Macon Republican,* Nov. 6, 1851.
[15] *Ibid.,* Nov. 27, 1851.

admitted that a reunion of the Democrats in Alabama would kill the Whig Party.[16]

The Alabama legislature assembled on November 10, 1851, with the two new parties—Union and Southern Rights—retaining their names but with the leaders of the old parties attempting to control the election of the officers of the two houses. The Democratic leaders and press appealed to the Union Democrats and the Southern Rights Democrats to unite and elect Democrats.[17]

The results, however, were partially favorable to the Unionists who elected Charles McLemore, a Unionist and a former Whig, president of the senate. J. D. Rather, who was supported by the Southern Rights group, was elected speaker of the house by a vote of fifty-three to forty-two over Nathaniel Davis, of Limestone County.[18]

These elections encouraged the Whigs to hope that they might be able to maintain the Union Party and remain in power over their old Democratic rivals. The *Southern Advocate* stated that the old party lines were ignored in these elections and that the Union Party was never better organized than at that time.[19]

Hoping to maintain the Unionist advantage, A J. Liddell, a strong Unionist from Talladega County, introduced a resolution in the house on November 17, to bring on the election of a senator for the seat held by Senator Clemens whose term was not to expire, however, until March, 1853. The plan was to reelect Clemens while the legislature was controlled by the Unionists. A vote on a side motion showed that a majority of the house favored Liddell's resolution, but the minority by dilatory tactics was able to prevent a vote on it during the day. At the next meeting of the house a change had taken place in the attitude of the members and the resolution was defeated by a vote of fifty-one to forty-seven.[20]

---

[16] *Alabama Journal,* Nov. 26, 1851.

[17] *Montgomery Advertiser,* Nov. 8, 1851.

[18] Garrett, *op. cit.,* pp. 546-47.

[19] *Southern Advocate,* Nov. 19, 1851.

[20] Garrett, *op. cit.,* p. 548. Garrett said that this change was a surprise to many who had no knowledge of the manner in which it was brought about and at the time of the compilation of his book (1872) he did not feel it necessary to give the explanation.

All of the votes for postponement of the election were old Democrats; fifteen Democrats joined thirty-two Whigs to make the election at once. Most of the old Union Democrats of north Alabama voted with the regular Democrats and every Whig, with the exception of Mr. Byrd, of Marengo, who was absent, voted for the resolution as a party measure.[21]

The Union papers were disappointed at the result. The *Alabama Journal* stated that the Union and compromise majority in the legislature was forty, but that political treason or bad management had resulted in the will of the people being defeated. It claimed that the gallant Union Senator, Clemens, had been sacrificed by the men from his own section, whereas, south Alabama had supported him to the east.[22]

The disappointment of the Unionists was expressed in a letter written from Union Springs, Macon County, to the *Alabama Journal* by a Unionist from his observations made in Montgomery. The writer was disgruntled that the legislature had elected M. A. Baldwin, who was a close friend of the "secessionist," John Cochran, for attorney general. The writer said that he saw Nathaniel Davis and he wondered if Fitzpatrick had made old "Thanny" think that he, Davis, was to be the next governor. Fitzpatrick was certainly busy and was "as smiling as a basket of chips." The speaker (Rather) "is *some pumpkins.*" The "Fire Eaters" would use him also, though the writer. He concluded his letter by insinuating that Governor Collier was in the confidence of the Democratic leaders.[23]

The old Democratic newspapers, such as the *Montgomery Advertiser* and the *Huntsville Democrat,* were elated over the results up to this time as they foreshadowed the future success of the Democratic Party.

On November 19, the Unionists, through the committee on foreign relations, introduced a resolution in the senate to put that body on record as favoring the Georgia Platform. The Whigs were behind this resolution and its rejection or adoption was considered a question of party strength. John A. Winston, later gov-

---

[21] *Montgomery Advertiser,* Nov. 27, 1851.
[22] *Alabama Journal,* Dec. 13, 1851.
[23] *Alabama Journal,* Dec. 13, 1851.

ernor, led the opposition to this resolution, and in the words of the *Montgomery Advertiser,* "the Old Coon" made the "fur fly" in his attack upon the Whigs. Winston warned the Democrats that the resolution was only a scheme of the Whigs to throw a firebrand into the ranks of the Democrats. He attacked the Whigs for forcing a debate on an issue which the Democrats had ceased to agitate since the election of 1851.[24]

This resolution passed the senate by a vote of sixteen to fourteen. In February, 1852, it was defeated in the house, however, by a vote of forty to thirty-seven, with twenty-three members not voting. Of those not voting, fourteen were opposed to the resolution and nine favored it.[25] This was another defeat for the Unionists.

In the senate the Unionists of northeast Alabama voted with the regular Democrats of south Alabama against the resolution. In the house the hill counties of northeast and east Alabama united with those which bordered on Mississippi against the resolution, while those of the western Tennessee Valley and the Black Belt favored it. The vote indicates plainly the tendency of the Democrats of north Alabama to return to the old Democratic Party and of the Unionists of the Black Belt to return to the Whig Party.[26]

Soon after the legislature convened in November, the Democrats began to make plans for their state convention which was to meet in Montgomery on January 8, 1852. Fifty prominent leaders, including ten senators, of whom seven had been Southern Rights men and three Unionists in 1851, thirty members of the house, and ten non-members of the legislature, issued an appeal to the Democrats in every county to send full delegations to the state convention.[27]

The *Alabama Journal* attempted to discredit the efforts of the Democrats to get unity in their convention. It claimed that many of the signers of the appeal had been elected to the legislature as Unionists and it expressed the hope that their constituents would punish them later for their betrayal of a trust. It was a painful exhibition

[24] *Montgomery Advertiser,* Nov. 24, 1851.
[25] *Journal of the House,* 1851-52, pp. 405-13; *Montgomery Advertiser,* Feb. 3, 1851.
[26] *Alabama Journal,* Feb. 21, 1852; *Montgomery Advertiser,* Feb. 3, 1852.
[27] *Alabama Journal,* Dec. 6, 1851.

of fickleness on the part of the signers, to some of whom party divisions had recently been a special abhorrence. Now they were trying to restore party organizations and at a time when the South was trying to avoid all connection with national party alliances. The *Journal* concluded this attack by sarcastically wishing the Democrats success with their free soil associates of the North.[28]

The Whig press in defense began to reorganize their old party soon after the legislature convened. Daniel Sayre, editor of the *Macon Republican,* was defeated for clerk of the house. Sayre then began to make charges that Union Whigs were being discriminated against in getting appointments to offices, and he began to urge the Whigs to return to their old party.[29] The *Alabama Journal* opposed this proposal for a time but soon became convinced that the Whigs could get no patronage as Unionists. The *Journal* finally admitted the failure of the Union Party in the following editorial:

> It is plainly apparent to all "outsiders" that the multiplicity of officeholders has been the cause of the failure to organize the Compromise party in Alabama. Office seeking was the string which skillful politicians of the anti-compromise party made to vibrate for their own party purposes, as seen by results, and a great principle declared by the people at the ballot box has been set aside for the purpose of advancing personal aims of a few individuals for which the great mass of the Union party cared nothing. There is a difference of opinion as to how far the Compromise party is prostrated. We admit there are some members elected from strong Union counties who have gone over to the enemy—to the party which will not recognize the Compromise or Union principles. They will be called to account.[30]

On December 15, the *Alabama Journal* printed a call, signed by forty-two men, for a meeting in January for the purpose of maintaining a Union party. Thirty-six of the signers were members of the legislature of whom twenty-four were Whigs and twelve were Democrats. Of the twelve Democrats, seven had been elected as

---

[28] *Alabama Journal,* Dec. 6, 1851.
[29] *Macon Republican,* Dec. 3, 1851.
[30] *Alabama Journal,* Dec. 13, 1851.

Unionists from Whig counties. To avoid the charge of being called submittionists, the reorganized party was to be named the Southern Rights Union Party.[31]

The *Montgomery Advertiser* ridiculed this attempt to give new life to the old Whig Party by the use of a new name. It declared that Senator King would not advocate such a movement.[32]

The *Advertiser* at this time was using the political prestige of King and Collier, both of whom had been strongly inclined towards Unionism in 1850, but who were leaders in the reorganization of the Democratic Party in 1851, to inspire confidence in the Democratic Party.

By January, 1852, the legislature was completely under control of the old Democrats. Just prior to the day on which Democratic state convention was to meet in Montgomery, they passed a resolution to adjourn the legislature in order that the Democrats could use the house chamber for sessions of the convention.[33]

In February, just before adjournment, a bill passed the legislature which rearranged the state senatorial districts in such a way as to give an advantage to the Democrats. This act combined Whig counties in the Black Belt to form fewer Whig districts, and made an increase in the number of Democratic districts in north Alabama. The result was a net gain of three senators for the Democrats. Bills were introduced to change representation in the lower house and to readjust the congressional districts but these bills failed of passage.[34]

The senatorial apportionment law was severely criticized by the Whigs. The *Alabama Journal* claimed that it was a regular gerrymander and that its passage was due to the absence of Whig mem-

---

[31] *Alabama Journal,* Dec. 15, 1851; *Montgomery Advertiser,* Dec. 23, 1851.
[32] Issue of Dec. 22, 1851.
[33] *Southern Advocate,* Feb. 4, 1852. A writer who signed his name "Wiggle" in a letter from Montgomery, January 21, 1852, gave the *Advocate* information on the Democratic convention. He said that the "fire-eaters" and their newly found Union allies met, and that the former pushed the latter forward by giving them the promise of offices. "Wiggle" said that he would tell later how the "fire-eating Copperheads" had been able to steal off some of the Union members.
[34] *Montgomery Advertiser,* Feb. 14, 1852.

bers from the House when the vote was taken.[35] The *Journal* later stated that the Whigs yielded, even though the act deprived them of several senators, in order to prevent an extra session of the legislature.[34]

The *Montgomery Advertiser* was delighted with the act as it indicated the approaching end of the Whig Party in Alabama. In an editorial it said:

> Their (Whigs) writhings and contortions were pitiful, as they scanned the Senate apportionment bill, and behind it the winding sheet of federal whiggery. The heroic, the grave, the dignified, the farce, were all jumbled together in the most ludicrous confusion, by the Whig portion of the Senate. Col. McLemore, the President of the Senate, was the first to give way. ****
>
> Their remarks were like the last tonic spasmodic efforts of an effete party; whose grave yawned before them, and they shuddered at the sight.[37]

Two other measures were introduced which were voted upon as party questions. Thomas B. Cooper, of Cherokee County, a Unionist and a former Whig, introduced a resolution in the house to thank Senator King and Senator Clemens for their support of the compromise measures in the United States Senate. After a week of debate, this resolution was defeated, the division of votes being along old party lines.[38]

Later the legislature voted, and again on old party lines, for candidates for certain state officers. John D. Phelan, a former Democrat, was elected by a vote of sixty-seven to fifty-eight over A. R. Manning, who had been a Whig senator in 1849-50, to a seat on the Alabama Supreme court. The *Montgomery Advertiser* pointed to this election as evidence that the Democratic Party was waking up to its rights.[39]

Garrett summarized the work of the legislature of 1851-52 by saying that it had been a long session and that it accomplished

---

[35] *Alabama Journal*, Feb. 14, 1852.
[36] *Ibid.*, Feb. 21, 1852.
[37] *Montgomery Advertiser*, Feb. 17, 1852.
[38] *Macon Republican*, Dec. 11, 18, 1851.
[39] *Montgomery Advertiser*, Jan. 8, 1851.

very little.[40] It passed 425 bills, of which 410 were local bills and 18 were joint resolutions. An elaborate state aid bill sponsored by Mr. Phillips, of Mobile, failed of passage. Party strife and factionalism took up so much of the session that constructive legislation was impossible.[41]

The *Montgomery Advertiser* which was waging a fight to reduce the number of laws said that the best work of the legislature was what it refused to do, rather than what it did. Among these were: its refusal to commit the state to an endorsement of the $2,000,000 issue of bonds for railroad construction; the refusal to pass the silly resolutions on Federal relations, known as the Georgia Platform; its defeat of the efforts made to bring on the election of a United States senator; and above all, its refusal to deliver Alabama to Federal Whiggery.[42]

The *Alabama Journal* was pleased that the Phillips Internal Improvement bill had failed of passage. But this paper was disappointed that the Unionists had been defeated in their efforts to carry a Whig program through the legislature. It characterized the session as a "humbug," politically.[43] The *Journal* realized that the failure of the plan to reelect Clemens to the senate and the gerrymandering of the senatorial districts were disastrious setbacks to the Whigs.

Outside the state legislature, the old party lines were being reestablished. In 1851 Kossuth, the great Polish patriot, had visited the city of New York. Senator Clemens opposed an official reception to him in the city, whereas, Senator King had attended a dinner in his honor and had made some complimentary remarks about him.[44]

In the spring of 1852 Kossuth visited Alabama and spoke in Mobile and Montgomery. The same divided attitude was taken respecting the reception of Kossuth in the state as had been taken by the two senators in Washington. The Whig papers, such as

---

[40] Garrett, *op. cit.*, p. 554.
[41] *Southern Advocate*, Feb. 18, 1852.
[42] *Montgomery Advertiser*, Feb. 21, 1852.
[43] *Alabama Journal*, Feb. 14, 1852.
[44] *Alabama Journal*, Jan. 24, 1852.

the *Mobile Advertiser* and the *Alabama Journal* were unfriendly to him, and the Democratic papers were friendly. The *Montgomery Advertiser* said that there was nothing in Kossuth's speech in Montgomery to startle such indignation as was true in certain quarters.[45]

As a result of the efforts of the Democratic leaders and the measures which they put through the legislature, the reorganization of the Democratic Party was practically completed by the spring of 1852. Yancey who had favored secession in 1850 was now making speeches advising the people to accept the principle of the Georgia Platform. This attitude put him in the same position of Governor Collier and Senator King, neither of whom had ever been a secessionist.[46] During the session of the legislature the Union Democrats of north Alabama had voted regularly with the Democrats of south Alabama who had been for Southern Rights in 1850. The lack of complete reorganization was the refusal of a small group of extreme Unionists in north Alabama and a group of irreconcilable Democrats of the Black Belt, who were still advocating secession, to cooperate with the regular Democratic Party. The secession group was represented by four newspapers, namely, the *Hayneville Chronicle, Dallas Gazette, Camden Republican,* and the *Spirit of the South.* All of these papers were in the Black Belt.

This was the situation in the Democratic Party when the time approached to nominate a candidate for the presidency in 1852.

---

[45] *Montgomery Advertiser,* Apr. 10, 1852.
[46] *Alabama State Guard,* cited in *Alabama Journal,* Mar. 20, 1852. The *State Guard* and other Whig papers were pointing out the different positions which Mr. Yancey had occupied since 1848 and taking jibes at him for his political inconsistencies.

CHAPTER V.

DEMOCRATIC PARTY SUCCESSES, 1852-54

The Democratic Party in Alabama approached the presidential election of 1852 with every assurance of success. It had accomplished a reorganization on the basis of an acceptance of the Compromise of 1850. The nomination of Franklin Pierce for president and Senator King, of Alabama, for vice-president by the national convention, and the adoption of a plank in the national platform, opposing all efforts in or out of Congress to renew any aggressions on the South, presaged the success of the Democratic ticket. The character of the Democratic electors was such as to inspire confidence in the ticket as they were among the most prominent Democrats in the state.*

The Whigs in their county meetings were united on their adherence to the compromise measures but were divided on their choice of a candidate, and even on the advisability of their participating in the Whig national convention, which was to meet at Baltimore, since it was generally thought that this .convention would be controlled by the Northern Whigs, many of whom were considered to be abolitionists by the Southern Whigs. A majority of the Alabama Whigs favored the nomination of President Fillmore for president and sent a delegation instructed for him to the national convention.[1] Two of the party leaders, however, Alexander White and James Abercrombie, both of whom had been elected to Congress in 1851 as Union Whigs, refused to go to the convention as delegates.[2]

The nomination of General Winfield Scott by the Whig convention was a severe blow to the hopes of the Alabama Whigs. Both White and Abercrombie refused to support him, claiming that he

---

*The Democratic electors were: John A. Winston, of Sumter; James E. Saunders, of Lawrence; F. S. Lyon, of Marengo; C. W. Lee, of Perry; Lewis M. Stone, of Pickens; James Armstrong, of Lawrence; C. C. Clay, Jr., of Madison; James F. Dowdell, of Chambers.

[1] *Alabama Journal*, May 29, 1852.
[2] *Macon Republican*, May 27, 1852.

was not as good a compromise man as was Pierce. The attitude of these two men is significant in that it shows that men who were elected to Congress, where they came closely in contact with the abolition propaganda, soon became more outspoken for the Southern attitude on slavery than were their constituents back home.[3]

The nomination of Scott was used by the regular Democrats to induce the Union Democrats of north Alabama to vote the Democratic ticket by claiming that Pierce was a better Unionist than was Scott. Price Williams, elected to the legislature in 1851 as a Southern Rights man, wrote to James E. Saunders, one of the Democratic electors:

> I am glad to hear that you are doing such good work in the canvass. It is noticed in the Register and in the Advertiser & Gazette of Montgomery. The North Alabama people are afraid of and opposed to dissolution of the Union. Therefore they must vote for Genl. Pierce. But the election of General Scott would be a dangerous precedent—And I think would endanger the permanency of the Government.[4]

As has already been stated, some of the extreme Southern Rights men refused to return to the Democratic Party after its acceptance of the compromise measures in 1851. The most interesting phase of the campaign of 1852 was the activity of this group, under the leadership of Yancey.

On January 19, Yancey and forty-eight of his followers, representing several of the Black Belt counties, made a call for a Southern Rights convention to meet at Montgomery.[5] The convention assembled March 4, and contrary to general expectations, the general tenor of the convention was conservative, and curiously enough Mr. Yancey was one of the most conservative of the members. He spoke against secession and in favor of an acceptance of the Georgia Platform, but the convention did not pass resolutions favoring this position.

---

[3] *Ibid.*, July 20, 1852.
[4] Saunders Papers, in possession of J. G. Sanderson, Courtland, Alabama. Letter dated Mobile, Sept. 9, 1852.
[5] *Southern Advocate,* Feb. 11, 1852.

The convention passed a resolution to maintain a separate party organization but, due to the influence of Yancey, voted down a resolution to make separate nominations for the presidency and the vice-presidency. A standing committee was appointed, consisting of Mr. Yancey as chairman, and John A. Elmore, Jefferson Buford, Percy Walker, and J. G. Gilchrist as members.[6]

On July 12, Southern Rights delegates from eleven Black Belt counties met at Montgomery but again adjourned without making nominations.[7]

On September 13, sixty-two delegates from eight Black Belt counties met at Montgomery and nominated General Troup, of Georgia, for president, and General John A. Quitman, of Mississippi, for vice-president. Yancey attended this convention but opposed these nominations, expressing the opinion that Pierce would protect the slavery interests of the South.[8]

Yancey did not take the stump for the Southern Rights candidates during the campaign. While in attendance at court in Autauga County, he received a letter from George W. Gayle informing him that the Southern Rights men were alarmed at his silence in the campaign, and stating that it was being rumored that he would vote for Pierce. Yancey replied that he would vote for Pierce if his vote were necessary to prevent the election of Scott, but that he conceived of no such necessity, therefore he would vote for Troup and Quitman, who in every respect represented his views.[9]

Mr. Yancey's position in this campaign was an anomalous one. He found himself in line both with the conservative Whigs of the Black Belt, who were opposed to Scott, and with the regular Democrats, who were supporting Pierce. The strong Whig paper, the *Alabama Journal*, was defending Yancey and his position. This paper agreed with Yancey that it was useless for the Southern Rights men to fight for an abstraction. It stated that Mr. Yancey's speech in the Montgomery convention was cool and deliberate, and that his political motives had more honesty in them than

[6] *Spirit of the South*, Mar. 16, 1852.
[7] *Montgomery Advertiser*, July 13, 1852.
[8] *Southern Advocate*, Sept. 22, 1852; *Montgomery Advertiser*, Sept. 22, 1852.
[9] DuBose, *op. cit.*, pp. 269-70.

some of his old Democratic friends were then conceding to him.[10]

Yancey's attitude was criticized by the old Democrats. The Democratic editors pointed out that he was in agreement with the principles of their party and that he had confidence in Pierce, but that he was refusing support for the ticket. John Hardy, editor of the *State Guard,* of Wetumpka, suggested that Yancey's attitude might be due to his desire for revenge for the insult which the Democratic Party had given him in 1848 by refusing to follow his leadership.[11]

According to a statement made by the *Montgomery Advertiser* in 1858, when the *Advteriser* was supporting Yancey for United States senator, Yancey was at a distant court on business on election day and did not vote in the election of 1852.[12] His refusal to participate in the campaign for the Southern Rights ticket indicated that he was almost prepared to return to the Democratic Party, which he did in 1856. It took him about four years to make the transition from the Southern Rights Party to the Democratic Party—a transition that Fitzpatrick, Seibels, and other political leaders made within a few months.

During the campaign of 1852 the press employed the usual campaign methods, printing political charges against their opponents and stirring political songs, but the people refused to become greatly excited over the candidates or the issues. The leaders and press of each party asserted that their candidate would protect Southern Rights if elected. By this time the Alabama Whigs had given up advocacy of a protective tariff as an issue in presidential elections, which tended to remove the fundamental differences which had separated the two parties heretofore.[13]

Most of the Whig leaders and press supported Scott, but there was a strong feeling among some of them that the Northern branch of their party was too strongly tainted with abolitionism, and this belief lessened their support for the national ticket.

Most of the Democrats likewise supported their own ticket. Senator Clemens, a north Alabama conservative, J. J. Seibels, a

[10] *Alabama Journal,* Mar. 20, 1852.
[11] *State Guard,* cited in *Alabama Journal,* Mar. 20, 1852.
[12] *Montgomery Advertiser,* Oct. 13, 1858.
[13] Letter from "Talleyrand" in *Sumter County Whig,* Sept. 28, 1852.

secessionist of 1850, and Fitzpatrick, of the "Montgomery Regency," all came together in their support of Pierce and King. Every old Democratic paper except five supported the Democratic ticket. These five papers—the *Spirit of the South, Hayneville Chronicle, Grove Hill Herald, Guntersville Eagle,* and the *Dallas Gazette,* supported Troup and Quitman.[14]

The election returns showed a complete victory for the Democrats. Pierce received 26,881 votes; Scott received 16,038; and Troup, 2,174.[15] Pierce carried forty-two counties; Scott carried eight, almost all of which were in the Black Belt; and Troup carried two Black Belt counties.

Troup's small vote proved the futility of any attempt to organize a third party in Alabama at this time. His supporters were mainly Democrats, although a few Whigs voted for him. Professor Cole states that "in Alabama many Whigs supported Quitman and Troup as an alternative to voting for either Scott or Pierce."[16]

The Whig papers pointed out that the vote for Pierce was four thousand less than Cass had received in 1848; this they interpreted as an indication of the success for the Whigs in 1853, provided they could effect a reorganization by that time.[17]

The vote for Scott, however, was fifteen thousand less than Taylor had received in 1848. The stay-at-home vote showed that there was a large group of voters in each party who were dissatisfied with the principles of their parties. The total vote, which was forty-four thousand, was twenty-three thousand less than the total vote cast in the congressional elections in 1851, and was only about forty-five per cent of the number of those eligible to vote.[18]

The meeting of the presidential electors in Montgomery brought to the city and to south Alabama a young political leader from north Alabama who was to play an important part in the political

---

[14] *Macon Republican,* Oct. 17, 1852.
[15] Hodgson, *op. cit.,* p. 337.
[16] A. C. Cole, *Whig Party in the South,* p. 274.
[17] *Sumter County Whig,* Nov. 9, 1852; *Alabama Journal,* Nov. 30, 1852.
[18] There were 93,808 white males in Alabama in 1850 who were 21 years of age and over. Compendium of U. S. Census 1850, p. 50.

history of the state during the remainder of the decade. This was C. C. Clay, Jr., elector from the Huntsville district, who was elected to the United States Senate in 1853. From this time, no man in the state exercised a more important leadership than did Clay. From Montgomery, Clay wrote a letter to his wife, who was a niece of Governor Collier, which throws an interesting light on the political methods of the times. Clay wrote:

> The town is full of office-seekers & other strangers. I have been besieged by seekers of offices. Their name is legion. Your uncle Collier, with his accustomed ponderence (?), is at home, having performed his duties about certifying the election returns & vamoosed, in advance of the arrival of the office seekers. ****
>
> I have only seen Col. Seibels & Mr. Dowdell, among the electors,—all of whom I understand are here.—Tomorrow we will meet in the capitol at 12 noon, cast the vote & elect a messenger. **** [19]

The election results in 1852 showed that a majority of the people of Alabama were willing to trust the Democratic Party to protect their interests. It was the last presidential election in which the Whigs presented a regular party opposition to the Democrats. In spite of the earnest efforts of its leaders and press, it was never able to develop the strength which it had had prior to 1850. For its reward in contributing to the defeat of secession in 1850-51, it was soon to disappear as a party. Some Whigs had gone into the Southern Rights Party in 1851; some became Southern Rights members of the American or Know Nothing Party in 1855 and supporters of Breckinridge in the presidential election in 1860.

The year 1853 marked the entrance into politics in Alabama of two new issues, namely, the question of whether the state should contribute funds and its credit to the development of internal improvements, and the restriction of the sale of liquors in the state by legislative enactment.

Since the latter forties a great interest in building new means of transportation, principally railroads and plank roads, had developed. The secession agitation of the early fifties and the first enthusiasm of the people for internal improvements retarded any

---

[19] Clay Papers.

organized opposition to state aid for railroad building for several years. By 1853 there had developed a strong opposition against state aid and this opposition caused it to become an issue in the election of that year.

The other issue, the regulation of the sale of liquors, arose from the prevalence of drinking in Alabama and from a wave of moral reform which swept over the state in the early fifties. Travelers and writers bear testimony to the frequency of intemperance at that time. Saloons or dram shops were located at every cross-roads. Not infrequently ministers carried flasks of brandy in their saddle-bags while making their trips around their circuits, quoting Paul's injunction to Timothy as a justificaton for this habit.[20]

In 1847 a group of temperance reformers assembled at Decatur and organized the Sons of Temperance of Alabama. This was a secret order which had a ritual with ceremonials and passwords, put on torch light processions, in which the members wore richly colored regalia, and attracted the curious minded by maintaining an air of mystery around itself.

The Sons of Temperance grew rapidly and by 1850 was claiming a membership of 16,000. From this time there was a decline in membership and interest and the leaders decided to revive the order and secure temperance reform through a new policy, that of legislative enactment. In order to formulate a program, a Sons of Temperance convention met at Selma in November, 1852. This convention worked out a local option bill which provided that a group of voters could petition for an election to prohibit the sale of liquor within a town, precinct or county. This policy of the temperance reformers was made an issue in the election of a governor and the members of the legislature in 1853 and again in 1855.

The Democratic county conventions and press in the spring of 1853 indicated a very strong sentiment in favor of John A. Winston as the Democratic candidate for governor. Winston was born in Madison County, had removed to Sumter County, where he had become an influential planter and political leader, and had made

---

[20] B. F. Riley, *Memorial History of the Baptists in Alabama*, pp. 114-15.

a fine reputation as state senator from Sumter County. In 1852 he had been a presidental elector on the Pierce and King ticket.

Winston favored a conservative attitude toward state aid for internal improvements. This he indicated in a letter to Y. L. Royston, a prominent planter and lawyer of Perry County, in March, 1853.[21] This letter arrayed the advocates of a strong state aid policy against Winston and made him definitely the leader of the conservative state aid group. He had been an aggressive Southern Rights man in 1851 and, in consequence, was now being opposed by many of the Union Democrats of north Alabama. Most of the press of this section urged the people to send delegates to the state convention in order to nominate a man who would be more acceptable to north Alabama.[22]

The Democratic state convention met at Montgomery on May 2, 1853, to nominate a candidate for governor. The interest of the people in the convention had not been great and only thirty-eight of the fifty-two counties had sent delegates to it; the missing counties were in the northern and southeastern parts of the state. Lack of full representation was partly due to poor transportation facilities and partly due to the feeling that no opposition could defeat Winston. The *Alabama Journal* claimed that the selection of Winston had been decided upon by a few prominent Democrats who met with the members of the electoral college in Montgomery in November, 1852.[23]

Four candidates received votes for the nomination in the convention: Winston, Judge Thomas A. Walker, of Benton, Congressman S. W. Harris, of Coosa, and J. L. F. Cottrell, of Lowndes. Cottrell received sixteen votes from delegates representing Autauga, Coosa, and Lowndes counties; his name was withdrawn after the third ballot. Harris who was not a candidate received thirty-four votes from seven counties, principally in southeast Alabama. The plan to make Harris governor and then elect Bolling Hall, a member of the "Montgomery Regency," to his seat in Congress is described later. The real contest in the convention

---

[21] Garrett, *op. cit.*, p. 622.
[22] *Guntersville Eagle,* cited in *Sumter County Whig,* May 17, 1852.
[23] *Alabama Journal,* Nov. 30, 1852.

was between the north Alabama delegates, who were supporting Walker, and the south Alabama delegates, who were supporting Winston. Winston received almost the necessary majority on the seventh ballot and was nominated by acclamation on the eighth.[24]

The nomination of Winston was generally disapproved by the old Union Democrats of north Alabama who considered him a tool of the "Montgomery Regency."[25] The *Mobile Register* and most of the Democratic papers of south Alabama approved the nomination.[26] The *Montgomery Advertiser,* a strong supporter of Winston, stated that the convention was all harmony and conciliation and that "everything for principle, nothing for men was the predominant sentiment." It stated that the nomination of Winston would be hailed with joy by the Democratic Party as Winston was

> chivalrous in all his movements—a gentleman, in the true conception of the word—a warm and generous friend—a bold and magnanimous opponent—an uncompromising Democrat of the Jefferson and Madison school—quick to decide and prompt to act—he combines in himself more of the characteristics of "Old Hickory" than any public man we have among us.[27]

The Whigs could not present a united party against the Democrats in this campaign. Some of the Whig papers, among which were the *Selma Reporter* and the *Southern Advocate,* favord uniting with the Union Democrats in support of a Union Democrat for governor, with the belief that no Whig could be elected, and that it would be better to neutralize the evil of a Democratic administration by forcing the nomination and election of a Democrat who would support a policy of state aid for internal improvements.[28]

A Whig state convention met at Montgomery on June 1, 1853, to make their nomination for governor and to adopt a platform. The platform which was adopted opposed any future annexations of territory, unless the rights of the South were secured in such

---

[24] *Montgomery Advertiser,* May 11, 1852. Three of the ballots resulted as follows: first, Winston 134; Walker 42; Harris 34; Cottrell 16; third, Winston 135; Walker 66; Harris 24; Cottrell 3; seventh, Winston 151; Walker 65; Harris 18; Cottrell 0.

[25] *Southern Advocate,* May 18, 1853.

[26] *Mobile Register,* in *Montgomery Advertiser,* May 7, 1853.

[27] *Montgomery Advertiser,* May 5, 1853.

[28] *Huntsville Democrat,* June 9, 1853; *Selma Reporter* in *Southern Democrat,* Jan. 26, 1853.

territories, favored internal improvements by state aid, and the election of all state judicial officials by the people. The popular election of court officers would enable the Whigs to elect Whig officials in counties in which they were in a majority. This had hitherto been impossible as the legislature was always Democratic on joint ballot and could elect Democrats throughout the state, even in Whig counties. Richard W. Walker, of Lauderdale County, was made the nominee for governor.[29]

Walker made a speech of acceptance which had in it some elements of real statesmanship. He said that Alabama must get away from worn out and irrelevant national issues with which the state had nothing to do. He felt that the state should concentrate on the development of her own resources through internal improvements, better agricultural methods, larger commerce and manufacturing, and a better system of education.[30]

During the campaign, Walker was forced to retire, due to illness; the Whigs then supported W. S. Earnest, of Jefferson County. Some of the mountain Democrats supported A. Q. Nicks, of Talladega County, who was a Union Democrat, in preference to Winston. The Democratic papers criticized Nicks and the Union Democrats for refusing to close the breach in the party. The *Huntsville Democrat,* in particular, was bitter against Union Democrats.

During the campaign the Sons of Temperance injected their program as an issue by sending questionnaires to the three candidates asking their attitudes on the proposed local option law. Winston and Nicks refused to take a definite position, replying that they would approve any laws passed by the legislature on this question; Earnest accepted the position of the Sons of Temperance by saying that he favored local option with beats as the election units. The order thereupon held a state convention and approved Earnest as their candidate.[31]

Winston was elected by a vote of over thirty thousand to an opposition vote of about seventeen thousand. Winston's vote was

[29] *Macon Republican,* June 9, 1853; *Sumter County Whig,* June 9, 1853.
[30] *Southern Advocate,* July 13, 1853.
[31] *Southern Advocate,* July 13, 1853.

about four thousand more than Pierce had received in 1852; the total Whig vote was five thousand less than the vote Scott had received. The principal Whig strength was in the Black Belt where Earnest carried three counties. Nicks carried four counties of the mountain section; Winston carried the other forty-five counties. The stay-at-home vote in this election was about twenty thousand as compared with about thirty thousand in the presidential election of 1852.

The results of this election emphasize the growing supremacy of the Democratic Party in Alabama, and the hopeless condition of the Whig Party. The Whigs failed to get any advantage by attempting to make state aid and local option issues. The people voted largely according to their party affiliations prior to 1850. The small vote of Nicks indicated that the fusion between the two groups of Democrats was almost completely accomplished by 1853. DuBose, Yancey's biographer, summed up the election in these words: "So complete was the reconciliation between parties that the Secessionist, John Anthony Winston, was chosen Governor without appreciable opposition."[32] It should be added that secession was not an issue in this election.

The Democratic success in the congressional elections was almost as sweeping as in the gubernatorial election. They won six of the seven districts, the successful candidates being equally divided between Union Democrats and Southern Rights Democrats. James Abercrombie, in the Montgomery district, was the only Whig to be elected.

Philip Phillips, a Southern Rights Democrat, was elected in the Mobile district over Lockwood, a Whig Unionist, by a majority of about one hundred, which was fourteen hundred less than the majority of the Southern Rights candidate in this district in 1851. The Whig papers explained the defeat of Lockwood as a defection of the Whigs, due to a promise made by Phillips to support a harbor and river bill for the improvement of the port of Mobile.[33]

The campaign in the Montgomery district was interesting and hard fought. James Abercrombie, who had been elected a Union

[32] DuBose, *op. cit.*, p. 273.
[33] *Southern Advocate*, Aug. 17, 1853.

Whig in 1851 and who had refused to support the Whig national ticket in 1852, was opposed by David Clopton, a lawyer of Tuskegee. The district was strongly Whig but the past political instability of Abercrombie gave the Democrats hope of electing Clopton. A writer in the *Montgomery Advertiser* pointed out the various political positions which Abercrombie had occupied as follows: in 1832, he favored South Carolina and its nullification; in 1844, he was for Whig Federalism; in 1849-50, he supported Southern Rights in the Alabama legislature; in 1850, he was a delegate to the Nashville convention and soon after this convention he began to oppose the Southern Rights movement; in 1852, he refused to support the Whig nominee for the presidency.

The old Whig papers—the *Alabama Journal* and the *Macon Republican*—gave Abercrombie only a moderate support. The *Montgomery Advertiser,* which was strongly for Southern Rights, put party welfare foremost and supported Clopton as a party duty. The *Spirit of the South* and a group of Southern Rights men in the southern counties of the district supported Abercrombie on the ground that he was a stronger defender of the rights of the South than was Clopton.[34]

Abercrombie won by a majority of more than sixteen hundred, which was practically his majority in 1851. He lost about one thousand Whig votes in the three Black Belt counties in the district, but gained almost an equal number of votes in the white counties in the lower part of the district as compared with his vote in 1851. The *Montgomery Advertiser* in commenting on the results stated that the Whigs voted against Abercrombie in order to punish him for his lack of party loyalty in 1852. The *Advertiser* said that such lack of party fidelity *"strikes at the very vitality of all parties."*[35]

S. W. Harris, whose name had been placed before the state convention as a candidate for governor in May, was reelected easily in the Wetumpka district over his Whig opponent, Moore, by a majority of almost 4,800. In 1851, Harris had carried the district by less than six hundred.

An effort had been made in the spring to break Harris' political control over the district by the nomination of Bolling Hall, of

---

[34] *Alabama Journal,* Apr. 5, 1853; *Montgomery Advertiser,* Apr. 16, 1853; *Spirit of the South,* in *Montgomery Advertiser,* May 7, 1853.

[35] *Montgomery Advertiser,* Aug. 17, 1853.

Autauga County, as the Democratic candidate in place of Harris. It appears to have been a part of the plan to remove Harris as a competitor by securing the nomination for governor for him. Hall was a close political friend of Fitzpatrick and the other members of the so-called "Montgomery Regency." It is impossible to determine whether this plan was originated by Hall or by his friends. The details of the plan are interesting and they illustrate the methods of these political leaders so well that they are given in full.

Early in January, 1853, John Hardy, who had been editor of the Wetumpka *State Guard,* went to Selma, which was in the most western county of the district, and established a newspaper which Hall was to finance.[36]

In a letter from Cahaba, January 28, 1853, Hardy informed Hall of the political outlook in the district. He was of the opinion that both Union and Southern Rights Democrats in the district were opposed to Harris; that if a convention were called, Harris would never "touch the bottom" and that Hall's chances of getting the nomination would be good. Hardy added that he had written an article to the Hayneville paper, in Lowndes County, advocating a district convention in May or June. He had done this, he wrote, as a partial reply to an article which had appeared in the We- *State Guard* signed by "Autauga." Hardy advised Hall not let it be known that his paper, the *State Sentinel,* was being financed by Hall as it would paralyze Hardy's efforts for him. He said that he had let Dorsey into the plan and that Dorsey was also advocating the calling of a convention.[37] Dorsey had succeeded Hardy as editor of the Wetumpka *State Guard* and his paper also was receiving financial aid from Hall.

About the time that Hardy set up the *State Sentinel* in Selma, there appeared in the *Montgomery Advertiser* a letter signed by "Dallas Democrat" which named the qualifications which the Democratic nominee for governor in 1853 should have. The writer stated that the "gifted and eloquent S. W. Harris of Coosa" fulfilled all the requirements mentioned. This letter had the earmarks of having

---

[36] Bolling Hall Papers; *Montgomery Advertiser,* Feb. 5, 1853.
[37] Bolling Hall Papers.

been written by Hardy as a part of the plan to send Hall to Congress by securing the nomination for governor for Harris.[38]

About this same time there appeared some activity in southeast Alabama to nominate Harris for governor. It was announced that Coffee County had come out for Harris. This county was under the political control of Gappa T. Yelverton, who was a close political friend of Hall and Fitzpatrick.[39]

In April, Hardy made a visit to Wetumpka, his old home. While returning to Selma, he wrote to Hall that he was full of fear that Harris would get the nomination for Congress, even though a convention were called at Selma. He based his opinion on resolutions which had been passed by several county meetings in the district. He promised Hall that he would try to manipulate the Selma convention for him, and, in the meantime, Hall must see to it that a delegation friendly to himself be selected in Autauga County and sent to the convention. Hardy, in conclusion, advised Hall to be a candidate for reelection to the state legislature.[40]

After Hardy returned to Dallas County he wrote Hall that if the Selma convention were discreetly directed he felt that Hall would get the nomination. He stated that the Southern Rights men were opposed to Harris and that the Union Democrats were supporting Judge G. D. Shortridge for Congress.

The Selma convention gave the nomination to Harris, Hardy then wrote that the situation during the convention had made him doubt the advisability of putting Hall's name before it, and that Major Elmore, another member of the "Regency," had agreed with him in this opinion. He warned Hall not to expect any gratitude from Major Harris. He informed Hall that he would bring him out as a candidate for speaker of the lower house of the legislature.[41]

We resume now the account of the elections in the remaining congressional districts.

---

[38] *Montgomery Advertiser,* Jan. 15, 1853. There is no evidence that the *Advertiser* was a party to this plan.

[39] *Spirit of the South,* cited in *Montgomery Advertiser,* Feb. 9, 1853.

[40] Bolling Hall Papers, letter dated April 23, 1853, and written on board the *Magnolia* on the Alabama River.

[41] Bolling Hall Papers, May 13, 1853.

The contest in the Tuscaloosa district was complicated. Two candidates—General Sydenham Moore, a Southern Rights Democrat, and S. F. Hale, a Whig—opposed the reelection of William R. Smith, who was a Union Democrat. Smith received a plurality of seventy-one over Moore, his nearest opponent. Smith carried only Fayette and Tuscaloosa counties, but each gave him a majority of about seven hundred over Smith which was sufficient to elect him.[42] Smith's majority in 1851 had been fifty-nine.

G. S. Houston was reelected without opposition in the Florence district.

C. C. Clay, Jr., opposed W. R. W. Cobb in the Huntsville distrist. Both were Democrats but Cobb was more strongly Unionist and received the support of the Union Democrats and the Whigs, which enabled him to win by a majority of fourteen hundred. He carried every county in the district, except one, by substantial majorities.[43] The *Huntsville Democrat,* edited by J. Withers Clay, brother of the defeated candidate, attributed the defeat of Clay to the support which the Union Democrats gave to Cobb. This election convinced the *Democrat* that a Union Democrat was no better than a Whig.

In the Talladega district the candidates made an issue of the question of whether secession was an abstract or a revolutionary right. Thomas G. Garrett, the Union Whig candidate, held to the revolutionary right of secession; James F. Dowdell, the Southern Rights Democrat, claimed that secession was an abstract right. The Whigs were at a great disadvantage in this campaign because their leader, Alexander White, who had been elected to Congress in 1851, had refused to support Scott for president in 1852 and was still at odds with his party. The district was nominally Democratic but it had elected a Union Whig in 1851, due in part, to the unpopularity of the Democratic candidate. In this election the district returned to the Democraic fold by a majority of about 2,800.[44]

The legislature which convened in November, 1853, was composed of fifty-nine Democrats and forty-one Whigs in the house, and twenty Democrats and thirteen Whigs in the senate. The

---

[42] *Southern Advocate,* Aug. 17, 1853.
[43] *Ibid.,* Aug. 24, 1853.
[44] *Dadeville Banner* in *Sumter County Whig,* July 12, 1853.

Democrats elected without opposition William Garrett, of Coosa County, speaker of the house. In the contest for president of the senate, the Democrats elected J. P. Frasier, of Jackson County, over William B. Martin, of Benton County, who was supported by the Whigs. The two old parties had by this time again taken their old party names and the Whigs were in a hopeless minority. The safe majorities of the Democrats in each house enabled the party leaders to concentrate on constructive measures, rather than on measures for party advantage, and more constructive legislation was passed at this session than had been passed at any session since the one of 1847-48.

One of the important matters before the legislature was the election of two United States senators. Senator Clemens' term had expired in March, 1853, and the term of Senator Fitzpatrick, who had been appointed to fill the vacancy caused by the election of Senator King to the vice-presidency, was to expire in March, 1855.

Clemens was entirely out of favor with the Democrats as he had not cooperated with the party since he had become a Unionist in 1851. And the charges that he had made promises to the Whigs to secure their support for him in 1849 were being repeated. The *Montgomery Advertiser*, which had lead the fight to prevent his re-election by the legislature in 1851, printed in April, 1852, a letter which, it claimed, exposed the bargain by which Clemens had been elected in 1849. This letter, dated November, 30, 1849, was said to have been written by a Whig member of the legislature from an important south Alabama county and was addressed to a Democratic colleague. This letter was as follows:

> You will observe with what integrity we voted for Judge H(opkins) for the long term, and with nearly unanimity for the 2nd term on the 2nd day against Gov. F(itzpatrick)—F. lacked only 1 vote & would have got *it* had another ballot been *taken*—we got adjournment; that night talked it over & **** made a new move. * * * *

> I feel constrained to let you guess, or find out elsewhere, whether we made overtures to the Taylor *democrat,* Jere Clemens, or his friends to us, or *he* to us—suffice it is to say that all parties in the premises, and all parties but one are pleased. We have gained a supporter of the Administration.

North Alabama has obtained a geographical representation, and the Hunkers are glad that their own choice is defeated.[45]

Among the Democrats it was generally agreed that Senator Fitzpatrick was to be elected. The only problem was to determine what Democrat of north Alabama should be awarded the seat of Clemens. For this place there were a number of candidates—Clemens, William Acklen, L. Pope Walker, and C. C. Clay, Jr., all of Madison County; D. C. Humphreys, of Morgan; David Hubbard, of Lawrence; and Congressman Houston, of Limestone.

Hubbard had been connected in some capacity with the state government almost from its beginning and possessed the elements of character requisite for leadership. But in the thirties he had been a supporter of Calhoun and his nullification principle and this now operated against him in his section where Jacksonian Democracy was strongly accepted.[46] Acklen, Walker and Humphreys had not been able to develop much strength, and it was thought that the contest would become one between Houston, who had the support of the Union Democrats, and Clay, who was being supported by the Black Belt Democrats, when the legislature should meet in November.

Two months before the legislature was to assemble, Clay had undertaken to get the support of the Montgomery group of political leaders. In September, he wrote a full and frank opinion of the senatorial situation to Bolling Hall. He felt sure, he stated, that Fitzpatrick would be elected one of the senators, which should be, to vindicate Fitzpatrick and to rebuke those who had defrauded him of his rights by electing Clemens in 1849. The other senator should be from north Alabama as this would tend to harmonize the party. But this senator must be from the States Rights wing of the party as the Whigs were determined to unite with the *Union Democrats,* whom them termed *conservatives,* and crush the Southern Rights group.

Clay said that the greatest danger to the Democratic Party was not the opposition of the Whigs, but that of the Union Democrats

---

[45] *Montgomery Advertiser,* April 17, 1852.
[46] Garrett, *op. cit.,* pp. 297-98.

in north Alabama who were able to get the support of the Whigs against States Rights Democrats. He emphasized this menace by pointing out some election returns in north Alabama in the recent election for governor. Winston was beaten by the Union Democratic candidate in DeKalb and Marshall; he received a bare majority in Madison; and the least majority a Democrat ever received in Blount, Jackson and St. Clair counties. And yet, there was a regular Whig candidate who received only three votes in Madison out of a total vote of 1800. Clemens voted an open ticket for Nicks, the Union Democratic candidate; Cobb refused to declare how he voted.

Clay said that Cobb's political control over north Alabama must be broken; the Whigs had hitherto elected him and would continue to do so unless his control over the masses could be broken. He would always be able to command the votes of the people of the country, who could not or would not read, against any lawyer, townsman or States Rights man—all of whom were considered suspicious characters by the Cobb followers. The Whigs in the legislature were using Cobb as they had used Clemens—as a means of defeating better Democrats. Cobb and Clemens, as individuals, could not mislead the people, but as congressmen, their votes were potent with the people. Clemens was closely affiliated with the Whigs and with Cobb. The States Rights Democrats will have to take steps to counteract their influence.

Clay then presented his claims to the high honor. He stated that he was a good party man and that no man of his age had worked harder for the party than he had. He wanted to redeem himself for his defeat in the congressional election of 1853 at the hands of "that ass" Cobb, who had defeated Clay by getting the support of the Whigs and the pseudo-Democrats and by claiming that Clay was a disunionist, simply because Clay stood for Southern Rights. Whether they could keep him down, Clay admitted, would depend upon his friends in south Alabama.

Clay ended his letter by giving Hall permission to show it, in confidence, to any of his friends.[47]

---

[47] Bolling Hall Papers.

The Whig press and leaders realized that they would not be able to elect a Whig to the Senate. The *Southern Advocate* admitted that there would be no hope for a Whig if the "Montgomery Regency" selected a Democratic candidate in a caucus. This paper advised the Whigs to hold aloof, in the hope that the Democrats would do the "Kilkenny act" of killing each other off.[48] The *Alabama Journal* felt that the Whigs should adopt the policy of attempting to force the Democrats to elect an anti-Pierce Democrat.

When the election of the senators came up in the legislature, the idea embodied in Clay's letter to Hall was carried out. Fitzpatrick was elected for the term which was to expire in March, 1855, receiving one hundred seven votes. Later in the session, Clay was elected to succeed Clemens, receiving eighty-five votes. Forty-three votes were cast against Clay, of which R. W. Walker received thirty-seven and Clemens six.[49]

The election of Fitzpatrick and Clay was considered a triumph for Southern Rights by the Unionists and the conservative Whigs, who considered both of them as "fire-eaters."[50]

Despite the defeat given to Clemens by the Democrats in 1853, he continued to have a large political following in north Alabama. An effort was made shortly before his term as senator ended to secure for him an appointment to the cabinet of President Pierce. Ex-Governor Clay wrote to his son, Senator C. C. Clay, Jr., on January 9, 1854, that

> it has been rumored that he (Clemens) would get into the Cabinet in a certain contingency—but I have maintained that it was impossible that a man who had betrayed his party and gotten into the Senate by private pledges to the Whigs—to say nothing of his bad moral habits and principles—could receive from such a President as Franklin Pierce, such high wideness of confidence and trust. It may be that the President is not fully informed of the character and conduct of that reckless and unprincipled man—if so you who desire to preserve the integrity and purity of the party—should place him in possession of the facts, the damaging facts of his political

[48] *Southern Advocate,* Aug. 17, 1853.
[49] Garrett, *op. cit.,* p. 582.
[50] *Southern Advocate,* Dec. 7, 1853.

course. In a word, to appoint Jere to any high office, would be, in effect, to offer a premium for political tragedy.[51]

Clay concluded his letter by asking that his regards be given to Senator Fitzpatrick and to Congressmen Harris and Phillips. He suggested that Fitzpatrick be permitted to read the political portions of the letter.

Senator Clay replied that Clemens did not stand well with the cabinet members; Davis, Marcy and McClelland disliked him very much. He said that Pierce had been reckoned Clemens' personal friend, but that he was probably displeased with Clemens' position on the Kansas bill.[52]

After the election of two Democratic senators, the next political issue which was presented in the legislature was a bill, introduced by the Whigs, to change the principle upon which congressional districts were laid out. The principle which had been used since 1843 was known as the White Basis, because in reckoning population in the formation of congressional districts the white population alone was counted, slaves not being considered. This principle gave the white counties of north Alabama an advantage in representation as compared with the counties of the Black Belt. It was maintained, however, by a combination of the Democrats of the Black Belt with those of north Alabama as a party measure against the Whigs. The Black Belt Democrats furnished the leadership and the north Alabama Democrats furnished the numbers which gave the Democrats political control of the state.

The White Basis had been advocated by Governor Fitzpatrick in his message to the legislature in 1842 and had passed almost entirely by a party vote.[53] An unsuccessful attempt was made during the session of 1843-44 to change to the Mixed Basis principle which would count slaves in the formation of congressional districts.[54] During the session of 1859-50, Mr. Blevins, a Whig of Dallas County, introduced a bill to change to the Mixed Basis. During the debates on this bill the Whigs made the argument that the very safety of the South depended upon a recognition of

[51] Clay Papers.
[52] Clay Papers, Mar. 14, 1854.
[53] Garrett, op. cit., pp. 246-50.
[54] Ibid., pp. 340-41.

slavery by counting slaves in laying out congressional districts. They quoted Mr. Calhoun who had claimed that the White Basis was "the entering wedge of abolitionism." Calhoun contended that if the South did not carry out the clause in the Constitution which provided for the counting of negroes as three-fifths in apportioning representation, he did not see why the South should criticize the North for refusing to do so.[55] Blevins' resolution failed of passage by a strict party vote.[56]

Another attempt to change to the Mixed Basis was made during the session of 1851-52 and was defeated. The *Huntsville Democrat,* an advocate of the White Basis, claimed that the Mixed Basis would give the Black Belt politicians control of the state and would possibly lead to secession.[57]

The Whig press renewed the agitation for a change to the Mixed Basis during the political campaign of 1853. The following arguments were advanced in favor of it:

1. The Constitution of the United States puts representation on a population basis, reckoning ngroes as three-fifths of the whites.

2. All Southern states except Alabama have the Mixed or Federal Basis.

3. Alabama might get two additional congressmen by counting slaves in ascertaining population.[58]

The *Alabama Journal* lead the fight to get the legislature in 1854 to adopt the Mixed Basis. The *Journal* pointed out the injustices to the Black Belt counties of the White Basis by making a comparison of the Mobile and the Huntsville congressional districts.

In the Mobile district there were 61,381 white people and 87,254 slaves—a total population of 148,635—with 15,588 voters and one congressman. In the Huntsville district there were 60,164 whites and 20,109 slaves—a total population of 80,273—with 11,455 votes and one congressman. Thus with 1217 fewer white population and 57,145 fewer slaves, the district composed of white counties

---

[55] *Alabama Journal,* Jan. 22, 1850.
[56] *Ibid.,* Feb. 16, 1850.
[57] *Huntsville Democrat,* in *Southern Advocate,* Nov. 26, 1851.
[58] *Sumter County Whig,* July 5, 1853.

had the same representation in Congress as had the district with the large slave population. To state it another way, 57,145 slaves of the Mobile district had no representation in Congress as compared with the Huntsville district. And this discrimination, according to the *Journal*, was made against a district which paid $145,000 taxes into the state treasury in 1852 as compared with $36,604 which the Huntsville district paid for the same year.[59] The *Journal* did not think that the slaveholders should surrender this great principle in order to gain some party strength in some county or district.

During the debate on this question in the legislature, the *Montgomery Advertiser* and most of the Democratic papers of the Black Belt were silent on the proposed change.

On January 20, 1854, the Senate by a vote of nineteen to fourteen defeated the bill which provided for a change to the Mixed Basis. The vote was largely political and sectional. Only one Whig and two Democrats broke party lines in their votes; the Whig counties of the Black Belt voted for the bill and the Democratic counties of north and south Alabama opposed it.[60]

During the session of the legislature of 1855-56 another attempt to change to the Mixed Basis was defeated and the White Basis remained the basis for the formation of congressional districts through the remainder of the decade.

The Democrats not only defeated the Whigs on the White Basis principle in this legislature, but strengthened their political control over the state by rearranging the congressional districts by an act which had the earmarks of a gerrymander.

The greatest changes were made in the Montgomery, Wetumpka and Talladega districts—all located in the central and eastern parts of the state. Montgomery, Macon and Russell—three important Black Belt counties which had been in the old Montgomery district (the second)—were placed in the third district which was carried by the Democrats in the election of 1855. Lowndes and Butler were put in the second district; this district also gave the Democrats a majority in 1855. By these changes the "Montgomery Regency" was able to control two important districts in which

---

[59] *Alabama Journal*, Feb. 18, 1854.
[60] *Ibid.*, Jan. 28, 1854.

their control had formerly been threatened by the Whigs. In this readjustment, Dallas County was placed in the Mobile district, which elected an American to Congress in 1855.

This reappointment act was largely a party measure but some of the Whigs voted for it as they considered it no worse than the districting act of which it took the place—a Democratic act which had been passed in 1843.[61]

The *Alabama Journal* claimed that the act was a gerrymander. It pointed out the injustice of the act by showing that, although the Whigs numbered forty per cent of the population of the state, they could elect only two congressmen out of the total of seven under this act.[62] The *Montgomery Advertiser* did not deny that the apportionment was favorable to the Democrats and admitted that it would not give the Whigs a single congressman if it could prevent it.[63]

This reapportionment act of 1854 did not give the Democrats a net gain in congressmen but it enabled them to elect congressmen in a Black Belt district which had been the stronghold of the Whigs.

Late in the session, David Hubbard, who had been a strong Southern Rights advocate in 1850, introduced in the house a resolution which had been prepared in the committee on Federal relations which stated that if the interests of the South were threatened by hostile legislation of Congress, Alabama would resist this legislation. The debate on this resolution showed that it was not regarded as a party question. Mr. Belser, a Whig of Montgomery, agreed that if the Nebraska Bill were passed with any feature of it in violation of the constitutional rights of the South, he, for one, would be in favor of resistance to it to the uttermost. This speech brought applause from both Whigs and Democrats. Some of the members felt that it was not best to agitate the question but the resolution was passed by a vote of forty-two to fourteen.[64]

[61] *Alabama Journal,* in *Sumter County Whig,* Feb. 22, 1854.
[62] *Alabama Journal,* Mar. 4, 1854.
[63] *Montgomery Advertiser,* in *Alabama Journal,* Mar. 4, 1854.
[64] *Montgomery Advertiser,* Feb. 16, 1854.

The debates in Congress in the spring of 1854 on the Kansas-Nebraska question caused much excitement in Alabama. The Democratic press as a rule opposed Douglas and his popular sovereignty policy. They were taking the position that the Constitution protected all of the slavery interests of the South and that there was no constitutional method of limiting the extension of slavery—the same attitude which the Supreme Court later took in the Dred Scott decision. The Whigs as a rule opposed a repeal of the Missouri Compromise and a reopening of the question of slavery extension.[65]

The political position of the Whigs was an embarrassing one. Hilliard, T. H. Watts, and the other leaders were attempting to maintain the Whig Party on the principles of the Compromise of 1850, but their efforts were made almost void by the activities of the Whig abolitionists of the North. Hodgson expressed the difficult position of the Whigs by writing that no mortal "could brook the assaults which New England was hurling at the South and live.[66]

The Whigs were being driven gradually into an acceptance of the Southern Rights principles. Most of them were not ready by 1855 to cooperate with the Democratic Party, however. A majority of them went into a new party which was being organized in Alabama in 1854, and which was to play a large part in the politics of the state for the next two years. This new party was the American Party, or Know Nothing Party, as it was more commonly called.

---

[65] *Montgomery Advertiser,* May 20, 1854; *Alabama Journal,* Mar. 25, 1854.
[66] Hodgson, *op. cit.,* p. 343.

Chapter VI

THE KNOW NOTHING CAMPAIGN OF 1855

The Know Nothing movement was initiated in the North as early as 1849 as a protest against the further immigration of foreigners into this country, and as an attack upon the Catholics within the country.[1] Know Nothingism was spreading in the early fifties when the various reform movements and *isms*—abolitionism, temperance reform, woman's suffrage, feminism—were sweeping over the country, and it fused with these movements.

The Know Nothing movement first became evident in Alabama about 1854. It soon attracted many people, even though foreigners made up only two per cent of the entire population of the state and Catholics less than two per cent of it. The leaders used subtle methods to attract followers. They would approach the editor of a newspaper or a political leader and present arguments against foreigners, pointing out that these people were ignorant and intemperate, and were the tools of political demagogues, and that they banded together in the cities to break down persons who dared to oppose them.[2]

The claim of the Know Nothings, or Americans as they called themselves, that they advocated Americanism made a strong appeal, as it still does, to certain classes. The secrecy features attracted many members and was particularly fascinating to young men, radicals and to men who had been unsuccessful in politics.

The leaders attempted to give prestige to the order by reporting that certain prominent men of the state were members. John Cochran, a leader in the "Eufaula Regency," was claimed at one time to be a member, and at one time John Forsyth, editor of the *Mobile Register,* had to deny a statement made by the *State Sentinel* that he was the grand scribe of the American lodges in the state.[3]

-----

[1] Rhodes, *History of the U. S.,* II. 6-13.
[2] *Dallas Gazette,* May 25, 1855.
[3] *Alabama Journal,* Feb. 2, 1855.

There was a rumor that Yancey was a member but he denied this in a letter written from Montgomery on June 23, 1855, to W. H. Thorington, although he admitted that he believed in some of the aims and purposes of the order. He disclaimed any intention of participating in the approaching campaign.[4] Later Yancey stated that there was no difference between the attitudes of the Democrats and the Americans on the power of Congress to regulate slavery expansion.[5]

From the first, the regular Democratic leaders looked with suspicion on the Know Nothing movement, as they considered it a scheme of the Whigs to defeat the Democrats.[6] The secrecy features were sufficient to frighten the Democrats, and they began to portray the dangers which a secret order carried with it. The Democratic press claimed that the order was attracting people who sought crooked ways of accomplishing any aim or purpose, and those who wanted to work out their deeds in darkness, and that the order was becoming the refuge of the malicious and the violent. The editor of the *Dallas Gazette* felt that the teachings of the order were as dangerous as had been those of the Jacobins of Paris during the French Revolution. He believed, however, that only a small proportion of the members of the order were dangerous men, but feared that ultimately the minority might get control of the order and, through it, get control of the government. To say the least, this editor wrote, the whole period of the French Revolution with its mob rule should be a warning to the people of Alabama.[7]

The *Montgomery Advertiser,* although hostile to the order, expressed a less gloomy opinion of the aims of its members. It stated that the Know Nothings had a new interpretation of the Declaration of Independence and that the purpose of government to them was to secure "life, liberty, and the pursuit of Irishmen."[8]

The warning of the *Dallas Gazette* and other papers did not seem groundless as violence had marked the first election in Alabama in which the American Party had participated. Rioting had taken

---

[4] *Dallas Gazette,* July 13, 1855; DuBose, *op. cit.,* pp. 294-97.
[5] *Alabama Journal,* July 14, 1855.
[6] *Dallas Gazette,* May 18, 1855.
[7] *Dallas Gazette,* June 8, 1855.
[8] *Montgomery Advertiser,* Mar. 20, 1855.

place in the city election in Mobile n the fall of 1854.[9]   A masked
mob had severely beaten a Catholic priest near Mobile and the
American press had partially defended the action of the mob on
the ground that the priest had been guilty of wrongdoing.[10]

The Americans were successful in the first elections in Alabama
in which they had participated.   In the fall of 1854 this party had
elected mayors in both Mobile and Montgomery over Democratic
candidates.   In Montgomery the American candidate, C. R. Hansford defeated P. H. Brittan, the Democratic candidate, by a vote of
339 to 134.   The defeat was particularly humiliating to the Democrats as Brittan was associated editor of the *Montgomery Advertiser,*
the leading Democratic newspaper in the state.   The *Montgomery Mail,*
a leading American paper, stated that Brittan was popular, but
that the Know Nothing strength was sufficient to defeat any
Democrat.[11]

Encouraged by these local successes, the Americans began to
organize for the state elections of 1855.   In January they held a
convention in Mobile for the purpose of organizing a party, adopt-
ing a platform and nominating a candidate for governor.   The
convention adopted a policy of attempting to make a fusion with
the Democrats who were opposing Winston and his state aid
policy.   It made no nomination for governor but discussed the
candidacy of four men, all of whom were Democrats.   The convention was divided over the advisability of nominating a state aid
man as there was strong opposition to state aid in the country districts.[12]   The convention took no definite action on the question of
temperance which was being agitated at this time.

The great weakness of the American movement, which became
so evident later, was apparent at this time.   This was the impossi-
bility of satisfying the various groups in their various demands,
and of fusing the factions into a real unified party.   Party traditions and party principles upon which a majority of the members
of the convention could agree were lacking.[13]

---

[9] *Mobile Register,* in *Dallas Gazette,* Sept. 15, 1854.
[10] *Mobile Advertiser* in *Dallas Gazette,* June 8, 1855.
[11] *Montgomery Mail,* Dec. 7, 1854.
[12] *Alabama Journal,* Jan. 27, 1855.
[13] *Mobile Register,* in *Alabama Journal,* Jan. 20, 1855.

During the spring of 1855 the Whig leaders were hopelessly divided on what should be the future policy of the party. The influential Whig papers of the Black Belt— the *Alabama Journal, Chambers Tribune, Macon Republican,* and *Selma Reporter*—were attempting to maintain the old Whig Party by calling a state convention to nominate a Whig candidate for governor. Other Whig papers and leaders were advocating a fushion with the Americans and anti-Winston Democrats.[14]

The *Alabama Journal* thought that the only way to defeat Winston was to nominate a regular Whig. It opposed fusion with the state aid group and putting the leadership in the hands of the latter. It would be disastrous to make state aid an issue, as only a small group of Democrats favored this policy, and most of the Whigs were opposed to it as it offered railroad speculators the opportunity of making raids on the state treasury. The *Journal* urged the Whigs to nominate Hilliard, whom it considered the best man in the party, and to appeal to all Whigs to support him on the basis of party loyalty.[15] The *Journal* was opposed at this time to any fusion with the Americans.

The *Journal* was not hostile to Winston; it favored his attitude towards state aid, but it refused to support a Democrat, due to its opposition to the national Democratic Party with its "loco-humbuggeryism."[16]

The *Sumter County Whig,* probably the most influential Whig paper in the western part of the Black Belt, was willing to support a state aid Democrat, if, by doing so, it might defeat Winston.[17] The cross purposes of the leaders show the hopeless condition in which the Whigs found themselves in 1855.

The first candidate to be suggested for governor by the state aid Democrats was Robert A. Baker, a prominent planter of Dallas County, who was brought out by John Hardy in an editorial in the

---

[14] *Alabama Journal,* Mar. 24, 1855.

[15] *Ibid.,* Jan. 13, 1855.

[16] *Alabama Journal,* Jan. 14, 1855. The Whigs often referred to the Democrats as the "Locos" or "Loco Focos."

[17] *Sumter County Whig,* Oct. 18, 1854. The *Whig* later suggested one of the following as a suitable candidate on a state aid-Whig ticket: Robert A. Baker, G. D. Shortridge, A. J. Pickett, R. W. Walker, L. Pope Walker, Percy Walker.

Alabama State Sentinel. After Hardy's failure to elect Bolling Hall congressman in 1853, he seems to have lost his affiliation with the political leaders of Montgomery, and by 1855 he had become a convert to state aid and was fighting the Democratic Party on this issue. Hardy printed a petition signed by eighty-three men, representing Whigs, Democrats, state aid men, and temperance reformers, urging Baker as the candidate. Baker owned a commission house in Mobile and this, together with his planting interests in Dallas County, made him the logical candidate for the support of these strong state aid. coutnies.[18]

The *Dallas Gazette* interpreted the Baker boom as a scheme to beat Winston and the Democratic Party. It pictured Baker as the embodiment of every kind of *ism,* just exactly like a New England abolitionist. The *Gazette* admitted that Baker was clever, upright, pious to fanaticism, especially on the liquor question, and that he was an excellent singer at church revivals.[19]

The *Montgomery Mail* came out for Baker, but the *Alabama Journal* and *Macon Republican* refused to support him. The *Journal* felt that the people of the state were with Winston in his opposition to state aid, and it believed the only way to defeat him would be to nominate a Whig who could get the support of the disaffected Democrats.[20]

During the spring, the Democrats were having no difficulty in determining a policy and selecting a candidate for the approaching campaign. The laws which the Democratic legislature of 1853-54 had passed, and the policy of Governor Winston in vetoing state aid acts and temperance acts, had been received with approval by a majority of the Democrats, through resolutions passed by county meetings and by the press, and even by many Whigs. Gradually the Democratic policy for the campaign became embodied in three principles which had been adopted by a county meeting at Cahaba, Dallas County, in January. These principles were: support of Winston for governor; opposition to any collateral issue, and adherence to Democratic faith only; and opposition to state aid.[21]

---

[18] *Dallas Gazette,* Jan. 5, 1855.
[19] *Dallas Gazette,* Jan. 12, 26, 1855.
[20] *Alabama Journal,* Jan. 20, 1855.
[21] *Dallas Gazette,* Feb. 2, 1855.

Winston was popular not only with the Democrats, but also with the old Southern Rights men and with many of the Whigs. The *Macon Republican* stated that he had poise and good sense and was practical, and that he did not run after every *ism* which came along in order to get popularity. This paper admitted that a majority of the people supported him in his opposition to state aid and in his attitude towards the liquor question, which was one of conservation and of opposition to the radical resolutions of the Selma Convention of 1852.[22] As early as the fall of 1854, the *Spirit of the South* and the *Dallas Gazette,* two old secessionist papers of 1850, had announced their support for Winston.[23]

By June, the support for Winston by the Democrats had become so unanimous that he was given the nomination without the formality of calling a convention, and he soon took the stump against state aid and in defense of his administration. This was before the opposition had been able to concentrate on any platform or candidate.

The Know Nothings finally organized for the campaign in a state convention which assembled at Montgomery on June 12, 1855, when one hundred and fifty delegates met behind closed doors. Most of the delegates were Whigs.[24] The convention nominated Judge George D. Shortridge, an old Democrat of Shelby County, for governor on the American platform. The main provisions of the platform were:

1. Only native Americans were to be elected to office.

2. Opposition to the immigration into the United States of paupers and criminals.

3. Opposition to granting political franchise to foreigners in any territories prior to their naturalization.

4. The right of all persons to freedom of worship, and opposition to the election of any man to office who recognizes the claim of any church to political power greater than that of the United States.

---

[22] *Macon Republican,* cited in the *Gainesville Independent,* Feb. 10, 1855.
[23] *Dallas Gazette,* Nov. 24, 1854.
[24] *Montgomery Advertiser,* June 14, 1855. The *Advertiser* made the estimate that two-thirds of the convention were former Whigs.

5. The non-intervention by the Federal Government with slavery, except for the protection of the constitutional rights of the South.

6. Perpetuity of the Union upon the principles of the Constitution; the full exercise by the states of all powers not delegated to the United States by the Constitution.

7. Purity of the ballot box and the enforcement of law and order.[25]

This platform was admirably adapted to attract all groups which were disaffected towards Winston and the regular Democratic Party. The first four provisions made an appeal to the people who were opposed to foreigners and Catholics. This was good campaign material, praticularly among people whose lack of education made them susceptible to racial and religious prejudice. The fifth plank was a bid for support from the slaveholding group; the sixth was an appeal to the states rights men; and the seventh was an appeal to the various reform groups. No reference was made to state aid which was a highy controversial question. The platform was a model of political ingenuity.

Shortridge was expected to appeal to several groups. He was classed as an advocate of state aid which would give him a strong following in Mobile, Selma and Tuscaloosa, and in a number of counties which were along the proposed routes of railroads. This was a group of considerable proportions. Some of the most prominent leaders of both the old parties were included within this group. He was acceptable also to the reform group and to the Americans. If Shortridge could get the support of these groups he might be able to defeat the Democrats. The problem was to fuse diverse groups, which had diverse interests, into a well organized political party. This was a difficult undertaking as the later history of the campaign showed.

Most of the old Whig papers which had advocated the nomination of a Whig for governor gave a reluctant approval to the nomination of Shortridge. The *Alabama Journal* could not approve the secret features of the American Party but claimed that the platform did not provide for religious proscription. This paper stated that Shortridge was a Democrat of the "old panel," but that he

---

[25] *Independent American*, June 12, 1855.

was stronger than Baker and that he had some ability. This attitude indicated that the *Journal* was about ready to support a candidate who favored state aid, which the *Journal* strongly opposed, and to line up with Americanism, which it did not favor, rather than to support a Democrat who stood largely for the principles which it advocated. Party feelings and traditions were stronger with the *Journal* than principles.[26]

Shortridge opened his campaign in Selma, the southern terminus of the Alabama and Tennessee railroad and the stronghold of state aid, on June 14, the day after the nomination by the Montgomery convention. He claimed that north Alabama had not been represented in the Democratic state convention in 1853 which had nominated Winston for governor, and attacked Winston for being a candidate for reelection without a nomination having been given to him by a convention. It was only the determination of Winston to be a candidate, in the face of strong opposition to him, that he, Shortridge, had consented to be a candidate.[27]

Shortridge then launched into the state aid issue. He claimed that the people had elected Winston in 1853 under the impression that he was a friend of state aid, and that he had betrayed this trust. He pointed out that there was a million dollars in the state treasury, which he, if elected governor, would lend to the railroads on such security that the state would not lose a cent of it. He pledged that he would not make any appropriation to any proposed railroad which would cause an increase of taxation on the people.[28]

During the campaign, Shortridge's speeches were confined largely to the state aid issue and to the counties of central and western Alabama where there was a strong sentiment for state aid. In Tuscaloosa he made a strong speech for state aid; in Pickens County, which was divided on the issue of state aid, he represented his position as being not greatly different from that of Winston. In a joint debate in Tuscaloosa, in July, between the two candi-

---

[26] *Alabama Journal*, June 16, 1855.

[27] *Sumter County Whig*, June 27, 1855. The *Montgomery Advertiser*, June 26, 1855, was able to show that Winston's nomination had been as regular as Collier's or that of any other Democratic candidate. There was seldom a state convention in which north Alabama was fully represented.

[28] *Sumter County Whig*, June 27, 1855.

dates, Winston accused Shortridge of occupying a double position with respect to this issue. In commenting on this debate, the *Southern Advocate,* an old Whig paper which was now supporting Winston, stated that Winston spoke better than it had expected and that Shortridge did not come up to expectations. Winston's speech was much the more effective.[29]

Shortridge, while claiming to a friend of state aid, disclaimed all intention of increasing the direct taxation upon the people in carrying out of this policy.[30]

The Know Nothings played an important part in the campaign. The secret features of the order attracted a large following and enabled them to develop morale by claims of an enormous membership. In July, Lewis A. Middleton, Secretary of the Alabama Council of the American Party, circulated a handbill which claimed a membership of 35,000 in the state. If this claim were correct, the Know Nothings had a good prospect of success as this number was larger than the vote any Democrat had ever received in Alabama and was eight thousand more than the number of votes which Pierce had received for president in 1852. The *Dallas Gazette* denied this claim, stating that ten thousand members had quit the order since June.[31]

Many people who favored some of the issues for which Shortridge stood did not approve of the secrecy of the Know Nothings. The Know Nothings attempted to remedy this weakness by making the charge that Democratic legislators practiced secrecy by holding secret caucuses to make nominations for officers which were to be elected by the legislature.[32]

The religious issue which the Americans injected into the campaign made it extremely bitter. Protestant ministers, of whom two-thirds were Know Nothings, according to the estimate of the *Gainesville Independent,* from their pulpits attacked the Catholic Church and urged their congregations to defeat the Democratic ticket.[33]

---

[29] *Southern Advocate,* July 25, 1855.
[30] *Tuscaloosa Monitor,* in *Southern Advocate,* July 25, 1855.
[31] *Dallas Gazette,* July 25, 1855.
[32] *Montgomery Mail,* Aug. 2, 1855.
[33] *Gainesville Independent,* Sept. 22, 1855.

The Americans claimed that the Catholics and foreigners were menaces to American institutions. They quoted figures to prove that a large per cent of the paupers in this country were foreigners, and that the criminality of that class was eight times as great as it was among native-born Americans. It was claimed that peddlers were almost entirely foreigners; that they were a serious menace to the planters by selling trinkets to the slaves and encouraging incendiarism among them; and that they often set fire to buildings in towns in order to rob other houses during the excitement. The charge was made that Bishop Hughes of the Catholic Church had sold his congregation to the Democrats.[34]

The Americans claimed to be the more moral of the two parties They took pride in the passage in Montgomery of a city ordinance which made Sunday a "real God-ordered day of rest and strict Sunday observance," instead of an open Sunday, as it had been under Dmocratic rule.[35]

But the religious issue was not an unmixed good to the Americans. The Primitive Baptists, or "Hard-Shells," a sect which was numerous in south and west Alabama, were opposed to all secret and temperance societies, and even to all organizations, other than the "Church of God."* They were ultra-conservative, and were

---

[34] These charges were contained in a letter in the *Independent American,* on October 3, 1855, in reply to Judge A. B. Longstreet, of Georgia, who was advising the preachers not to participate in politics.

[35] *Alabama Journal,* Feb. 17, 1855.

*In North Carolina, three Primitive Baptist preachers were expelled from their church, by a vote of 70 to 29, because they became members of the Sons of Temperance. The majority then voted to expel the minority of twenty-nine who had voted to sustain the three preachers. *Crystal Fount,* of Tuscaloosa, Nov. 28, 1851, cited from the *Methodist Protestant,* of Baltimore.

It is impossible to give the exact membership of the Primitive Baptists as the census figures make no distinction between the various groups which composed the Baptist Church. Miller, *History of Alabama,* p. 140, states that the Primitive Baptists were fourth in membership in Alabama. A study of the numbers given for Butler, Greene and Marengo counties, in Little, *History of Butler County,* pp. 237-39, Snedecor, *Directory of Greene County,* Tharin, *Directory of Marengo County,* together with figures in the Compendium of the U. S. Census for 1850, p. 138, leads to the belief that there must have been 20,000 Primitive Baptists in Alabama in 1855.

In some counties in south Alabama, the Primitive Baptists outnumbered any other church; some communities were almost entirely of this group. In the fall of 1855, Reverend Moses W. Helms announced that he would establish a Primitive Baptist newspaper, the *Lone Star,* at Elba, in Coffee County. No copies of this paper have been found. *Spirit of the South,* Oct. 23, 1855.

opposed to all of the *isms* of the day. They were opposed to church missions, an educated ministry, and the establishment of church papers. But they did have a real denominational consciousness, and, so far as can be ascertained, voted practically as a unit for the Democratic ticket. Due to their numbers, they played an important part in electing Winston.

The American press ridiculed the Primitive Baptists, picturing them as having the faith of the backwoods of the last century. One writer said that they had the same kind of faith as that which adorned "his satanic majesty with the eyes of a saucer, tail like an elephant's, and cloven foot like an ox. Verily they are fit instruments in the hands of a Foreign Party leaders to preach Republicanism and Americanism."[36]

Such criticism of the Primitive Baptists embarrassed the American press and political leaders in south Alabama where this church was strong in numbers. The American papers explained that such comments were not directed towards the entire body of the Primitive Baptists but only against those preachers who were "rampant politicians," and that most of the members of the sect themselves disapproved of their preachers getting into politics.[37]

The Primitive Baptists pointed with pride to the fact that none of their members had ever been abolitionists—not even in the North—and this was more than the Americans could say of their Northern members.[38] They took pride in the fact that temperance and the other reforms of the fifties did not get any support from their church.

An important element in the American Party was a group of Southern Rights men. Some of these men had come to the conclusion that the South could get her rights only by the disruption of all national parties and the union of all parties and factions of the South into a sectional Southern Rights party. They believed that secession would be forced upon the South and that the South would have to break with the national Democratic Party in order to assure secession. They believed that disruption of the Democratic Party might result from its defeat by the Americans. The

[36] *Georgia Citizen* in *Dallas Gazette,* July 25, 1855.
[37] *Independent American,* July 4, 1855.
[38] Letter in *Memphis Appeal,* copied in *Southern Advocate,* Sept. 5, 1855.

most prominent leaders of this group were the *Montgomery Mail* and the *Independent American,* of Troy

Both the *American* and the *Mail* had been established during the early period of the Know Nothing movement. The *Mail* was edited by J. J. Hooper, a former prominent Whig and editor of the *Chambers Tribune,* and J. A. Holifield, a preacher. Hooper expressed the program of the Southern Rights group in the *Mail* in an editorial entitled "Everything in Subordination to the Rights of the South:"

> The *Mail* set out a year ago with the chief political idea to further the advancement of Southern interests, all other creeds, questions, being subordinated. Time strengthens our conviction—not only as to principle—but as to necessity—*unity of acton of the South.* Yet there are difficulties in the way. There was never yet the man who did not *underestimate* the strength of long-continued party associations and affinities. Stultification of the South in the past on vital questions due to *party associations*—the Slave holder has not seen the condition and the relation of slavery as a *slave-holder* but as a *Whig* or as a *Democrat,* so his vision has been untruthful. * * *
>
> We must look abolitionism in the face. We want people to curse, in their hearts, all those party combinations for spoils, which, in turn, *practically* whatever may be their *theories,* have contributed to lessen the power and degrade the political condition of the South. The South must throw *Whig and Demoocratic* views and politics to the winds, and ask themselves what are *their rights* boldly, and maintain them.
>
> It is the mission of the truly independent *Southern Press* to war against old party associations so far as they are calculated to affect the sentiment of the South on Slavery.
>
> Of all the Southern papers, we know of only two or three which *avowedly* hold all party obligations in subordination to the highest requirements which Southern Patriotism can make.****
>
> We took the above sentiments as our policy a year ago, and it is to be our program for the coming year. From "our youth up" we have belonged to the Union organizations. We performed our part in 1851. Disunionism is the work of the North and the devil who makes the plea to remain in the Union under the Constitution.**

---

[39] *Montgomery Mail,* May 3, 1855.

The Southern Rights group became the core of the opposition to the Democratic Party after 1857.

In the early part of the summer the Democrats were disturbed by the rapid increase in membership of the Know Nothing lodges. The *Dallas Gazette,* which was anti-Know Nothing, later admitted that at one time less than twenty native white men out of a population of one hundred and forty white males over twenty-one years of age in Cahaba were not members of the order, and that one thousand of the 1870 white males over twenty-one years of age in Dallas County were members.[40] The *Gazette* stated that some men were actualy afraid not to join it, and that the "brothering" among the members was an appeal to join it which the young men could not resist.

Had the election occurred at the end of June, the Americans probably would have won. As the campaign progressed, many who had become members of the Know Nothing lodges from honest motives and others who had become members from curiosity became disgusted and deserted the order. Some bad characters had joined the order to shield themselves from punishment for their wrongdoing. The Democratic press gave wide publicity to these facts and to other information that might injure the Know Nothings, who were kept busy denying charges which were being made against them.[41]

A favorite campaign method used by the *Montgomery Advertiser,* and adopted by some other Democratic papers, was to print in each issue a list of the "come-outers," those who had quit the order. The *Gainesville Independent* reported an exodus of members from the "oath-bound, dark-lantern, clap-trap, hypocritical, truth-stretching, abolition-hatched party." Often the resolutions of a lodge which was disbanding were printed. Those of the lodge at Rockford, Coosa County, which was disbanded on July 27, 1855, were as follows: seventy-five per cent of the Catholics of the United States live in the North, therefore the religious question is not vital in Alabama; the American Party is un-American; the method of re-

[40] *Dallas Gazette,* July 20, Dec. 21, 1855.
[41] *Sumter County Whig,* July 18, 1855; *Gainesville Independent,* July 14, 1855.

stricting Catholics, if there is a danger from them, is for Congress to make naturalization laws stronger.[42]

The campaign propaganda which the Democratic press printed tended to allay the fears of the people that there was danger of political domination by the Catholics, and caused desertions from the order. The Americans were forced to admit that there were some withdrawals from the order, but they usually gave some explanation for them. They accused the Democrats of organizing a Know Nothing lodge and then disrupting it in order to give publicity to the disruption. The following were often listed as deserters from the order: disappointed office-seekers, men who returned to the Democratic Party who had been taught to follow leaders through "tergivisations" and "lofty sommersettes," and political soldiers of fortune who were seeking to better their conditions.[43]

As the election approached, wild rumors were circulated and the excitement became intense. Winston was accused of being a Know Nothing. The rumor was that T. H. Watts had spread this report. Winston pronounced this report a lie and, according to the rumor, challenged Winston to a duel, but Winston declined, giving as a reason that Watts "was not a gentleman."[44]

The *Montgomery Advertiser* charged Shortridge with having borrowed money from the old State bank, which had gone into bankruptcy, but this charge was never proved. Winston was charged with having used the state's money in his commission house in Mobile, and also with subsidizing the *Dallas Gazette* and the *Montgomery Advertiser* with state money in return for their support in the campaign. It was rumored that Senator Fitzpatrick was buying votes in Autauga County for Winston with state funds.[45]

The *Troy Bulletin* reported that the Know Nothings had distributed a hand-bill in Pike County calling for the organization of "Vigilance Committees" to bring out the American vote and to watch at the polls on election day. The *Bulletin* was indignant at this insult to American freemen and it warned the people to beware of the Know Nothing spies. It quoted from the French *Marseillaise* to express its indignation at the spying methods employed by the Know Nothings.

---

[42] *Montgomery Advertiser*, July 31, 1855.
[43] *Independent American*, July 4, 1855.
[44] *Dallas Gazette*, Sept. 7, 1855.
[45] *Ibid.*, Aug. 1, 1855.

O, Liberty, can man resign thee,
Once having felt thy generous flame,
Can dungeon, bolt or bar confine thee,
Or whips thy noble spirit tame?[46]

Wild rumors were circulated about foreigners and their participation in the election. The *Independent American* asserted that two railroad companies in Virginia had carried eight thousand Irish laborers into Virginia just prior to an election, and that it was the votes of these men which had defeated the American candidate in that state, and it feared such an occurrence in Alabama.[47]

The American papers in Mobile claimed that the naturalization papers of five thousand deceased naturalized foreigners in New Orleans had been obtained by the Democrats, who were giving these papers to foreigners and bringing them into Mobile to vote them for the Democratic ticket. Statements were made that as many as fifteen hundred of these transient foreigners had been brought into Mobile.[48]

The situation in Mobile was made more tense by the organization of the foreigners, principally Germans, into a secret society which was called the Sag Nichts. This society was said to be opposed to temperance and prohibition and in favor of an open Sabbath, and was said to be the branch of a secret Democratic organization of Ohio.[49] The *Montgomery Mail* said that the Sag Nichts were strong in Mobile and that their purpose was to oppose Americanism.[54]

There was some rioting in the southern part of Mobile a few days prior to the election, which was begun by some foreigners being attacked and beaten by mobs.[51]

On election day, the Americans stationed twenty watchers at every polling place in Mobile; the Democrats in defense organized their watchers into groups and assumed the name "Red Warriors" for these groups. Despite all the excitement and rumors of the campaign, the election passed off without rioting.[52]

---

[46] *Troy Bulletin,* in *Independent American,* Aug. 1, 1855.
[47] *Independent American,* Aug. 1, 1855.
[48] *Mobile Evening News,* in *Dallas Gazette,* July 30, 1855.
[49] *Ibid.*
[50] *Montgomery Mail,* Aug. 2, 1855.
[51] *Montgomery Advertiser,* Aug. 22, 1855.
[52] *Ibid.,* Aug. 4, 1855.

Winston won by a vote of 42,000 to 30,000 for Shortridge. Shortridge carried only fifteen counties, of which twelve were in the Black Belt, two, Mobile and Baldwin, were in the southwest, and Lawrence, in the Tennessee Valley.

Winston carried the eighteen north Alabama counties by an aggregate majority of ten thousand. His majority in the counties south of the mountains was less than two thousand. North Alabama voted largely on party lines—party traditions playing a more important part in the result than the Know Nothing, temperance, and the other issues. The large majorities given Winston in the "Avalanche" counties saved the state for the Democratic Party. The election figures in the white counties of both north and south Alabama indicated that the Democrats were absorbing the old Whig vote in these counties.

Shortridge failed to get the support in the state aid counties which he had hoped to get. He did not carry the state aid counties of North Alabama through which a railroad was being built from Selma to the state of Tennessee, nor the counties of the Tennessee Valley, which were interested in securing aid from the state for the completion of the Memphis and Charleston railroad.

Shortridge's effort to straddle on the state aid issue caused some of its advocates to conclude that Winston was as safe on this issue as Shortridge was, and that he was more sincere than was Shortridge. The *Southern Advocate,* published in a section of the state which wanted state aid, supported Winston, claiming that his position of being willing to make loans to the railroads of the funds which were in the state treasury, provided the loans were properly secured, was a safe policy for the state and also a just policy to the friends of internal improvements.[53]

The *Alabama Journal* supported Shortridge, but it believed that his position on state aid did not get him a great amount of support.[54] The *Mobile Advertiser,* the leading American paper of Mobile, said that the defeat of Shortridge was due to the weak support given him by the state aid group.[55]

---

[53] *Southern Advocate,* Aug. 29, 1855.
[54] *Alabama Journal,* Sept. 5, 1855.
[55] *Mobile Advertiser,* in *West Alabamian,* Feb. 20, 1856.

Mobile, Tuscaloosa, Dallas, Sumter, and the other counties situated in the lower basins of the Alabama and Tombigbee rivers, favored state aid, and most of them gave majorities for Shortridge.* These were old Whig counties and party traditions may explain, to a great extent, their votes. Shortridge, however, did not carry all of the old Whig counties in the eastern part of the Black Belt which were not so much interested in securing aid for the construction of any particular railroad.

During the campaign the Democratic press had claimed that the Know Nothing movement was only the "Whig Party in disguise" —a scheme of political trickery which the Whigs had worked out to get the support of certain Democrats who were opposed to the immigration of foreigners and to Catholicism, but who could never be induced to vote with the Whigs in the Whig Party. In proof of this charge, they cited numerous cases in which the Americans had nominated fusion tickets for the legislature, the personnel depending upon the political affiliations of a majority of the people of the county. In regular Democratic counties, the Americans placed Democrats on the tickets; in Whig counties, they selected Whigs; and, in counties in which the two parties were approximately equal in numbers, they selected Whigs and Democrats in equal numbers.[56]

The Whigs denied that the movement was political trickery on their part. They claimed that it was a real fusion of Democrats with the Whigs. In proof of this, they pointed out the number of prominent Democrats who had become Americans, among whom were S. F. Rice, G. D. Shortridge, W. R. Smith, Luke Pryor, T. B. Bethea, Jeremiah Clemens, Percy Walker, Reuben Chapman, and J. T. Morgan—an impressive list.[57] On the contrary, they claimed, only two Whigs of statewide prominence—R. W. Walker and E. J. Bacon—had supported the Democratic nominee.[58]

---

* The *Dallas Gazette,* Aug. 10, 1855, stated that a number of Irish laborers in Dallas County voted for Shortridge, with the belief that his election would assure the continuation of railroad construction and thus provide work for them. This, if true, was in contrast to the generally accepted belief that foreigners were Democrats.

[56] *Sumter County Whig,* July 4, 1855; *Independent American,* Aug. 15, 1855, discuss party realignments of the campaign.

[57] *Montgomery Mail,* July 5, 1855. The *Mail* gives a long list of the Democrats who were supporting Shortridge.

[58] *Dallas Gazette,* Aug. 24, 1855.

The *Southern Advocate,* a former Whig paper which supported Winston, was of the opinion that one-third of the Whigs in Alabama voted against the American ticket. The *Advocate* had opposed a fusion between the Whigs and the disaffected Democrats and it felt that the Whigs had made a serious mistake in thinking that they could defeat the Democrats by joining the Know Nothings. It believed that the fusion was a "Whig trick."[59] Later the *Advocate* estimated that the American vote was composed of Whigs and Democrats in equal numbers.[60]

The *Alabama Journal* agreed with the *Advocate* that the Whigs had invariably lost by attempting to catch disaffected Democrats in the Know Nothing movement.[61]

The *Dallas Gazette* stated that hardly thirty Whigs in Dallas County had voted the Democratic ticket. They could not resist the temptation to vote for their old Whig friends who were Know Nothing candidates, even though they were opposed to the principles of Know Nothingism.[62]

There is no evidence that the temperance question aided the American ticket to any great extent in this campaign. The temperance movement was strong in the early fifties, but the leaders were never able to elect men to office who ran on a temperance platform. This movement was considered as having the same source as the abolition movement of the North, and was thus looked upon with suspicion by the people of Alabama. The Know Nothings attempted to identify intemperance with the foreigners, it being a common charge that this group, who were brought into the state to build railroads, were intemperate and that they spent their wages in dram shops.

The religious issue cannot be said to have strengthened the American cause in this campaign. The votes which were gained were offset by those which were lost due to this issue. The Americans recognized the mistake of attempting to use religious preju-

---

[59] *Southern Advocate,* Aug. 29, 1855.
[60] *Ibid.,* Oct. 17, 1855.
[61] *Alabama Journal,* in *Southern Advocate,* Sept. 12, 1855.
[62] *Dallas Gazette,* Aug. 10, 1855.

dice as an issue, and later abolished all ceremonials, secrets, and passwords of the order.[63]

In the congressional elections the Democratic victories were more pronounced against the Americans than they had been against the Whigs in 1853.

In the Mobile district, the American Party elected Percy Walker over J. A. Stallworth, a Democrat, by a majority of about five hundred. The *Sumter County Whig* said that Walker's election was a distinct triumph for Americanism which was unknown in Alabama twelve months prior, and this was particularly gratifying as Americanism was a definite issue in the campaign.[64]. The *Dallas Gazette* claimed that Walker's election was a victory for Southern Rights, as he had been a Southern Rights Democrat, and it felt that Walker would vote with the Democrats in Congress because he had repudiated the principles of the national American Party as outlined in the Philadelphia platform.[65]

Walker's support came from Southern Rights men, the state aid group, and Americans, the combined vote of which was sufficient to elect him.

The old Montgomery district had been greatly changed by the redistricting act of 1854. Montgomery, Macon and Russell counties had been taken from the district and Butler and Lowndes had been added. This change had put the leadership of the second district in the hands of the Eufaula political leaders, who had been strongly Southern Rights since 1850, and who had voted for Abercrombie in 1853. One of the leaders of this "Eufaula Regency," Eli S. Shorter, was nominated by the Democrats to oppose Julius C. Alford, the American candidate. The *Spirit of the South,* which had been secessionist since 1851, supported Shorter.

Early in the campaign Shorter was accused of having joined the Know Nothings. He at first refused to reply to these charges, but finally admitted that he had begun to take the degrees in the order,

---

[63] DuBose, *op. cit.*, p. 312. The *Dallas Gazette*, September 21, 1855, had an article which gave the character of the religious literature which caused so much bitterness.

[64] *Sumter County Whig*, Aug. 22, 1855.

[65] *Dallas Gazette*, Aug. 24, 1855.

but that he had refused to go through all of the degrees after he had learned what the order stood for.[66]

Alford had been a Union man in 1851, was later a Georgia Platform man, and was now claiming to prefer a disruption of the Union to further compromises. He was in favor of resistance within the Union if the Federal government refused to admit Kansas, repealed the Fugitive Slave act, or committed any other aggressive act against the South. He attacked Shorter as being a secessionist.[67]

Shorter denied advocating secession and claimed that he was a States Rights Democrat on the Georgia Platform.

J. L. Pugh, who had left the Whig Party in 1849, stumped the district for Shorter. He had great influence in the "Cow" counties. Shorter proved to be a good campaigner. He made the argument in the lower counties that he would be able if elected to get mail routes established in the district because he would have the support of the Pierce administration.[68]

The principal support for Alford came from a group of leaders at Troy, in Pike County, led by Reverend A. N. Worthy, J. McCaleb Wiley, and E. L. McIntyre, who had established the *Independent American* as an American paper early in the year. They proudly pointed to Alford as the "Old War Horse," due to his good record in the Creek Indian War in 1836[69]

Shorter won by a majority of twelve hundred. Both candidates were Southern Rights men. Know Nothingism was not a clear cut issue as Alford denied being a member of the order, although he was supported by its members. Democratic traditions and the political influence of the leaders of Eufaula were sufficient to elect Shorter.

The campaign in the Montgomery district was interesting, due to changes made by the redistricting act and to the personality of the two candidates. J. F. Dowdell, of Chambers County, was the Democratic candidate opposed to Thomas H. Watts, a former Whig of Montgomery, who had become an American.

---

[66] *Spirit of the South,* in *Independent American,* July 11, 1855; *Independent American,* Aug. 11, 1855.

[67] *Independent American,* July 18, 1855.

[68] *Ibid.,* Sept. 3, 1855.

[69] *Independent American,* June 27, 1855.

Most of the counties of this district were anti-state aid and the Democratic press used the state aid issue effectively against Watts who was a state aid man.   He was also attacked for having voted for the repeal of a clause in the Alabama Code which permitted men who could not read and write to sit on juries.   It was claimed that the next step which Watts would take would be to deny to those who could not read and write the privilege of voting.[70]

The defense of the Americans was that state aid could not in any way be an issue in a congressional election.   They claimed that Watts was only trying to protect the poor farmers from the jury law which took them from their crops and forced them to serve for only $1.50 a day, whereas their expenses as jurors were two dollars a day, besides much loss to their crops.[71]

Dowdell could not use the secrecy issue against Watts as he himself had been a member of the Sons of Temperance in the early fifties.   He now stated that temperance was dead as a political issue, and that he was now advocating education as a means of removing intemperance, instead of through legislation.[72]

Dowdell won by a majority of 534.   Watts did not get the whole-hearted support of the Whigs as he had not been sufficiently energetic in working for the reorganization of the party after 1851. Some of the Southern Rights Whigs voted against Watts, claiming that he favored the slavery attitude of the national American Party, which was against the rights of slavery.[73]   Lack of party organization of the Americans as contrasted with a strong Democratic organization, also explains the defeat of Watts.[74]

W. R. Smith was elected over Sydenham Moore, who had been an officer in the Creek Indian War, in the Tuscaloosa district by a majority of almost two thousand.   Smith had been a candidate for the nomination in a Know Nothing convention in Tuscaloosa, but had been defeated; he had then become an independent candidate

---

[70] *Montgomery Advertiser,* July 16, 19, 1855.
[71] *Alabama Journal,* July 28, 1855.   The census figures for 1850 showed that there were 1,333 white men of voting age in the counties of the Montgomery district who could not read and write.   All of these would have been debarred from jury service by Watts' proposal.
[72] *Montgomery Mail,* Aug. 2, 1855.
[73] *Alabama Journal,* Sept. 8, 1855.
[74] *Ibid.,* Aug. 11, 1855.

against S. F. Hale, who was the regular nominee of the convention, and Moore, the Democratic candidate. Hale, who had been a candidate in this district in 1853, withdrew and the Whigs then supported Smith.[75] Smith's success was due to his personal popularity and the combined support of the Whigs and Americans for him.

George S. Houston, who was an anti-Know Nothing Democrat, was reelected without opposition in the Florence district.

W. R. W. Cobb was reelected by a majority of over twenty-five hundred over James M. Adams in the Huntsville district. Americanism was not an issue in this district. Adams said that he was an anti-Know Nothing; Cobb denied being a member of the order but said nothing to offend them.

In the Talladega district, S. W. Harris, whose home county, Coosa, had been transferred by the redistricting act of 1854, was elected over William B. Martin, a former Democrat, who ran as an independent. Martin denied being a Know Nothing although he received the support of the order. He claimed that good government depended upon a rotation in office, and he thought that Harris had been in Congress long enough. He also opposed the Democratic method of making nominations by conventions and caucuses.[76]

The regular Democratic candidates won in five of the seven districts of the state. In only three districts—the Mobile, Eufaula, and Tuscaloosa—did the Americans make a real fight. They won in the Tuscaloosa district, due to Smith's personal popularity and to the union of the Whigs and the Americans. Their victory in the Mobile district was due to Walker's advocacy of state aid and the support which he received from the old Whigs.

In the districts and the counties in which there was a clear-cut campaign between an American and a Democrat, the results were practically the same as the votes for the candidates for governor. The people in this election voted largely along old party lines. Party traditions and personalities were still powerful factors in state politics.

The legislature which assembled in November, 1855, was composed of sixty-one Democrats and thirty-nine Americans in the house, and twenty Democrats and thirteen Americans in the sen-

---

[75] *Tuscaloosa Observer*, cited in *Alabama Beacon*, July 27, 1855.
[76] *Montgomery Advertiser*, June 21, 1855.

ate. B. C. Yancey, a Southern Rights Democrat, and a brother of
W. L. Yancey, was elected president of the senate. R. W. Walker,
who had been nominated the Whig candidate for governor in 1853,
but who had voted the Democratic ticket in 1855, was elected
speaker of the house.[77]

The *Alabama Journal* tried to get some comfort out of the selection
of Walker, claiming that it was a victory for the Whigs. It was,
however, rather an indication of the drift of the Whigs into the
Democratic Party. About this time, R. M. Patton and Nicholas
Davis, two of the most important Whig leaders in north Alabama,
changed their allegiance to the Democratic Party.[78]

A legislative program was suggested by the *Gainesville Independent,*
which was generally considered the organ of Governor Winston.
The suggested program was: Alabama must meet the abolition
storm, and show that she has made her last compromise on slavery;
she must pass an act to revive the state militia; and she should
pass an act to modify the school act.[79]

Much talk was indulged in during the session regarding the relations of the state to the Federal Government. Most of the legislation, however, related to the affairs of the state and did not affect
the status of political parties or groups.

One of the important matters before the legislature was the election of a United States senator to succeed Senator Fitzpatrick,
whose term had expired in March, 1855. The Americans attempted
to defeat Fitzpatrick by giving their support to F. S. Lyon, a Democrat who was more acceptable to them; their plan failed, however,
and they finally supported Luke Pryor, a member of the house from
Limestone County. Twenty senators and fifty-eight members of
the house voted for Fitzpatrick; ten senators and thirty-five members of the house voted for Pryor. The vote was closely along party
lines.[80]

The opposition to Fitzpatrick came from the Southern Rights
Democrats and the old Whigs, who opposed him because he was

[77] *Alabama Journal,* Nov. 20, 1855.
[78] *Southern Advocate,* Nov. 21, 1855.
[79] *Gainesville Independent,* Sept. 29, 1855.
[80] *Journal of the House,* 1855-56, pp. 44-46.

such a strong party man. The *Spirit of the South* said that it was time, whether the politicians had discovered it or not, when all party lines must be put aside, and men must resist the inclination to vote for party interests and must unite in defense of Southern Rights.[81]

The opponents of Fitzpatrick criticized the caucus which had nominated him. They claimed that resorting to the caucus was evidence that the Democrats, who were urging all parties to unite with them by posing as the champions of the South, were playing politics and were putting party success above interests of the South. Hooper's *Montgomery Mail* criticized the Democrats for using the caucus with its secrecy in the following lines:

> Old King Caw is a jolly old cuss,
> And he gets his friends out of many a muss;
> He hasn't a "lodge" but a sly old Hole,
> And it's there the old King calls his roll!
> King Caw! King Caw!
> Caw! Caw! Caw! Caw!
> Is the jolly old cock that makes the law.[82]

---

[81] *Spirit of the South,* Nov. 20, 1855.
[82] *Montgomery Mail,* Nov. 22, 1855.

CHAPTER VII.

THE PRESIDENTIAL CAMPAIGN OF 1856

The vote polled by the American Party in the election in 1855 was the largest one which had been cast against the Democratic Party since the presidential election of 1848, when the Whigs came within less than a thousand votes of carrying the state. It appeared that this new party would succeed the Whig Party and that the two-party system would be maintained in Alabama. But this condition was not to be. The groups in the American Party were too diverse and their interests too varied to hold together, and the fifteen months after the election of 1855 was a period of rapid disintegration of the party.

The first break in the party came when a group of Know Nothings met in a convention in Montgomery, in November, 1855, abolished all passwords and ceremonials of the order, declared for a strict construction of the Constitution, and demanded religious freedom for all men. These resolutions put the state party in an irreconcilable attitude towards the national American Party.[1]

In an effort to keep their party alive in Alabama, the state council of Americans held a meeting at Montgomery on February 14, 1856. The leaders in this meeting were J. E. Belser, B. S. Bibb, J. H. Clanton, J. J. Hooper, A. F. Hopkins, C. C. Langdon, L. E. Parsons, Daniel Pratt, T. H. Watts, and B. M. Woolsey. These men were former Whigs and all of them lived in or near Montgomery, except Hopkins, who lived in Mobile, and Parsons, who lived in Talladega County.[2] This convention selected electors, pledged to support ex-President Fillmore for president in the national convention of Americans which was to meet in Philadelphia in February, and adopted resolutions on slavery extension, one of which took similar ground to the "Alabama Platform" of 1848. DuBose states

---

[1] DuBose, *op. cit.*, p. 312.
[2] *Montgomery Advertiser*, Feb. 1, 1856.

that the demands for Southern Rights would not have been stronger, even though Mr. Yancey had drawn them up.[3]

But the Fillmore party in Alabama was handicapped by the refusal of its leaders to approve the platform, adopted by the American national convention at Philadelphia, which did not take a satisfactory attitude towards slavery extension and which declared that Americans must rule America. Congressman Alexander White and Judge Shortridge opposed the Philadelphia platform, and Judge A. F. Hopkins and B. F. Porter, old Whig "war-horses," took the stump for the Democratic ticket[4] Percy Walker, elected as an American to Congress from the Mobile district in 1855, left his party and stumped his district against the principle of religious proscription of the American Party, as typified by C. C. Langdon, his former political ally.[5]   Even Jeremiah Clemens, who had been attacking the Democratic Party after his defeat for reelection to the Senate in 1853, admitted that he believed that the Philadelphia platform was unwise, and that he could find no objection to Pierce other than that he "was all things to all men." For this reason, Clemens thought it better to support Fillmore than Pierce.[6] Luke Pryor, member of the house from Limestone County, and Jones M. Withers, mayor of Mobile, were two other prominent American leaders who refused to support the American nominees.[7]

The American papers were no more successful in securing united effort against the Democrats than were the political leaders. The *Montgomery Mail,* established as an American paper in 1854, supported the platform but was opposed to Fillmore for the candidate and finally gave him only a reluctant support.[8]

The *Alabama State Sentinel,* the most aggressive American paper in the state, held a similar opinion.[9]

The *Independent American* was strongly advocating Southern emigration to Kansas, which the *Montgomery Mail* was opposing. The *Mail* however, was demanding protection for Southern Rights. It ex-

---

[3] DuBose, *op. cit.,* p. 313.
[4] *Clarke County Democrat,* Sept. 18, 1856.
[5] *Ibid.,* Sept. 25, 1856.
[6] *Independent American,* cited in *Alabama State Sentinel,* June 4, 1856.
[7] *Montgomery Advertiser,* Aug. 13, 1856.
[8] *Southern Advocate,* Feb. 27, 1856.
[9] *Ibid.,* Mar. 12, 1856.

pressed the opinion that Charles Sumner deserved every bit of punishment which Preston Brooks inflicted upon him for his speech on "Bleeding Kansas."[10]

The *Alabama Journal* supported Fillmore on the ground that he was not a member of the Know Nothing order which the *Journal* was denouncing. The *Southern Advocate* supported Buchanan.

Soon after the election of 1855, most of the old Whig papers which had supported Shortridge began to urge the Whigs to reorganize the Whig Party. The *Alabama Journal* stated that the disintegration of the Whig Party had driven many conservative men of the North from the arena of politics which had left political power in the hands of fanatics. Consequently, hosts of men, it continued, had come to the belief that the only way to save the country was to reorganize the old Whig Party on the acceptance of the Compromise of 1850 as a finality.[11]

The *Southern Advocate* which had not supported Shortridge favored a reorganization of the Whig Party on the basis of the Georgia Platform. It thought that either old party, Whig or Democratic, would assure the safety of the South, and that there should be a fusion of these parties against the American Party, with its abolitionism.[12] Later the *Advocate* admitted that the Whigs could no longer hope to exist as a party, because its national issues—tariff and public lands—were relegated to the past, and that the only issue for them now was to united to save the South.[13]

The Southern Rights group realized the futility of attempting to continue as a separate party and began to cooperate with the Democrats as a matter of expediency. The attitude of this group was expressed by the *Dallas Gazette*, which stated that it was in favor of secession, but that it was useless to press its views as a majority of the people were in favor of unionism. The problem then was how to maintain Southern Rights in the Union. The *Gazette* believed that this could be done only through one of the great political parties. The Union Party of 1851 could not do this as it had died, due to the desertion of its own members; the Whig Party had been swallowed

---

[10] *Independent American*, June 4, 1856.
[11] *Alabama Journal*, Sept. 7, 1855.
[12] *Southern Advocate*, Oct. 17, 1855.
[13] *Ibid.*, Nov. 28, 1855.

up by the Know Nothings; the American Party had abolitionists for leaders in the North; therefore, concluded the *Gazette,* the Southern people must look to the Democratic Party for protection of their rights.[14]

Early in 1856, the Democrats began to organize for the presidential election of that year. Democratic clubs were organized to study the current political questions as a means of defense against the aggressions of the abolitionists of the North. In one of these clubs the *Mobile Register* was used as a textbook and files of it were kept for reference.[15]

The Democrats utilized the glamor which still hung over the name of Andrew Jackson in Alabama by holding their state convention in Montgomery on January 8, 1856, with the capitol brilliantly illuminated in honor of the victory of the "Old General" over the British at New Orleans. A number of anti-Know Nothing Whigs attended the convention. Yancey, who was sitting in the audience as a spectator, was called upon for a speech. He made a strong plea for a permanent union between the anti-Know Nothing Whigs and the Democrats and suggested that the fusion party be called the Democratic and Anti-Know Nothing Party.[16] This attitude on the part of Yancey pleased the old Whigs, to whom the name Democrat was obnoxious, but who were willing to cooperate with the Democrats under the new name. Many of them did support the Democratic ticket in November.[17]

The convention approved the Pierce administration and recommended him for reelection. A platform, which was modeled on one adopted in Georgia in November, 1855, was approved. This platform demanded civil, religious and political equality, and the right of the people of the slaveholding states to the protection of their property in the states and in unorganized territories. It stated that the American Union was secondary in importance to the rights which it was designed to perpetuate, and that the people of Alabama would be bound to it only so long as these rights were protected. With respect to legislation by Congress, the platform

[14] *Dallas Gazette,* Sept. 14, 1855.
[15] *West Alabamian,* Aug. 29, 1855.
[16] *Independent American,* Jan. 23, 1856.
[17] *Southern Advocate,* Jan. 16, 1856.

stated that Alabama ought to resist, even to a disruption of the Union, any action by Congress impairing the slavery rights of the South.[18]

The convention selected for the approaching election a state executive committee whose personnel gave almost equal representation to the Southern Rights Democrats, the Union Democrats, and the Whigs.[19]

During the spring, Mr. Yancey became very active in an effort to get the leadership of the Democratic Party. When the state convention met in Montgomery in May for the purpose of appointing delegates to the Democratic national convention and district electors on the electoral ticket, an interesting change in the personnel of the delegates, due to Yancey's efforts was noticeable. The old leaders of the "Montgomery Regency," such as Seibels and Fitzpatrick, were absent and a group of younger men made up the convention.

The convention made Yancey chairman of the committee on resolutions; choose him unanimously an elector at large; adopted his "Alabama Platform" of 1848; and instructed the delegates to vote for no man for president who was not unequivocally opposed to the Wilmot Proviso and the squatter sovereignty methods of limiting slavery.[20]

Democracy was united in this campaign, but under leaders different from those of the early fifties. Yancey had been forced to wait six years for the Democratic Party to accept his political philosophy. He was destined to wait four more before he was able to get the state to follow him into secession.

Conditions in Kansas and the speeches of abolitionists in Congress aided the Democrats in Alabama in getting support for their ticket. They used the plea that the Pierce administration was a

---

[18] *Clarke County Democrat,* Jan. 31, 1856.

[19] *Southern Advocate,* Jan. 16, 1856. The personnel of the committee was as follows: Southern Rights Democrats, B. C. Yancey, of Cherokee; J. L. M. Curry, of Talladega; W. L. Yancey, of Montgomery; L. Pope Walker, of Madison; Union Democrats, A. B. Meek, of Mobile; John G. Barr, of Tuscaloosa; John D. Rather, of Morgan; old Whigs, James L. Pugh, of Barbour; E. J. Bacon, of Chambers.

[20] DuBose, *op. cit.,* pp. 320-21. DuBose gives a full account of the campaign of 1856.

friend to the South, and that this section could expect no relief from a national American Party, since the Americans of the North were opposed to Southern Rights.

Late in the campaign there developed a feeling in Alabama that the Republicans might win the presidency. This was indicated in several letters written to Senator Clay from his constituents.[21] This fear caused some old Whigs and Americans to vote for Buchanan as it was believed that he had a better chance of defeating Fremont, the Republican candidate, than Fillmore had.

The expedition of Jefferson Buford, of Barbour County, to Kansas to aid in establishing slavery there aroused great enthusiasm in south Alabama. Even Americans and old Whigs supported this expedition. Reverend A. N. Worthy and other American leaders of Pike County spoke at a Kansas emigration meeting in Troy and contributed to the Kansas fund.[22] Hilliard was in sympathy with the project and participated in the reception given to Buford's men in Montgomery where they made a stop on their way to Kansas. The enthusiasm for Buford had a stimulating effect upon Democrats in Alabama.

Senator Clay, who has been elected to the Senate in 1853, was arousing enthusiasm for Southern Rights by his speeches in the Senate. In April, 1855, he made a speech on "The Plan and Purpose of Black Republicanism," which was a severe arraignment of abolitionism, and which had great influence in causing his constituents to realize that their best hope for the protection of their slave property was in the Democratic Party.

Clay was doing much also by his correspondence with Democratic leaders in Alabama. The information and advice which he gave to them was valuable in enabling them to attack the opposition during the campaign. A typical letter received by Clay was one written by C. R. Woods, of Eufaula, as follows:

> Some of our old Whig and Know Nothing friends are very much in the fog, and I am anxious to put them right. I know I can do but little, but I am willing to that little, at any time, and anywhere. **** It is said that Mr. Clemens will be down this way after a while, when he comes Col. Pugh will take him

---

[21] Clay Papers.
[22] *Independent American*, Feb. 20, 1856.

in hand and put him through this district. Now Sir you can have no doubt as to my object in writing to you an entire stranger. I trust you will pardon the liberty as I am one of your admirers & constituents as well as a worker in trying to kill off Know Nothingism & Black Republicanism. In this I trust in God we may succeed to our hearts content. I am Sir one of your well pleased constituents.[23]

Clemens took the stump in north Alabama against the Democrats. He attacked the Pierce administration for excessive expenditures and for appointing foreigners to office. His influence in the Tennessee Valley was strong and his speeches were very effective. John D. Rather, speaker of the house in 1851, heard Clemens make a speech at Decatur, in which he quoted figures on the appointment of foreigners to office and expenditures of both the Fillmore and Pierce administrations. Rather wrote to Senator Clay asking information regarding these matters. He also asked information on the national campaign—what the North was doing, how many free states Buchanan would carry, and whether Fillmore had much support.[24]

Late in the campaign, Yancey was sent into north Alabama to meet Clemens in joint debate. The discussion of the issues by these men at Huntsville, Tuscumbia, Florence, and Courtland, was the most spectacular feature of the campaign in Alabama. Great crowds attended the debates, barbecues were held, and excursions were run on the railroads to the speaking places.

Yancey defended the Pierce administration and all of the measures regarding slavery which the Democratic Party had supported since 1848. He pointed out that the platform upon which Buchanan had been nominated had been the position of all parties in the South—Democrats, Whigs, and Americans—and that this position had been considered a settlement, in substance and in principle, of the slavery question. The theme which ran through the speeches of Yancey was that all parties in the South must unite on a defense of Southern Rights and that the national Democratic Party was the party through which a defense of these rights must

---

[23] Clay Papers. Letter dated July 28, 1856.
[24] Clay Papers. Letter dated July 29, 1856.

be secured. He made no radical utterances nor threats of secession.

The *Southern Advocate* said that it could not do justice to the beauty and strength of Yancey's speech in Huntsville. "Great as was his reputation he more than maintained it, and high as were the expectations of our people they were fully realized by Col. Yancey's efforts. He won a place in their hearts, and the name of *William Lowndes Yancey* has become a household name dear to them."[25]

Clemens confined his speeches largely to attacks on Pierce, Buchanan and the national Democratic Party. He was handicapped for a following due to the belief that he had betrayed the Democratic Party, while in the Senate, and to his personal life after he had retired to private life in March, 1853.[26]

The *Southern Advocate* commented as follows on Clemens' speeches: "Not one who has heard Col. Clemens in other days and who listens to him now, can fail to realize that 'Richard is not himself'—that he is mangled by the cause that he is attempting to sustain."[27]

During the latter part of the campaign, Hilliard made a speaking tour through north Alabama for the American ticket. At Huntsville, in September, he defended Southern Rights in a speech which the *Southern Advocate,* which had been Democratic since 1855, called the strongest defense of Southern Rights which the editor of this paper had ever heard. Hilliard stated that the South must resist further aggression by the North; that the election of Fremont by the "Black Republicans" in the condition the country was then in would be the inauguration of a series of aggressions against the South; and that the South ought to resist in case of the election of Fremont.[28]

---

[25] *Southern Advocate*, Sept. 11, 1856.

[26] Clay Papers. Senator Clay wrote to his father, ex-Governor Clay, on March 14, 1854, that Clemens was giving expensive dinners, and that he was drinking and gambling heavily. Clay wrote the facts of a recent fight which Clemens had had with Representative Harriss of Mississippi. Clemens was in a drinking house in company with Representative Ewing, of Kentucky. Harriss came in drunk. Ewing offered to introduce him to Clemens but Harriss declined. Clemens then asked him what he meant, and Harriss replied that he did not want to know him any better, or something of that sort—whereupon Clemens struck him with a heavy pistol on the head, stunning him badly. Harriss either challenged him or threatened to do so, when their mutual friends interposed and made up some terms of reconciliation.

[27] *Southern Advocate*, Sept. 11, 1856.

[28] *Southern Advocate*, Oct. 2, 1856.

The *Southern Advocate* was pleased with Hilliard and the tenor of his speech. It said that when a speaker inculcated such a doctrine, it had no great censure for him, even though he deemed it best to support Fillmore. "For we are satisfied," the *Advocate* stated, that "when the struggle comes, as it may come, he will be found at his post true to the South and ready to imperil all to secure her safety."[29]

The speeches made in north Alabama by Yancey and Hilliard were important for later developments. They brought about a better political understanding between the two sections of the state, and made advocates for Southern Rights in a section where unionism had previously been very strong.

After the adjournment of Congress in August, Senator Clay, Congressmen Cobb and Houston, and other Democratic leaders of north Alabama made speeches in their section for the Democratic ticket. In October, Governor Andrew Johnson, of Tennessee, was brought to Alabama and made speeches for the ticket at Huntsville and Tuscumbia.[30]

The campaign was made bitter, as had been the one of 1855, by the injection into it of the religious issue. Sermons were preached urging support for the American Party, the claim being made that it was the party of reform and morality. The anti-Americans claimed that the ministers preached "Douglas and him damned," instead of "Christ and him crucified." The *Southern Advocate* stated that the Baptists were the most energetic in preaching politics, but that those who were contaminated with politics were not the old Baptists, familiarly known as "Hard Shells," who had never been infested with any of the *isms* of the day, but the regular Baptists.[31]

The Democrats carried the state by a vote of 46,000 to 28,000, and won forty-four of the fifty-two counties. Buchanan received sixty-two per cent of the vote cast, and a majority larger by six thousand than Winston had received in 1855. The greatest Democratic gains were in the Mobile and Tuscaloosa congressional districts. In the former, an American majority of about five hundred

---

[29] *Ibid.*
[30] *Southern Advocate,* Oct. 9, 1856.
[31] *Ibid.,* Dec. 4, 1856.

in 1855 was changed to a Democratic majority of about fifteen hundred; in the latter, an American majority of about seventeen hundred in 1855 became a Democratic majority of about five hundred. The losses of the Americans were in the counties which had given a heavy vote to the American candidate in 1855, due to his advocacy of state aid, which was not an issue in 1856. Some notable gains were made by the Democrats in the eastern counties of the Black Belt. From this time, this section became more strongly and uniformly Democratic.

The Americans polled their largest vote in the counties of the Montgomery district where some of the old Whig leaders, such as Hilliard, Watts, W. P. Chilton, and R. A. Baker, made speeches for the ticket. But they lost ground here as the ticket received a defeat greater by fifty votes than Watts had received for Congress in 1855.

The Democrats carried the north Alabama counties by the usual large majorities.

The Democrats had carried Alabama by urging party loyalty and by convincing the people that the national Democratic Party would give sufficient protection to the slaveowners against abolitionism. The people of the state had come to the position which was expressed by R. M. Patton, a north Alabama conservative, in a letter which he wrote to Alabama from New Haven, Connecticut, on August 19, 1856. Patton stated that he was surprised to find so many people there who were as strongly pro-slavery as were the Southerners, and who felt that the only conservative national party was the Democratic Party. And it was strange to Patton that any man in the South would "fool away" his time, at this critical moment, talking about Americanism or Mr. Fillmore. He ended his letter by asking that his friends cease representing the claims of Fillmore.[32]

The Democrats received the news of their victory with great rejoicings. Cannon were brought out and fired during the great meetings which were held to celebrate the victory. The papers carried cuts of roosters crowing and cannon being fired. The *Montgomery Advertiser* carried its engravings of the "cannon of vic-

---

[32] *Southern Advocate,* Sept. 4, 1856.

tory," under which were placed the words, "Bring out the Baby Waker."
Some of the papers burst into poetry. The *Wetumpka Dispatch* car-
ried this exultation to express its joy over the downfall of Know
Nothingism: "No North, No South, No East, No where, Know
Nothing."[33]

This defeat marked the end of the American Party in Alabama,
though the Americans continued to hold some of the county offices.
This party had always been stronger in county politics than in
state or national politics.[34]

Soon after the election the Alabama Democrats took steps to
further strengthen national Democracy in the state by attempting
to secure the appointment of an Alabamian to the cabinet of President Buchanan. The *Montgomery Advertiser* preferred Senator
Fitzpatrick, but felt that Senator Clay, Congressman Houston, or
John Bragg, ex-congressman from the Mobile district, would be a
good choice.[35] Some of the Democratic papers were urging Yancey
for a cabinet position.[36] The objection to Yancey was that his views
had been so extreme that his appointment might embarrass Buchanan and the Democratic Party in the North. Yancey realized this,
as indicated in a letter to Senator Clay in February, 1856:

> I am sincerely obliged to you for the kind words spoken to
> B— Mr. Dowdell will inform you that I desire him, if proper,
> to let Mr. B— be disembarrassed of all considerations respect-
> ing me. I have long felt that I should have prevented my
> friends urging my name in connection with a cabinet appoint-
> ment. I feel even now, crippled for future usefulness, if ever
> we shall be forced to act against Mr. B— ****[37]

The election of 1856 was a significant turning point in the movement which culminated in secession in 1861. This campaign
brought into prominence a group of young leaders who gave to the
Democratic Party more aggressive leadership than it had formerly

---

[33] *Wetumpka Dispatch*, Dec. 5, 1856.
[34] *Macon Republican*, May 15, 1856. In May, 1856, Americans were judges of
probate in sixteen counties and Democrats held this office in eighteen counties. The
party affiliations of the other eighteen were unknown.
[35] *Montgomery Advertiser*, Dec. 3, 1856.
[36] *Dallas Gazette*, Jan. 23, 1857.
[37] Clay Papers, Feb. 15. No year is given.

had. These men, like the young "War Hawks" who brought on the War of 1812, took over the leadership of the Democratic Party, and finally lead it into secession.

The failure of the Whigs and Americans to organize a successful fusion party in opposition to the Democratic Party caused a continuation of the disintegration of the Whig Party. After 1856, Southern Rights Whigs and Americans began to unite with the Democrats. This left the Democratic Party without opposition from a regularly organized party.

The breaking up of party lines in Alabama was a step towards disunion. As long as there were two parties, fairly well balanced, secession was difficult because the campaigns centered, to a large extent, around party advantage. After 1856, the strongest contests in elections were for leadership within the Democratic Party, and this leadership was secured by the secession wing of the party in 1860.

CHAPTER VIII.

TRANSITION TO THE ONE-PARTY SYSTEM IN ALABAMA, 1857-59

The year 1857 was a kind of "era of good feelings" in Alabama politics. The Democrats had united in 1856 in support of their national ticket and had carried Alabama for Buchanan on the issue of maintaining relations with the national party. Mr. Yancey and the other Southern Rights leaders seemed satisfied to entrust to national Democracy the protection of Southern Rights. Soon after the inauguration, Hilliard probably the most influential Whig in the state, announced that he would support the Buchanan administration and other leading Whigs, and Americans began to take a similar attitude.[1]

For the first time since 1851, the Democrats in 1857 had no opposition from either the Whigs or Americans in the election of a governor. The campaign became a contest among several Democrats who represented various degrees of opinion regarding Southern Rights. Among the candidates were Judge John E. Moore, of Florence; Judge A. B. Moore, of Perry County; John Cochran, of Eufaula; William F. Samford, a planter of Russell County; and David Hubbard, ex-congressman of Lawrence County.

The two Judge Moores were rather conservative; Cochran, who had been defeated for Congress in 1851, was still strongly in favor of Southern Rights, and was being supported by this group in Barbour County; Samford and Hubbard were two of the most uncompromising Southern Rights men in the state.[2] Hubbard in a letter to the *Montgomery Advertiser*, claimed that the South was in a dual war—a war with the North which had Great Britain for an ally in

---

[1] Miss Toccoa Cozart, "Henry W. Hilliard," in *Transactions of the Ala. Hist. Soc.*, IV. 69. Hilliard later felt that he had made a mistake in uniting with the Democrats when Yancey and the secessionists gained control over the party. He supported Bell for president in 1860.

[2] John F. Comer, of Cowikee, Barbour County, in a letter, March 3, 1857, to Senator Clay shows that Cochran was brought out by the "Eufaula Regency." Clay Papers. Samford's position is given in an excellent monograph by Professor George Petrie, in *Transactions of the Ala. Hist. Soc.*, IV. 169-89.

its attacks on slavery, and a war against that portion of Southern statesmen who were not sufficiently aggressive in defending Southern Rights. To meet this situation, Hubbard favored a declaration of war against England and an attack upon her colonies in the Caribbean Sea.[3]

The Democratic state convention met at Montgomery on June 1, 1857, with two hundred thirty delegates in attendance. A. B. Moore was nominated on the twenty-sixth ballot. Harmony prevailed in the convention and three of the defeated candidates—Cochran, J. E. Moore, and Hubbard—made speeches after the nomination and pledged their support for the ticket. Hilliard, who was now regularly cooperating with the Democrats, also made a speech before the convention.[4]

The platform drawn up by the convention adopted the principle of the Cincinnati convention of 1856 and the Dred Scott decision as the attitude of the Alabama Democrats on slavery extension.

The Americans and Whigs attempted to nominate a candidate to oppose Moore but were unable to organize. The *Alabama Journal* stated that Moore was a man of fair ability and that his nomination was equivalent to his election. It stated that the Democratic convention was the most imposing and able body of men in appearance that had been seen in Montgomery since the days of the Clay Whigs, with the exception of the Grand Lodge meetings. It felt that the interests of the state would be safe in such hands.[5]

The greatest threat to the Democratic Party at this time came, not from an organized party, but from its own adherents, many of whom were beginning to believe that the Buchanan administration could not protect Southern Rights. The criticism of the administration was caused by the attitude which R. J. Walker who had been appointed governor of Kansas by Buchanan, was taking in the

---

[2] *Montgomery Advertiser,* April 21, May 7, 1857. This letter was written at Hubbard's plantation, "Kinlock." The subscription list of the *Advertiser* shows that it was read widely by the political leaders of North Alabama.

[4] *Southern Advocate,* June 11, 1857.

[5] *Alabama Journal,* cited in *Montgomery Advertiser,* June 10, 1857. Soon after this time, the *Journal* ceased publication. It was succeeded in January, 1858, by the *Montgomery Confederation,* which was set up as a Douglas paper and edited by J. J. Seibels, who had been the secessionist editor of the *Montgomery Advertiser* in 1851.

affairs of the territory. The Democratic leaders in Alabama held meetings to discuss this situation. In a meeting at Montgomery on June 27, 1857, a resolution of "undiminished confidence" in Buchanan was passed, but only after Yancey had been forced to admit that there was evidence tending to prove there was collusion between Buchanan and Walker, and after he had made a strong plea that Buchanan should not be deserted by the South until such collusion should be proved.[6]

The opposition refused to exonerate Buchanan for the events in Kansas. They claimed that the defense by the Democrats was due to a desire to maintain their party intact until after the election in August. The *Montgomery Mail* refused to believe that Mr. Yancey was sincere in withholding criticism of the President. It stated that "everybody that knows Mr. Yancey politically must feel that his loathing of Mr. Buchanan cannot be much less potent than his contempt for Governor Walker."[7]

There was much evidence during the state convention of sectional feelings over state aid for railroad construction. But the leaders refused to permit state issues to take precedence over the national issues, which were considered more important,and the contraversies over local interests were subordinated.

In the congressional elections, the Democrats elected their condidates in every district of the state and carried every county except four.

The Mobile district, which gave the Americans a majority of over five hundred in 1855, gave the Democrats a majority of twenty-seven hundred in this election.

The strongest opposition to the Democrats was in the Montgomery district where T. J. Judge opposed Dowdell. Judge ran as a States Rights Whigs but without a platform. He cited the inaugural speech of Walker as governor of Kansas, as well as the whole Kansas imbroglio, as proof that the national Democratic Party was not sufficiently aggressive in defense of the rights of the South in slavery extension.[8] The old Whig papers which supported Judge

---

[6] *Montgomery Mail,* June 29, 1857.
[7] *Montgomery Mail,* July 28, 857.
[8] *Montgomery Advertiser,* July 29, 1857.

referred to the Democratic Party as the "Free Soil Northern Democratic Party."[9]

Both Yancey and Hilliard were called upon to stump the district for Dowdell, and Robert Toombs was brought from Georgia to make speeches for him. The *Montgomery Mail*, which was supporting Judge and attacking the Buchanan administration, described the visit of Toombs to Alabama by saying that "the Philistines are coming on," and then expressing a wish for "the Ass with the best jaw-bone" with which to smite Toombs.[10]

Toombs, like Yancey, blamed Walker for affairs in Kansas and made the plea that criticisms of Buchanan be withheld until his views were made known in the presidential election.

In the Tuscaloosa district, the redoubtable W. R. Smith, who had represented this district since 1851, was beaten by General Sydenham Moore by a majority of over fourteen hundred. Smith's record in Congress was used against him. The charge was made that he had voted to censure Preston Brooks for caning Sumner; it was claimed also that he had opposed the efforts of Jefferson Buford and others to carry expeditions into Kansas to make a slave state of it.[11]

The *Independent Monitor,* an American paper, stated that Smith's defeat was such a political revolution as had rarely been known. It stated that Moore was chivalrous and honorable, and that his character was without blemish. He was an "old fire-eater" of 1850, which fault could be wiped away only by tears in the service of the Union. For him to have beaten Billy Smith, the *Monitor* concluded, was fame enough for an ordinary ambition.[12]

In the Florence district, Houston, who had had no opposition since 1851, was opposed by David Hubbard. Houston won, but by a majority of less than nine hundred votes. The result indicated a strong Southern Rights sentiment in the plantation counties of the

---

[9] *Montgomery Advertiser,* July 29, 1857.
[10] *Montgomery Mail,* July 20, 28, 1857.
[11] *Alabama Beacon,* July 24, 31, 1857.
[12] *Independent Monitor,* Aug. 6, 1857. Smith had held the following political positions since 1840: a Whig in 1840; then a Democrat; a Union Democrat in 1851; a Union Whig in 1853; an American in 1855; and an anti-Buchanan Democrat in 1857.

Tennessee Valley, which had not had a heated political congres--sional campaign since 1851.

J. L. M. Curry, who was a political disciple of Senator Clay, and who later became an important leader, was elected to Congress in the Talladega district.[13]

The Democrats increased their majorities in both houses of the state legislature. They elected twenty-seven of the thirty-three senators, and eighty-four of the one hundred members of the lower house.

The *Southern Advocate,* which had been the leading Whig paper in north Alabama up to 1855, carried a significant editorial on the political situation in 1857:

> The recent elections in the Southern States are almost unanimous for the Democracy. The people of the South, satisfied that there is no other party promising the least hope or guaranty for the protection of their rights, have rallied to its cause, and present nearly an undivided front in Congress. ****
>
> With occasional errors and departures from the true lines of duty, the Democratic party is and has been, true to the Constitution, the Union, and the rights of the States.[14]

This editorial stated correctly the political beliefs of most of the people of Alabama in 1857. The Democratic Party was supreme, but the diverse groups within the party, which lead to the split in the party in 1860, were becoming more and more apparent. The Democrats in Alabama in 1857 were speaking of Democratic beliefs and principles, but the opposition newspapers were probably more correct when they pointed out that party loyalty, not principles, held the party together. The *Montgomery Mail* described the "loathsome, discordant ingredients," which composed the Democratic Party as being the

> Eye of Toombs, toe of Van
> Heart of fogy Buchanan,
> Foot of Cobb, nose of Cass,
> Ears of Old Virginia's Ass.[15]

---

[13] Clay Papers. There are a number of letters from Curry to Clay in these papers.

[14] *Southern Advocate,* in *Alabama Beacon,* Aug. 21, 1857.

[15] *Montgomery Mail,* July 6, 1857.

That the Democrats differed among themselves on controversial subjects and then united for the support of their party at the ballot box was provoking to the *Mail*.

An effort was made during the session of the legislature of 1857-58 to elect Governor Winston to the United States Senate in place of Senator Clay, whose term was to expire in March, 1859. In June, Winston had announced his candidacy on an anti-state aid platform, explaining that the early announcement was due to the demand of many people that the legislature of 1857-58 elect a senator for the term which would begin in March, 1859. At the time of this announcement, the *Montgomery Advertiser,* which was generally considered a Winston organ, was demanding that anti-state aid men be elected to the legislature.[16]

When the legislature assembled Governor Winston sent to it his message, one point of which advocated a reapportionment law, based on the Mixed Basis, which would give the slave counties representation for their slaves. It was charged that this was a scheme of Winston to get the Black Belt counties to support his candidacy for the senate. North Alabama opposed Winston as it was the custom for this section to have one of the senators and the election of Winston would give both of them to south Alabama.[17]

Winston's candidacy failed and he then became more nationalistic and more conservative with respect to Southern Rights. In the spring of 1858, the *Montgomery Advertiser* was purchased by new owners and it then began to support Yancey for the senate.[18]

The legislature of 1857-58 confined its activities largely to questions of a domestic nature. Governor Winston set the example by devoting only one of the nineteen points of his message to the slavery question. The Governor defended the Southern position on the Kansas controversy and declared that the Union was not the paramount political good to Alabama and the South.[19]

In December, the senate passed resolutions unanimously requiring Governor Moore to call an election for delegates to a state con-

---

[16] *Independent Monitor,* July 9, 16, 1857.
[17] *Southern Advocate,* July 23, 1857. This paper, the *Huntsville Democrat,* and the *Athens Herald* opposed Winston strongly.
[18] *Independent Monitor,* Nov. 12, 1857.
[19] *Ibid.*

vention to determine what steps the state should take to protect its rights and honor. Later the house passed these resolutions with but two dissenting votes.[20]

The year 1858 was an "off-year" in politics in Alabama, but it was enlivened by an effort made by Mr. Yancey, who had been active in the Democratic Party since 1856, to get the leadership of the party in the state. His program embodied the following steps: a break with the national Democratic Party, and the organization of a Southern party; the election of Yancey to the United States senate by securing the defeat of Senator Fitzpatrick; and ultimately the secession of Alabama.[21]

As has been stated, Yancey had found it difficult to give his support to the Buchanan administration during 1857, due to the policy of Governor Walker in Kansas. The attitude of Senator Douglas towards the Lecompton constitution in the late fall convinced Yancey that the South could no longer rely upon the national Democratic Party for the protection of slavery rights, and that the safety of the South demanded the formation of a Southern party.

During the summer of 1859, Yancey took definite steps to disrupt the Democratic Party by the organization of Leagues of United Southerners, the purpose of which was to unite the Southern people into a sectional party.[22]

The constitution of the League was composed of a number of articles, none of which was intended to cause alarm for the safety of the Union. The purpose of the Leagues was to be the use of proper means to enforce the rights of the South in the Union; there were to be no more compromises of these rights, either in party platforms or in national legislation. The most interesting article of the constitution was the one which related to the political activities of the League. It stated that the League would nominate no candidate for any office, either state or federal, but demanded that its members should use all honorable means to secure the nomination, by the respective parties to which they belonged, of sound,

---

[20] *Journal of the Senate*, pp. 126-27; *Journal of the House*, p. 474.
[21] DuBose, *op. cit.*, p. 347, stated that Yancy was the leader of the Democratic Party in Alabama in 1856 and 1857. He interpreted the political maneuvering of these years as being efforts of J. J. Seibels, editor of the Mobile Register, to take the leadership from Yancey.
[22] *Clarke County Democrat*, July 29, 1858; *Dallas Gazette*, July 30, 1858.

able and pure men of the Southern Rights school. All candidates, of course, were to be Southerners.[23] The League would thus secure united effort on the part of the South, and at the same time would permit the old parties to retain their party names.

Some of the advocates of the League gave a more radical interpretation of its aims than Yancey gave. One of these was William F. Samford, who was one of the most aggressive secessionists in the state. From his home at Eyrie, in Russell County, Samford wrote three articles, which he called the "Leaguers against the Intriguers," in which he attacked allegiance to a party.[24] "To be bawling in the ears of freemen, 'the party'—'the party' like the town-crier is enough to disgust and insult the intelligence of free electors, who have a stake in 'the country' and cherish the patriots of 1776."[25]

Samford favored disruption of the national Democratic Party. He claimed that history proved the necessity for new parties. "Necessity had caused the development of the Southern Rights Party and if it fails of its purpose—if it turns a deaf ear to the South—because nationalized—then the League will unite all those who are willing to fight for the South. The SOUTH will then be the League!"[26]

Many Southern Rights Whigs and Americans, including the *Montgomery Mail,* were supporting the principles of the League. This gave the Democratic newspapers the opportunity of attacking the Leagues as a combination of defunct Know Nothings and disaffected Democrats whose purpose was to overthrow the Democratic Party. The *Clark County Democrat* pointed out the danger which lurked in a fusion with the Americans. In an editorial on the "Fire-Eaters of 1859" the *Democrat* said:

> In 1855 the Know Nothings gloried in the doctrine that the Union was the 'paramount political good.' Now in 1858 they are terrible 'fire-eaters' and can with difficulty be persuaded to

---

[23] The *Montgomery Advertiser,* Sept. 15, 1858, printed the constitution of the League and also a long letter from Yancey to R. A. Pryor, of the *Richmond South,* who was attacking the Leagues.

[24] These articles were printed in the *Montgomery Advertiser* in October, 1858.

[25] *Montgomery Advertiser,* Oct. 20, 1858.

[26] *Ibid.,* Sept. 15, 1858. Samford wrote under the pen name of Zeno.

remain in the Union. Democrats of the Dowdell, Shorter, Stallworth type and tame submittionists when compared with them. They 'snuff treason in the tainted air' and swear lustily that the South was sold in the recent adjustment of the Kansas problem. They are strong for Southern Rights only so long as the Democratic Party is in power. Efforts to weaken the Democratic Administration or impeach the motives of the Southern Rights men who supported the Kansas Conference Bill will fall harmless to the ground.[27]

Yancey was attacked by the regular Democrats who considered the Leagues a scheme to destroy the national Democratic Party, which they were trying to maintain.

The *Montgomery Confederation,* established in January, 1858, by J. J. Seibels, who was then a conservative, claimed that the Yancey group was agitating the Kansas and Minnesota questions for political advantage. This paper and Forsyth's *Mobile Register* were waging a vigorous campaign to select an Alabama delegation pledged to the support of Douglas for president in the national convention in 1860. The *Alabama Beacon* stated that Yancey had hoisted the banner of disunion, but that "we," as Democrats, "are not prepared to concur in his sentiments."[28]

Yancey denied that the organization of the League was a party move to unite the Know Nothings and disaffected Democrats in order to divide the Democratic Party. He claimed that the *Montgomery Mail* was the only American paper which was supporting the League, and, on the other hand, most of the Democratic papers were supporting it.[29] But the old Democratic leaders could not be driven from the attitude that "whatever is done for the South now, or in the future, is to come of the Democratic party, and that the cause of the South is injured as Democracy is weakened."[30]

While the discussions of the Leagues were going on, the campaign to elect Yancey to the Senate was in progress. The initiative was an editorial entitled "The Treachery of Douglas," which appeared in the *Montgomery Advertiser* shortly after its change in owner-

[27] *Clarke County Democrat,* June 10, 1858.
[28] *Alabama Beacon,* in *Montgomery Advertiser,* June 16, 1858.
[29] *Clarke County Democrat,* Sept. 16, 1858.
[30] *Ibid.,* June 24, 1858.

ship.[31] The *Advertiser* later began to attack Senator Fitzpatrick for supporting Douglas on a favorable report which he brought into the Senate from the committee on territories to admit Minnesota as a state.[32]

But Yancey was becoming too radical for some of the Southern Rights men. He took a leading part in the sessions of the Southern Commercial convention which met at Montgomery in May and attempted to get the convention to pass resolutions favoring the reopening of the slave trade.[33] He was also making speeches in support of William Walker and his filibustering activities against Nicaragua.[34] In the summer Yancey met Walker at a public dinner in Montgomery County and gave encouragement to him. The theme which ran through the speeches of Yancey at this time was that there was no hope for the South if it remained in the Federal Union.[35]

The *Dallas Gazette,* which had expressed a desire to see Mr. Yancey in the Senate, thought that his attitude on the slave trade and filibustering would seal his political doom. It said that if "the 'Southern League" is to be contaminated with filibustering, it will receive no favor at our hands; indeed we will fight against it.[36] Prior to this the *Gazette* had said that "Mr. Yancey has the reputation of being the ablest man in the Southern States—his honor and patriotism are unquestioned. He occupies an exalted position of all men."[37]

The *Montgomery Advertiser*, which in the spring had advocated Yancey for senator, began to look with misgivings upon him and his Southern clubs. It felt that too many Whigs and Americans were lining up under the banners of the clubs, and it feared that these two groups would get control of the Leagues and through

---

[31] *Montgomery Advertiser,* Feb. 15, 1858. The *Advertiser* on April 7 denied that the paper had been purchased by its present owners—N. B. Cloud and G. H. Shorter—to prevent "a certain man" from being elected United States senator.
[32] *Montgomery Advertiser,* Mar. 3, 1858.
[33] W. W. Davis, "Ante-Bellum Southern Commercial Conventions," in *Transactions of the Ala. Hist. Soc.,* IV.185-88.
[34] *Tuskegee Republican,* Feb. 4, 1858.
[35] *Dallas Gazette,* July 23, 1858.
[36] *Ibid.,* July 16, 1858.
[37] *Dallas Gazette,* July 9, 1848.

them would attack the Southern Rights Democrats. The *Advertiser* believed that the most efficient instrument for the promotion of the interests of the South was the Democratic Party.[38]

While Yancey was threatening to develop a schism between the Northern and Southern Democrats, Senator Clay was exercising an influence to maintain the party intact. Clay's attitude was not unfriendly to Yancey. He had offered, early in 1857, to use his influence to get Yancey an appointment in the cabinet of President Buchanan.[39] But Clay did not agree with the ultra views of Yancey and Samford. This was revealed in a letter which Samford wrote to Clay. Samford stated that he could not rely on Clay to fight the battles which had to be fought. He said that the Buchanan administration did not come up to his expectations as to a Southern Rights policy, and that he did not believe the Democratic Party could win the presidential election of 1860 on the achievements of this administration.[40]

With respect to local politics, Samford expressed opposition to Congressman Dowdell. He said that Dowdell "will not promise not to run" for reelection, but he was determined that "no man of the *Regency* shall run or be elected."[41]

A new angle was given to the senatorial situation in 1858 by the announcement of the *Gainesville Independent* that Winston would be a candidate for Fiztpatrick's seat in the Senate. The *Independent* claimed that the *Montgomery Advertiser,* which was supporting Yancey for the Senate, and the *Montgomery Confederation,* which was supporting Fitzpatrick, were not the Democratic Party, nor their candidates alone entitled to consideration. It claimed that to Winston "more than any other man do we owe the unexampled prosperity we enjoy, the soundness of our currency, and our exemption from public debt. The people know and admire him. **** He was the Cerberus who drove off the harpies that desired to deplete and plunder the treasury."[42]

---

[38] *Clarke County Democrat,* July 13, 1848.
[39] Clay Papers. This letter bears no date.
[40] Clay Papers, Samford to Clay, Oct. 22, 1858.
[41] *Ibid.*
[42] *Gainesville Independent,* Nov. 13, 1858.

The *Independent* attacked Yancey and denied that he was the sole champion of the assailed rights of the South. "It requires the good offices of a flapper," it said, "to remind the *Advertiser* that there are other men in Alabama besides Mr. Yancey and Mr. Fitzpatrick."[43]

During 1858 and 1859 the senatorial situation was widely discussed by the press, but no action was possible until the meeting of the legislature in November, 1859.

Yancey had worked tirelessly, but unsuccessfully, in 1858 to attain leadership of the Democratic Party in Alabama. His failure to accomplish this purpose is attested by the election of men who stood for national Democracy to the state and federal offices in the fall election in 1859.

In the gubernatorial election, the extreme Southern Rights group supported William F. Samford against Governor Moore, who was a conservative Southern Rights Democrat. Samford had received some support for the gubernatorial nomination from delegates of east Alabama in the Democratic convention in 1857. In 1858 he had warmly espoused the candidacy of Yancey for senator, and had aided in the organization of the Leagues of United Southerners. While Yancey was making speeches, Samford, whose health had been impaired early in life, remained at his plantation home and wrote letters to friends and articles for the press urging support for a Southern Party. Professor Petrie expressed the opinion that Samford did more, with the possible exception of Yancey, to mold the political thinking of the people than any other man in the state.[44]

Samford announced his candidacy as an appeal to the people against the politicians, an advocacy of principles as opposed to mere partyism, and all for the South.[45] He claimed that Governor Moore had betrayed the state when he refused to call a convention to give the people an opportunity to express an opinion regarding secession after the passage by Congress of the Kansas Conference bill.[46]

---

[43] *Gainesville Independent,* Nov. 27, 1858.
[44] George Petrie, "William F. Samford," in *Transactions of the Ala. Hist. Soc.,* IV. 169.
[45] Letter from W. H. Samford to Peyton H. Colquit, in *Southern Messenger,* June 8, 1859.
[46] *Southern Advocate,* July 7, 1859.

Governor Moore stated his defense, in reply to an inquiry from J. D. Phelan, of Montgomery. The governor wrote that the Southern people should do everything possible to secure their rights in the Union, but that they should submit to no more compromises. The security of the South and the fate of the Union would probably depend upon the next presidential election, which would probably be between a "Black Republican" and a national Democrat. The Democrats, he thought, would not nominate a man who was not sound on Southern Rights, and the South must support him in order to prevent the election of a Republican. A division of the Democratic Party at that time, he concluded, would be fatal.

Governor Moore then defended himself for not calling a convention when admission was refused to Kansas under the Lecompton constitution. He claimed that the disposition of the Kansas question by the Conference bill left him without authority to call such a convention.[47]

Moore was elected by a vote of forty-seven thousand to eighteen thousand for Samford, who carried only two counties, and these by a total majority of less than one hundred. Samford received only 2,500 votes in the sixteen north Alabama counties to 20,000 for Moore, and his vote in west Alabama was correspondingly small. His largest vote came from the old Whigs and Americans of the eastern Black Belt counties.[48]

The results of this election indicate that the people of Alabama still accepted the national Democratic Party as the defender of Southern Rights, and rejected the attempt of Yancey and Samford to organize a separate Southern Party. The regular Democratic leaders were looking to the Democratic Party to defeat the Republicans in 1860 and then protect the South.

The congressional elections were also victories for the national Democrats.

In the Mobile district, James A. Stallworth, an administration Democrat, who had voted for the Kansas Conference bill, was opposed by F. B. Shepard, a secession Democrat, and a denouncer of national Democracy. Stallworth's nomination was made in a dis-

---

[47] *Gainesville Independent,* June 25, 1859.
[48] *Southern Messenger,* July 29, 1859.

trict convention which met at Mobile, and which represented the sentiments of various county meetings which had passed resolutions approving the Buchanan administration.[49]

The old Whig papers made an effort to bring out a Whig candidate but failed to do so. Most of the support given Shepard came from Whigs and Americans.[50]

In the Eufaula district, James L. Pugh, the national Democratic candidate, was opposed by J. E. Sappington, who had been a Union Democrat, but who ran as a Southern Rights man in this election. In the card announcing his candidacy, Sappington stated that he favored cessation of all agitation except for a united South. He looked in vain for the Democratic Party to save the South. He wanted Southern Rights in the Union, or independence out of it. "In throwing my banner to the breeze I inscribe on it the motto of my gallant opponent, Pugh, 'Union among ourselves for the South.' I protest, like Samford, against any national party affiliation."[51]

The campaign in the Montgomery district was exciting as usual. T. J. Judge was again a candidate as a States Rights Whig, and was defeated by a majority of over two hundred.

A correspondent of the *Tuskegee Republican* wrote a vivid description of rallies of both parties held in Montgomery before the election and of celebrations held in the city on the night of the election.

> Each party had torch-light processions on Wednesday night and speaking; the Democrats in front of the Exchange Hotel; the Opposition in front of the Montgomery Hotel. But Saturday night was the great night—I never saw anything like it. Before night bonfires were lighted; stirring notes of music called the people from their homes. Just after dark the thunder of artillery awaked the echoes of the surrounding hills. Rockets pierced the dark ethereal. After the speaking came more music, more bonfires, more sky-rockets, cannon and torch-light processions.
>
> After perambulating several of the back streets, both processions spread themselves upon Market Street nearly up to the Capitol. The street was full of smoke, fire, dusk, hollowing

[49] *Clarke County Democrat*, May 2, 1819.
[50] *Mobile Advertiser*, in *Southern Messenger*, May 24, 1839; *Alabama State Sentinel*, Apr. 23, 1859.
[51] *Southern Messenger*, July 27, 1859.

fire, music, and rockets. The oldest inhabitants have never seen anything like it.[52]

The Whigs and Americans in the Tuscaloosa district held a convention and nominated Captain Jack F. Cocke, of Perry County, but this opposition movement broke down when the *Independent Monitor* refused to support the candidate. The *Monitor* had been an important Whig paper, but it opposed any factional opposition to Sydenham Moore, the Democratic incumbent. This paper was more interested in getting men elected to the legislature who would work to complete the proposed railroad through Tuscaloosa. This, it felt, was more vital to Tuscaloosa than the defeat of Moore.[53]

In the Florence and Huntsville districts, Houston and Cobb were reelected over Democratic opponents. One feature of the campaign in north Alabama was the strong appeal which was made by the *Southern Advocate* to maintain the national Democratic Party, with the idea that this was the only hope for the preservation of the Union.[54]

In the Talladega district, J. L. M. Curry, who was a supporter of the Buchanan administration was elected with only a scattering opposition.

National Democrats were elected in every district in the state. In some districts, the opposition candidates were stronger Southern Rights men than were the national Democrats; in others, they were stronger Unionists. The results indicate that the people were satisfied to be represented in Congress by men who were favorable to the Buchanan administration. In only the Montgomery district was there opposition from a Whig candidate.

The Alabama legislature assembled in November, 1859, with a distinguished personnel. In the house were ex-Congressman Percy Walker, Stephen F. Hale, S. F. Rice, John Forsyth, who had been a minister to Mexico, and W. P. Chilton, a former chief justice of the Alabama supreme court. A. B. Meek, of Mobile, was elected speaker of the house. Most of the members were young men who were aggressive for the rights of the South. These men were to play an important part in the final events which lead up to secession in 1861.

---

[52] L'Ecrire in the *Tuskegee Republican*, Aug. 4, 1859.
[53] *Independent Monitor*, in *Alabama Beacon*, May 13, 1859.
[54] *Southern Advocate*, Aug. 25, 1859.

The acts passed by this legislature were largely devoid of party partisanship. One act provided for the organization of a military corps of 8,000 men and the appropriation of sufficient money for their equipment. The author of this bill was W. P. Chilton, of Macon County, who was a Whig.

An important act—one which was directly related to secession—authorized the governor to call a state convention to determine what course Alabama should take in case of the election of an incendiary president in the November election.[55]

The most interesting political qestion before the legislature was a resolution to elect a senator to succeed Senator Fitzpatrick whose term was to expire in March, 1861. Fitzpatrick was a national Democrat and a supporter of Douglas for the nomination for president, which caused opposition to him from the Southern Rights group. The leaders of this group attempted to secure the election of Yancey but were defeated, not until strong feelings had been developed on both sides, however. The Montgomery correspondent of the *Tuskegee Republican* wrote to his paper that sons of Yancey and Fitzpatrick had gone to South Carolina to fight a duel over charges which had been printed regarding the election of a senator.

The details of the attempt which was made in the legislature to defeat Fitzpatrick were given in a letter from E. C. Bullock, senator from Barbour, to Senator Clay. This letter was as follows:

> I do not think that there is much probability that any further effort will be made to bring it on this winter. Baldwin, the kinsman & next friend of Gov. F. opined to me on the day after the decisive vote in the Senate that the attempt would not be renewed. Yancey who was at first anxious to bring it on, was afterwards discouraged by new developments which settled beyond question that fact that he could not be elected. Whether anybody else could or not, I think extremely doubtful. Gov. F. counted on 70 votes on the 3rd ballot, but I am certain that his calculations were not all correct & my own impression is that there would have been many ballotings but no choice. There was unquestionably a clear anti-F. majority if it could have been concentrated on any one man, but of this there was but slight probability. I think Gov. F. would have started off with about 58, Y. with about 50 & Winston with 22. W's friends with the balance of power, were too uncertain

---

[55] *Southern Era,* Mar. 6, 1860.

to hazard the result in their hands. There was more affinity between W. & F's partisans than between either of them & Y. Besides F's reelection would have afforded a chance for an earlier vacancy. He might, by one of those extraordinary freaks of fortune which so often raise small men to great places, be Vice President or even Prest, while Y. once in the Senate would be likely to stay there. These facts coupled with F's evident eagerness for the fight contributed largely to the postponement. Besides it was urged that the delay was itself a defeat after your triumphant reelection two years ago & again that future developments must strengthen & could not weaken the S. R. wing of the party. The immediate cause of Y's change of opinion was the defection of Saffold who after being elected Chancellor come out for F, when he was put down on our list as certain & the fact that the two members from Dale could not be induced to go for Y. One of them came out at one time for him, but had not backbone enough to resist (?) the local pressure (?). Gen. Bradford of Talladega reputed the best counter in legislative elections in the state, thought that there was but one man who could certainly beat Gov. F. & that was Walker **** who was quite right on the Douglas question. The wish may have been father to the thought, but for me I was quite willing to take the new candidate. The advice of one most discreet friend was to put off & it prevailed, not however without some difficulty. I was certainly committed as you know to the *business* or policy, being somewhat in the condition of the Irishman, who went so far in one day that he could not get back in two. Whether the danger of election a Douglas Senator would have been so inconsistent as to have made me sacrifice constituency to the exigencies of a bleeding country, it is unnecessary to say.

Bullock then explained that fortune so favored his group that by means of parliamentary tactics they were able to defeat the resolution in the senate to fix a day for the election of a senator, and at the same time they saved their pride in not revealing their weakness against Fitzpatrick. He concluded his letter by describing the chargrin of the conservatives over their defeat:

They were taken by surprise & blown up before they knew there was a grain of powder on the premises and forthwith Seibels (retaliated) **** by reading us out of the Democratic party in the Confederation. F. was there with Seibels & other retainers to see the consurrence. A more melancholy set of old fogies never darkened a Senate chamber.[56]

---

[56] Clay Papers. This letter was dated Dec. 13, 1859.

CHAPTER IX.

DISRUPTION OF THE DEMOCRATIC PARTY, 1860

The problem of the Democratic leaders in Alabama from 1857 to 1860 had been to prevent a break between the Southern Rights group and the national Democratic Party. The prominent Southern Rights leaders had refused to break with the national party and to support Yancey in the formation of a separate Southern Rights party. Yancey had been thwarted in 1859 in his effort to defeat Fitzpatrick, a conservative, for reelection to the Senate. But the break of Senator Douglas with President Buchanan had intensified the issue in Alabama between the supporters of Douglas and the Southern Rights group. Douglas' candidacy for the Democratic nomination for the presidency in 1860 was the issue around which most of the political activities of the year centered.

The initiative in the campaign to prevent the Alabama delegation from supporting Douglas in the national convention was taken by a county convention which met on October 17, 1859, in Perry County, with W. M. Brooks as chairman. This convention declared that it would not support Douglas nor any other man for president who did not affirm that slavery was expressly provided for in the Constitution, and that the only power conferred upon Congress was the right and duty of guarding the slaveowners in their rights.[1]

The Montgomery County convention which met later was dominated by Yancey and a delegation favorable to his platform was selected to go to the state convention, but only after strong opposition had been offered by the conservatives, who were led by Henry C. Sample, a supporter of Douglas, and a compromise had been made whereby one-third of the delegation were to be Douglas supporters.[2]

Eighteen other counties held conventions and passed resolutions similar to those of Perry County, although only about one-half of

---

[1] *Marion Commonwealth,* in *Montgomery Advertiser,* Nov. 2, 1859.
[2] DuBose, *op. cit.,* pp. 442-43.

them condemned Douglas by name. A few of them adopted resolutions which declared that the election of a "Black Republican" would be sufficient cause for secession.

Yancey was the leader of this movement to put Alabama under the control of the Southern Rights group. It was his plan to control the delegations in the state convention and to get this convention to select delegates to the national convention pledged to support his "Alabama Platform" of 1848. The Democratic state convention assembled on January 11, 1860, with representatives from every county in the state except Covington. Most of the delegates were Democrats, only a few old Whigs and Americans having been elected. One newspaper stated that the convention was "composed of the brightest and best intellects our state can boast, and bears the reputation at home and abroad, of having been the ablest political assemblage, in point of talent and energy, ever convened in Alabama."[3] The delegates were not the old Democratic leaders of the early fifties but a younger group. Among them were the following who later reached high positions in the political and military affairs in the state: W. C. Oates, of Henry; E. A. O'Neal, of Lauderdale; R. W. Cobb, of Shelby, all of whom became governors of the state; John T. Morgan, of Dallas, who became a United States senator; H. D. Clayton, of Barbour; S. D. Weakley, of Lauderdale; C. A. Battle, of Macon; T. H. Herndon, of Greene, and N. B. Powell, of Macon. W. F. Samford, of Russell County, an older leader, was also a delegate. Most of these men were lawyers.

In the organization of the convention a conflict developed between a group of conservative Democrats, led by Nicholas Davis, of Limestone, a nephew of the Whig candidate for governor, in 1847, and a Yancey group. A deadlock developed over the selection of a chairman, but F. S. Lyon, of Marengo County, upon the motion of L. Pope Walker, of Madison, was finally selected as a compromise man. The election was really a victory for the Yancey group as Lyon was a strong Southern Rights man, which was indicated in his acceptance speech, in which he said that nothing less than a

---

[3] *Independent American*, Apr. 11, 1860. Other young Democratic leaders were: Eli S. Shorter, John Gill Shorter, E. C. Bullock, all of Barbour; W. H. Forney, of Calhoun; A. B. Meek, of Mobile; J. L. M. Curry, of Talladega; and Hilary A. Herbert, of Butler.

protection of the rights of the South under the Dred Scott decision would satisfy the South.[4]

The convention adopted twelve resolutions which were to guide the Alabama delegates in the adoption of a platform and the nomination of candidates in the Democratic convention which was to meet at Charleston. One resolution provided for the withdrawal of the Alabama delegation from the convention in case the convention refused to adopt the "Alabama Platform" as one of its planks, and a second one declared opposition to the nomination of any candidate for president who did not believe in the principle of this platform. Only seventy-one delegates out of a total of four hundred forty-five opposed the withdrawal resolution and only twelve voted against the one pertaining to the nomination of a candidate. The other resolutions were adopted unanimously.[5]

The convention selected a state executive committee, composed of one member from each congressional district, which was authorized to call a state convention to consider what steps should be taken in case the Alabama delegation should withdraw from the Charleston convention. The members of this committee were: John T. Morgan, H. D. Clayton, J. F. Dowdell, J. S. Kennedy, of Lauderdale, Edward Wallace, of Jackson, A. C. Jones, of Greene, and Floyd Bush, of Calhoun. Dowdell was the only member who had been active in state politics in the early fifties.[6]

The thirty-six members of the Alabama delegation obeyed instructions and withdrew when the Charleston convention refused to adopt the principles of the Dred Scott decision in the party platform. With the return of the delegates from Charleston, the breach between the Democrats of north and south Alabama gradually widened. The withdrawal of the delegates was approved by the people of the four congressional districts of south Alabama who later sent seventeen of their twenty-four delegates to the anti-Douglas convention at Richmond, Virginia; whereas, the people of

---

[4] *Florence Gazette*, Jan. 25, 1860; *Clarke County Democrat*, Jan. 19, 1860.
[5] *Clarke County Democrat*, Jan. 19, 1860. DuBose, pp.443-44, gives a long account of this convention but does not point out the conflict between the two groups.
[6] *Clarke County Democrat*, Jan. 26, 1860.

north Alabama sent only three of their twelve delegates to the Richmond convention.[7]

From this time until secession was accomplished, south Alabama, under the leadership of Yancey, became more unified for secession, and north Alabama more unified in opposition to immediate secession. A number of north Alabama leaders, however, continued to cooperate with Yancey. Among these were Senator Clay, Judge John E. Moore, L. Pope Walker, and the three men who had been delegates to both the Charleston convention and the later anti-Douglas convention at Richmond—F. G. Norman, of Franklin, J. T. Bradford, of Talladega, and ex-Governor Chapman.

Soon after the Alabama delegates returned from the Charleston convention, the state executive committee, pursuant to the instructions of the state convention which had met in January, called a convention to meet in Montgomery on June 4, to "consider what is best to be done to protect the rights of the South. The committee urged the Democrats in every county to hold primary meetings to select delegates to the state convention.[8]

Some of the conservative newspapers, particularly the *Montgomery Confederation* and the *South Alabamian,* of Greenville, warned the Democrats against a final break with Douglas and the national Democrats, pointing out that this procedure would disrupt and bring ruin to the party.[9]

The Democratic state convention met at Montgomery on June 4, 1860, with delegates from forty-eight of the fifty-two counties in attendance. The personnel showed a preponderance of the Southern Rights group, only a few of the old Union Democrats being in attendance.[10]

Yancey attempted to get the convention to send delegates to the Southern Rights convention, which was to meet at Richmond; and to instruct them to reaffirm the platform which had been defeated in the Charleston convention, to nominate a candidate for president of the type of R. M. T. Hunter, and then to adjourn *sine die.* Most

---

[7] *Florence Gazette,* June 6, 1860.
[8] *Southern Champion,* May 18, 1860; DuBose, *op. cit.,* p. 74.
[9] *South Alabamian,* May 26, 1860.
[10] *Florence Gazette,* June 13, 1860; *Montgomery Advertiser,* Oct. 13, 1860. The *Advertiser* gave the names of the delegates.

of the delegates were not ready for a final break with the national party and the convention made a compromise by appointing delegates to the Richmond convention and instructing them to meet with the national Democratic convention which was to meet later at Baltimore.[11].

In the meantime, the conservative Democrats in Alabama were organizing to prevent Yancey and the Southern Rights Democrats from getting control of the Democratic Party and leading the state into secession. There were three groups of leaders in this movement, namely, the old Democrats of north Alabama who had been Unionists in 1850, the old leaders of the "Montgomery Regency," many of whom had been secessionists in 1850, and a group of old Whigs. Among the north Alabama leaders were Congressmen Cobb and Houston, O. H. Bynum, of Lawrence; Nicholas Davis, of Madison, and L. E. Parsons, of Talladega. The south Alabama leaders included Fitzpatrick, J. J. Seibels, John Forsyth, William Garrett, Bolling Hall, James E. Saunders, of Mobile, and ex-Governor Winston. The old Whigs who were supporting this movement were C. C. Langdon, editor of the *Mobile Advertiser;* E. A. Banks, of Montgomery; D. C. Humphreys, of Madison, and ex-Congressman Alexander White, of Dallas.

Soon after the return of the delegates from the Charleston convention, these leaders became active. Most of their attacks were directed against Yancey. The *Greensboro Beacon* stated that Yancey was the worst culprit in sectionalizing the party, and that he was a secessionist *par excellence.*[12]

The *Gainesville Independent* asked why Yancey, who had been whipped in 1848 and again in 1852, and who had then quit the political field should be considered the head of the Democratic Party, and why it should be *scandalum magnatum* to doubt his orthodoxy.[13] The *Dallas Gazette* said that a split in the national Democratic Party would throw victory to the "Black Republicans" and would be certain to bring on secession.[14]

---

[11] J. E. D. Yonge, "The Conservative Party in Alabama," in *Transactions of the Ala. Hist. Soc.,* IV. 153.

[12] *Greensboro Beacon,* in *Gainesville Independent,* Apr., 14, 1860.

[13] *Gainesville Independent,* Apr. 14, 1860.

[14] *Dallas Gazette,* Dec. 30, 1859.

In May, thirty-three leaders of the conservatives signed a call for a state convention to meet in Selma on June 4, and appoint delegates to the national Democratic convention which was to meet at Baltimore on June 18 and which was expected to nominate Douglas for president.[15]

On June 4, delegates representing twenty-eight counties assembled in Montgomery, to which city the convention had been transferred from Selma. All of the counties in the Tennessee Valley, except Morgan, about one-half of the Black Belt counties, and five of the counties of southwest Alabama were represented in the convention. The hill counties and the southeast counties were not represented. The editor of the *Southern Messenger*, which was supporting Bell for president, visited both this convention and the Southern Rights convention, which was being held in Montgomery on the same day; he was of the opinion that the latter was larger and composed of men of more ability than the former.[16]

Addresses were made before the convention by ex-Governor Winston, H. W. Hilliard, R. M. Patton, D. C. Humphreys, and Robert B. Lindsay, of Lauderdale. Resolutions were passed approving the principle of the Dred Scott decision and pledging to send delegates to the national convention at Baltimore. The delegates were not instructed, which left them free to support Douglas if they saw fit to do so.[17]

The movement for Bell in Alabama was initiated in the spring of 1860 in the western counties of the Black Belt by a group of old Whigs, who were bitterly opposed to Yancey and the secession Democrats, and whose unionism resembled that of the Douglas Democrats of north Alabama. But these Whigs refused to identify themselves with the Douglas Democrats as the latter had continuously, during the fifties, united with the Democrats of south Alabama to maintain the White Basis, which deprived the planters of representation for their slaves.[18]

The Bell movement was definitely launched by a call for a state convention which appeared in the *Selma Reporter* on May 23, eighteen

---

[15] *Southern Champion*, May 18, 1860.
[16] *Southern Messenger*, June 13, 1860.
[17] *Montgomery Confederation*, June 8, 1860.
[18] *Pickens Republican*, Apr. 19, 1860.

days after Bell had been nominated by a convention at Richmond, composed largely of old Whigs and Americans. The text of the call was as follows:

> We honestly believe that today there are over 30,000 honest conservative voters in Alabama who do not sympathize with or wish to vote for either wing of the Democracy of Alabama and who do not wish to vote for the Charleston nominee. They are men who are tired of continual agitation of slavery, since it has been settled by the Supreme Court decision and further agitation can do no good.
>
> That the disunion wing of Alabama Democracy has control of the party in Alabama is proved by the last State Convention of the party. Yancey and his right bowers have control, and unless conservative men rally around some sound National men, such as Bell and Everett, and put both wings of Democracy down, Alabama will be lost.
>
> We are no alarmist, but the signs of the times are ominous and Democracy has brought it upon us. Something must be done and done quickly. It will not do to trust Democracy longer. They have deceived the people and broken the pledges of 1856. Shall they be allowed to continue their warfare against the Union? Never! Never! Never![19]

A Constitutional Union convention, composed of supporters of Bell, assembled at Selma on June 27, 1860. Two hundred and four delegates, representing twenty-four counties and every congressional district, except the Huntsville, attended. Practically all of the delegates were Unionists, mostly old Whigs. The convention was predominantly a movement initiated in and confined to the western counties of the Black Belt. Not a leader of importance from east or north Alabama attended. Watts, Judge, Hooper, and Hilliard—all prominent Whigs—took no part in the convention, although Watts and Hilliard voted for the ticket in November.[20]

The convention repudiated the doctrine of popular sovereignty and claimed protection for slavery under the Dred Scott decision. It appointed presidential electors and an executive committee to promote the work of the party.[21]

---

[19] *Pickens Republican,* Mar. 29, 1860.
[20] *Southern Messenger,* July 4, 1860.
[21] *Ibid.* Four of the electors had been Americans or Whigs; the others were men of little prominence.

A fourth political movement was launched in the spring of 1860 by a group who called themselves the Southern Rights Opposition Party. The leaders of this party were G. W. Gayle, G. H. Short-ridge, S. F. Rice, and the two old American papers—the *Montgomery Mail* and the *Independent American.* Most of the leaders were former Whigs and Americans who refused to cooperate with the Constitutional Unionists or with either group of the Democrats.

Some of these leaders had advocated the formation of a new party as early as the summer of 1859, based on the principles of Yancey's Leagues of United Southerners.[22] They had approved the position taken by the Democratic state convention in January, 1860, but refused to affiliate with the Breckinridge party as they felt that it would reunite with the Douglas party if Douglas were elected president.[23]

The *Independent American* criticized Governor Moore for refusing to call a convention after Congress had betrayed the South in the Kansas controversy, and the party leaders had remained silent on the matter in order that "the harmony of the party" be preserved. This, according to the *Independent,* was wanton dishonesty.[24]

The *Montgomery Mail* approved the withdrawal of the seceders from the Charleston convention, but expressed the fear that it would only result in the erection of a new Democratic "wigwam" with a change of leaders, and this would not be acceptable to the Southern Rights organization. This paper wanted a party whose name would be broad enough "to furnish all a resting place for the sole of their political feet" as there were many men in south Alabama "who would never join any party called "Democratic." The feeling against the name was intensely strong, the *Mail* continued, and, as the party which a man has borne for thirty years becomes a part of him, he must not be merged into the name of his enemy organization when he surrenders his own party name.[25] The *Indepenedent American* agreed with this position.

A Southern Rights Opposition convention, composed of seventy-eight delegates from seven counties of the eastern Black Belt, as-

[22] *Clarke County Democrat,* June 2, 1860.
[23] *Independent American,* Apr. 11, 1860.
[24] *Ibid.,* Oct. 19, 1860.
[25] *Montgomery Mail,* in *Independent American,* May 9, 1860.

sembled at Estelle Hall in Montgomery on July 2, 1860. The convention passed strong resolutions regarding slavery extension, but split over a resolution, introduced by Mr. Watts, declaring that the views of Bell and Everett on slavery extension were satisfactory and pledging the support of the convention for them. Mr. Watts and a minority group left the convention and later supported Bell for president; the larger group finally accepted the leadership of Yancey and supported Breckinridge.[26]

During the campaign, some of the speakers for Breckinridge and Lane boldly advocated secession in case of the election of Lincoln. The leaders organized clubs of "Minute Men," who were pledged to carry out secession. The *Montgomery Mail,* which supported Breckinridge after the collapse of the Opposition movement, took a leading part in the organization of these clubs, which were confined largely to the eastern counties of the Black Belt.[27] The pledge of the "Minute Men" was as follows:

> We, the undersigned citizens of **** county, Alabama, in view of the impending crisis necessarily incident upon the election of a Black Republican to the Presidency of these United States, and in view of our duty to our section, ourselves, and our dearest right which must fall upon us in the event of the triumph of Northern fanaticism, hereby form ourselves into an association under the name and style of *Minute Men,* and do solemnly pledge ourselves, our fortunes, and our sacred honors, to sustain the Southern Constitutional equality in the Union, or failing in that, to establish our independence out of it.[28]

The Douglas and Bell men attacked the Breckinridge supporters as being dangerous secessionists. Douglas himself was claiming that the election of Lincoln would not be a sufficient cause for secession, and this attitude was being taken by his supporters in Alabama.[29]

---

[26] *Montgomery Mail,* in *South Alabamian,* July 7, 1860. The counties represented with the number of delegates from each were: Montgomery 32; Lowndes 17; Macon 12; Autauga 10; Butler 4; Pike 2; Russell 1. Not a county of West Alabama was represented.

[27] *Montgomery Mail,* Nov. 7, 1860; *Montgomery Post,* Nov. 7, 1860.

[28] *Alabama State Sentinel,* Nov. 14, 1860.

[29] *Alabama State Sentinel,* Oct. 10, 1860; *Pickens Republican,* Sept. 20, 1860.

In October, Douglas came to Alabama and made speeches in Huntsville, Montgomery, Selma, and Mobile. From ten to fifteen thousand people, according to a paper sympathetic to Douglas, attended these speakings. Four hundred people from Marshall County went to Huntsville to hear him, traveling on horseback, on wagons, or on foot. Many of them arrived the day before Douglas reached there.[30]

The Bell men, for the most part, were on the defensive, being forced to defend their candidate against the charge of being too submissive to the North. It was claimed that Bell had said in Nashville in the summer that he "would coalesce with the Black Republicans themselves to preserve the Union."[31] The Bell papers denied this and pointed out that Bell had held since 1848 the opinion that the government was obligated to protect the slaveowners in the territories, and that he believed slavery, as it existed in the South, to be sanctioned by the Bible.[32]

The Bell men in the preceding session of the legislature had voted against a bill providing for military defenses, and this was now embarrassing them.[33]

Late in the campaign, when it became evident that Breckinridge was the leading candidate, efforts were made to unite the two minority parties against him. The Bell leaders assembled in Selma on October 10, and passed resolutions instructing their electors to vote in the electoral college for any candidate who might be able to defeat Lincoln, provided the party of the candidate for whom this vote was to be cast should have passed similar resolutions.[34]

There was much bitterness exhibited during the campaign. Rumors were rife that abolitionists in the state were encouraging slaves to revolt, and even poisoning the wells of the slaveowners. Men who were reported to be abolitionists were tarred and feathered and driven from the community.[35] Letters were forged to incriminate men who were considered not sufficiently loyal to the South.[36]

---

[30] *Southern Advocate*, Oct. 31, 1860.
[31] *Southern Era*, Sept. 1, 1860.
[32] *Pickens Republican*, Aug. 16, 1860.
[33] *Clayton Banner*, Aug. 16, 1860.
[34] *Alabama State Sentinel*, Oct. 24, 1860.
[35] *Clayton Banner*, Sept. 27, 1860.
[36] *Montgomery Post*, Oct. 16, 1860.

The total vote cast was over ninety thousand. Breckinridge received a majority of seven thousand over the other candidates combined; Bell polled twice the vote of Douglas. Breckinridge received a majority in the Huntsville, Talladega, and Eufaula congressional districts—all bordering on the state of Georgia. He received a majority in thirty of the counties and a plurality in forty-two of them. Douglas received a plurality of about 1,600 in five counties; Bell received a plurality of about 400 in five counties. Douglas' strength was greatest in the Tennessee Valley, the stronghold of Unionism in 1851-52, and Bell's strength was greatest in the Black Belt. The vote in round figures was 48,000 for Breckinridge, 27,000 for Bell, and 13,000 for Douglas.[37]

When the result of the election was known, the secessionists in Alabama began to urge Governor Moore to call a convention to determine what the policy of the state should be in the crisis. A joint resolution providing for a convention in such a contingency had passed the two houses of the legislature, with only two dissenting votes, and the governor had approved it. A convention met in Montgomery on November 10, and appointed a committee of twenty-one, divided almost equally between the Democrats and the Whigs, to consult with the governor as to the advisability of calling a convention.[38]

Numerous county meetings were held, urging a state convention and passing resolutions for secession. The following brief resolution, adopted in a meeting in Selma, was typical: "We, the citizens of Selma, are opposed to living under a government with a Black Republican President."[39]

Many of the Bell and Douglas leaders became secessionists as a result of Lincoln's election. James Webb, a prominent Whig planter of the Black Belt and a Bell elector, wrote to Thomas H. Herndon on November 28, that having satisfied his mind "that our future career is to be one of eternal discord, and of angry crimination and recrimination, I conclude that separation, with all its consequences, is not only inevitable but desirable.[40]

---

[37] Official returns, in Alabama Archives Department.
[38] *West Alabamian,* Nov. 28, 1860.
[39] *Alabama State Sentinel,* Nov. 13, 1860.
[40] *West Alabamian,* Nov. 28, 1860.

T. H. Watts, a Bell supporter, wrote thus of the election of Lincoln:

> A piratical fanatical crew has taken possession, and now stands erect, in haughty defiance, on the deck of the old Ship Constitution! The black flag of abolition domination and Southern subjection will soon be hoisted at her mast head; and where Washington commanded, a Lincoln will rule****

With regard to the dilatory tactics which the cooperationists were advocating, Watts said:

> Why longer delay? What folly to talk about "forms of law" and "forms of constitutions," and "overt acts?" The vilest oppressions, and the grandest frauds and tyrannies the world ever saw, have been perpetrated under the forms of law and consitutions.[41]

Ex-Governor Winston, who had supported Douglas, came out for secession. He said:

> I look upon the position of those who talk about an overt act as a lame and impotent text to avoid the issue**** As for coordination, that is but a device of timidity and cowardice, or a piece of strategy for delay and postponement. My own views are that we should go into the convention and take steps for a separacy.[42]

About the middle of December, the Southern congressmen in Washington issued an address to their constituents, declaring that the Republican Party was resolute in its purpose to make no concession to satisfy the South, and stating that there was no hope for relief in the Union. The address ended with these words:

> We are satisfied that the honor, the safety, and the independence of the Southern people require the organization of a Southern Confederacy—a result to be obtained only by separate state secession—and that the primary object of each slaveholding state ought to be its speedy and absolute separation from a Union with hostile States.[43]

---

[41] *Southern Messenger,* Nov. 21, 1860.
[42] *Montgomery Advertiser,* Dec. 5, 1860.
[43] *Montgomery Confederation,* Dec. 21, 1860.

This address was signed by all of the Alabama congressmen except Houston and Cobb.

The churches became involved in the agitation. Dr. Basil Manly, president of the University of Alabama, introduced a resolution in the Baptist state convention at Tuskegee which claimed that the Baptist Church for the most part held aloof from political controversies, but as the Union had failed to answer the purpose for which it was created, the Baptists were prepared to defend the sovereignty and independence of Alabama. The convention was *"heartily, deliberately, unanimously,* and *solemnly united"* on the adoption of this resolution.[44]

A Methodist conference at Montgomery, although disclaiming any intention of meddling in politics, passed the following resolution: (a) African slavery as it exists in the South is wise, humane and righteous, and approved by God, and any measure looking to its overthrow can be dictated only by blind fanaticism; (b) that the election to the presidency of any man subversive of Southern rights can be considered only as a declaration of hostility; (c) that the conference members placed their lives and fortunes upon the altar of their state.[45]

Soon after the election of Lincoln, Governor Moore, in accordance with the resolution of the legislature, had called an election for December 24, to elect delegates to a state convention which was to meet in Montgomery on January 7, 1861, to determine what policy Alabama should adopt with regard to secession.

A few conservative leaders attempted to stem the tide of secession sentiment. They pointed out that secession was a very doubtful expedient, even admitting that the aggressions of the North justified this procedure. Senator Fitzpatrick, in reply to a request for his attitude, wrote that Alabama had a perfect right, acting in its sovereign capacity, to secede, but under the present circumstances

---

[44] B. F. Riley, *op. cit.,* pp. 141-32. Riley states that this declaration of the Alabama Baptists hastened secession.

[45] *Gainesville Independent,* Jan. 5, 1861.

he would not advise secession, "but would be opposed to this course on the part of the state alone, believing it unwise and unsafe."[46]

Judge John A. Campbell, who had been closely identified with Calhoun and the movement for secession in 1850, was counseling conservatism and opposing secession, except by cooperation with the other Southern states.[47]

The *Alabama State Sentinel* in an editorial headed, "Union Men to Your Posts," warned the people that there was a movement on to dissolve the Union, and it urged the friends of the Union to unite, irrespective of party, to oppose the secessionists. It stated that there was grave danger from the "Minute Men" who had signs and passwords and were pledged to disunionism. The *Sentinel* claimed that the secession movement was being encouraged by influences at Columbia, South Carolina, from which documents were being sent into Alabama.[48]

The strongest Union sentiment was in north Alabama. The first concerted action against secession was taken in this section in a convention at Leighton, Lawrence County, in the early part of December. This convention passed a resolution which became the principle advocated by the conservatives—opposition to separate state secession, but adherence to any action taken by a convention of all the Southern states.[49]

Gradually two parties developed which contested for delegates to the state convention, one party favoring separate state secession, and the other advocating secession only with cooperation with other states. There were various shades of opinion among the co-operationists, varying from unconditional unionism to an advocacy of secession with the promise from the other Southern states that they would give Alabama their support in case Alabama should secede.

In the election of December 24, the secession candidates carried twenty-nine counties for an approximate vote of 36,000; the cooper-

---

[46] *Montgomery Post,* Nov. 21, 1860.
[47] Letter from Campbell to Henry Tutwiler, Jan. 2, 1861, in Alabama Archives Department.
[48] *Alabama State Sentinel,* in *Selma Reporter,* Nov. 14, 1860.
[49] *North Alabamian,* Dec. 21, 1860.

ationists carried twenty-two counties for a vote of 28,000, and one other county, the vote of which is not available. Fifty-four of the one hundred members elected were secessionists and forty-six were cooperationists. In eight counties, principally in southeast Alabama, the secession candidates had no opposition.

The secessionists received majorities in the four congressional districts of south Alabama; the cooperationists carried the three north Alabama districts. Only one county, Calhoun, in north Alabama elected secessionists, and only one county in South Alabama, Conecuh, gave a majority for a cooperationist. The vote shows a distinct sectionalism between north and south Alabama.

The total vote was about 65,000, which was 25,000 less than the total vote in the presidential election in November. This decrease is partially accounted for by the fact that the cooperationists had little or no opposition in three north Alabama counties, and the secessionists had little opposition in fifteen south Alabama counties. In none of these counties was there a normal vote cast.

In the counties of the Tennessee Valley the cooperationist vote corresponded closely to the total vote cast for Douglas and Bell and the secession vote corresponded fairly well with the vote for Breckinridge, but in the mountainous counties, which were always strongly Democratic, the secession candidates ran behind the vote for Breckinridge. Nineteen counties which gave majorities for Breckinridge in November gave majorities against secession candidates. Lauderdale, Lawrence, and Madison which gave pluralities for Douglas gave about 2,300 majority for the cooperationists.

In some of the Black Belt and other counties of south Alabama the secession majorities were larger than were the majorities for Breckinridge. Apparently the Bell supporters joined the Breckinridge men in support of secession. In the five counties which Bell had carried in November, the secession majorities were more than 2,500 in December, and in two of these counties the secessionists had no opposition.

On January 7, 1861, two weeks after the election of delegates, the state convention assembled at Montgomery. The cooperationists used various tactics to prevent secession, or, at least, to try to delay it. After a session of four days the convention voted in favor of secession and the delegates returned home to face a future which was filled with gloomy forebodings. The Southern Rights movement had at last succeeded and had carried out the threat which had been made in Mr. Yancey's "Alabama Platform" of 1848.

CONCLUSION

The Democratic Party was predominant in Alabama politics from 1847 to 1860, with the exception of the year 1851. The period from 1847 to 1856 was characterized by party contests between two organized parties; the period from 1856 through 1860 by factional contests within the Democratic Party for party leadership.

The only thoroughgoing change which the Democratic Party passed through during the period was in 1850-51, when the party split over an acceptance of the compromise measures of 1850. The party easily reorganized in 1851, upon the principle of an acceptance of the Compromise of 1850, and continued in cooperation with the national Democratic Party up to 1860.

The Whig Party had a much more complicated history during the period. It was a minority party up to 1850, but won the elections of 1851, in fusion with the Union Democrats of north Alabama. This success of the Whigs was of short duration, because the party was never able to completely reorganize after 1851 and to muster the strength which it had had prior to 1850.

The Whigs seized the Know Nothing movement of 1854-56 to restore their party, but without success. During the years 1857-60, they were without a regularly organized party. Some of them became affiliated with the Democratic Party, some continued to oppose the Democrats under the name of the Opposition Party, and some abstained from politics. During the year 1860, Whigs were found in the ranks of the Southern Rights Democrats; the national Democrats, and the Constitutional Union Party of Bell. Many of them in the Black Belt had become strongly aggressive for Southern Rights by this time.

In general, party history from 1847 to 1860 was marked by changes and complications, both as to change in party names and the personnel of parties and party leadership. There was, however, less breaking of party affiliations than the various changes in party names and issues might indicate. The tendency to adhere to party, to vote as their fathers had voted, was strong among the men of both parties during the fifties.

Loyalty to party was probably no stronger among the Democrats than among the Whigs. But party successes and patronage of the former gave them an advantage in securing party allegiance. Twice during the decade—in 1851 when the Union Democrats joined the Whigs, and again in 1855 when many Democrats joined the Know Nothings—the Democratic Party was threatened with disaster. In both cases, however, the party was able to revive and to win presidential elections the following years. The strong traditions of the Democratic Party explain much of the political history during this period.

The Whigs failed to maintain their party but they retained much loyalty to party principles and traditions. Many of the Whigs disapproved of the alliance with the Know Nothings in 1855. After 1856, many old Whigs united with the Democrats, but, as a rule, they did not feel much enthusiasm for their newly formed alliance. The large vote which Bell received in 1860 in the old Whig strongholds attests to the inclination of the Whigs to remain loyal to their party principles.

The Democratic Party had better leadership in Alabama during the fifties than had the Whigs. This leadership during the early part of the decade was in the hands of a group of men, principally planters and lawyers, who lived in or near Montgomery. This group, the so-called "Montgomery Regency," exercised an important influence over the state legislature, the election of United States senators, and the election of governors.

The Democratic leaders of the Black Belt were able to defeat the Whigs in the election of state officers by making compromises with the conservative Democrats of north Alabama. One agreement between the two sections was for each section to have one of the United States senators; another was that the Black Belt Democrats should support the White Basis principle of representation which gave north Alabama an advantage in representation in Congress and in the state legislature. Only twice during the period were the Whigs able to get the support of the north Alabama Democrats against the Black Belt Democrats.

Planters shared with lawyers the political leadership of the early fifties. Many of the Democratic planters were aggressive Southern Rights men in the early fifties, but by the middle of the decade they were becoming more conservative. Yancey was never able to get such planters as Bolling Hall and Benjamin Fitzpatrick to follow his leadership.

By the middle of the fifties, the influence of the planter group in politics declined, and a group of young men, principally lawyers, came to the front as leaders. Many lawyers were editors of papers which gave them the opportunity for leadership. Their knowledge of laws and of government and their ability to set forth in glowing speeches the rights of the Southern people caused the people to look to them for leadership. This was the group of which Mr. Yancey became the leader. It would be no great exaggeration to speak of the conversion of the people of Alabama to the policy of resistance to the North as a lawyers' revolution.

There was a development from 1848 to 1860 which, although not always causing party changes, was important as culminating in the breaking up of parties and ultimately in secession. This was the gradual conversion of the people to the conviction that the formation of a Southern party was necessary for the safety of the South.

This feeling that there should be a Southern party, separate in all respects from any national party, was first advocated by Yancey after the rejection by the Democratic convention at Charleston of his "Alabama Platform," in 1848. The agitation over slavery extension from 1847 to 1850 gave Yancey and his group the opportunity of carrying out his plan, which he accomplished by the formation of the Southern Rights Party in 1850-51. The defeat of this party in the elections of 1851 and the return of most of the Southern Rights leaders into the reorganized Democratic Party left Yancey without a party. He took little interest in the elections in 1852 and 1855, and did not engage actively in politics until the presidential election of 1856, when he returned to his party in support of Buchanan for president. The work performed by Yancey in 1856 gave him high standing in the party. Again he attempted to organize a sectional party, this time through Leagues of United Southerners. But he was defeated for a seat in the senate of the

United States and was unsuccessful in the organization of his Leagues, and, consequently, was forced to bide his time.

The failure of the Charleston convention in April, 1860, to nominate a candidate, pledged to the principles of the "Alabama Platform," gave Yancey the opportunity for which he had been forced to wait ten years. The majority of seven thousand received by Breckinridge gave Yancey and his group for the first time political leadership in the state.

A great impetus was given to the efforts of Yancey to break up national parties by the activities of the Northern opponents of slavery and slavery extension. The policy of the Northern Whigs, some of whom were abolitionists, and of the Taylor administration caused the dissolution of the Whig Party in the early fifties. The attitude of the Americans in the North had a similar effect upon the American Party in Alabama in the middle fifties. The Whigs hoped as late as 1856 to revive their party, but could make no headway after the formation of the Republican Party.

The political party was an important factor in delaying secession sentiment in Alabama. The political leaders were strongly opposed to attacks on the slavery rights of the South, but they were willing to make compromises of principles in order to get party unity and welfare. This policy of compromises characterized the history of the Democratic Party as long as it had had opposition from another party. In 1860, when there was no longer opposition from any organized party, the secessionists won the leadership of the party and carried the state into secession.

APPENDIX A

TABLES OF ELECTION FIGURES

VOTE IN PRESIDENTIAL ELECTIONS, 1848-60

	1848		1852			1856		1860		
	Taylor (Whig)	Cass (Dem.)	Scott (Whig)	Pierce (Dem.)	Troup (S.R.)	Fillmore (Amer.)	Buchanan (Dem.)	Breckinridge (S.R.Dem.)	Douglas (N.Dem.)	Bell (Whig)
Autauga	553	471	196	322	205	475	·621	611	394	256
Baldwin	100	133	62	72		219	144	129	81	248
Barbour	1,205	614	297	309	571	857	1,445	1,715	9	644
Benton	566	1,272	74	918		443	1,687	2,347	54	364
Bibb	474	416	238	346	3	479	539	613	156	582
Blount	134	526	55	422		37	770	546	443	51
Butler	772	277	345	251		792	777	918	111	1,079
Chambers	1,323	689	668	616	21	967	1,141	1,017	157	918
Cherokee	630	921	242	735		455	1,537	1,706	223	527
Choctaw			227	334	2	404	643	542	158	472
Clarke	120	327	98	479	19	222	754	952	77	255
Coffee	192	174	113	239	18	301	703	878	2	394
Conecuh	426	231	216	287	15	408	425	348	205	338
Coosa	626	683	294	709	42	802	1,167	930	844	706
Covington	248	92	52	117		288	304	404	12	416
Dale	368	555	170	406	31	419	945	1,280	5	277
Dallas	860	618	386	440	244	676	831	833	339	620
DeKalb	257	650	139	501		130	900	649	202	204
Fayette	272	841	81	516		440	799	1,299	37	359
Franklin	510	795	462	993	5	711	1,056	902	460	715
Greene	1,088	712	694	555		784	694	696	157	765
Hancock			9	65		14	221	203	147	40
Henry	504	496	94	184	140	471	966	1,109	0	317
Jackson	136	1,589	83	1,154		97	1,790	1,760	565	130
Jefferson	288	385	114	339		196	697	831	77	245

County										
Lauderdale	695	772	441	803		555	1,141	706	790	444
Lawrence	663	656	512	588	5	631	699	370	576	525
Limestone	374	833	227	662		281	790	522	325	368
Lowndes	761	434	126	186	206	703	699	1,007	57	592
Macon	1,464	538	772	658	99	1,239	1,039	1,184	46	1,210
Madison	465	1,385	354	1,300		401	1,476	591	1,300	400
Marengo	739	553	450	526	20	567	789	838	63	512
Marion	193	514	118	467		*198	700	986	62	197
Marshall	246	708	111	568		89	883	441	763	165
Mobile	1,319	1,073	1,123	1,380	94	1,771	1,838	1,541	1,823	1,629
Monroe	479	216	264	260	45	469	604	530	222	446
Montgomery	1,176	669	717	557	98	1,158	1,100	1,555	133	1,034
Morgan	361	335	208	482	2	222	808	549	545	144
Perry	826	631	261	512	13	824	808	982	99	791
Pickens	1,044	931	568	752	9	669	1,037	1,211	16	619
Pike	935	663	379	703	71	1,178	1,262	1,581	84	1,227
Randolph	461	770	102	707	3	683	1,460	1,734	343	537
Russell	970	577	434	522	24	855	994	993	53	854
St. Clair	150	456	44	455		83	818	963	240	174
Shelby	557	368	317	315	3	468	787	853	186	570
Sumter	820	771	482	497	4	532	703	684	136	473
Talladega	869	820	372	672	4	896	1,134	1,307	74	1,091
Tallapoosa	972	920	351	845	19	1,276	1,478	1,451	298	1,274
Tuscaloosa	976	694	527	475	3	973	680	1,219	23	1,023
Walker	231	383	54	217		146	449	446	303	103
Washington	72	65	52	65	2	152	194	176	24	155
Wilcox	639	479	286	398	9	446	813	833	113	355
	30,109	30,895	15,061	26,881	2,040	28,552	46,739	48,671	13,613	27,834

Figures for 1848, 1852 and 1856 are from "A Political Textbook for 1860," New York, 1860, pp. 228-29; figures for 1860 are from official returns in the Alabama Archives and History Department.

CONGRESSIONAL ELECTIONS
FIRST CONGRESSIONAL DISTRICT
MOBILE

	1847				1849				1851				1853			
	Gayle, John (Whig)	Taylor, John (Democrat)	Majority	Party	Alston, W. J. (Taylor Whig)	Sellers, C. C. (Sou. Rts. Dem.)	Majority	Party	Bragg, John (Sou. Rts. Dem.)	Langdon, C. C. (Unionist)	Majority	Party	Phillips, P. (Sou. Rts. Dem.)	Lockwood, E. (Unionist Whig)	Majority	Party
Baldwin	156	196	40	Dem.	198	192	6	Whig	211	207	4	S. R.	143	178	35	Union
Butler	673	302	371	Whig	692	342	350	Whig	653	395	258	S. R.	314	823	509	Union
Choctaw																
Clarke	358	586	228	Dem.	216	609	393	Dem.	718	161	557	S. R.	515	240	275	S. R.
Conecuh	358	383	25	Dem.	416	343	73	Whig	377	433	56	Union	388	455	67	Union
Dallas																
Marengo	774	565	209	Whig	681	608	73	Whig	637	662	25	Union	664	538	126	S. R.
Mobile	1,280	1,117	163	Whig	1,343	1,192	151	Whig	1,678	1,225	453	S. R.	1,644	1,407	237	S. R.
Monroe	571	351	220	Whig	504	343	161	Whig	572	400	172	S. R.	408	603	195	Union
Washington	288	393	105	Dem.	308	379	71	Dem.	526	366	160	S. R.	154	85	69	S. R.
Wilcox	592	597	5	Dem.	564	580	16	Dem.	No Returns				650	448	202	S. R.
	5,050	4,490	560		4,922	4,588	334		5,372	3,849	1,523		4,880	4,777	103	

Figures for 1847—*Independent Monitor*, Aug. 17, 1847.
Figures for 1849—*Mobile Register and Journal*, Aug. 27, 1849.
Figures for 1851—Totals are official returns; figures for the counties are from *Macon Republican*, Aug. 18, 1851.
Figures for 1853—Official returns.

	1855				1857				1859			
	Walker, P. (American)	Stallworth, J. A. (Democrat)	Majority	Party	Stallworth, J. A. (Democrat)	McCaskill, J. (American)	Majority	Party	Stallworth, J. A. (Democrat)	Shepard, F. B. (Secess. Dem.)	Majority	Party
Baldwin	204	60	144	Amer.	203	225	22	Amer.	205	198	7	Dem.
Butler												Dem.
Choctaw	437	502	65	Dem.	697	376	321	Dem.	697	256	441	Dem.
Clarke	287	450	163	Dem.	742	192	550	Dem.	902	217	685	Dem.
Conecuh	360	446	86	Dem.	564	212	352	Dem.	576	313	263	Dem.
Dallas	906	617	289	Amer.	787	614	173	Dem.	779	469	290	Dem.
Marengo	618	632	14	Dem.	753	404	349	Dem.	651	381	270	Dem.
Mobile	1,760	1,162	598	Amer.	1,775	1,321	454	Dem.	1,925	1,578	347	Dem.
Monroe	517	557	40	Dem.	625	463	162	Dem.	710	296	414	Dem.
Washington	75	51	24	Amer.	202	130	72	Dem.	241	154	87	Dem.
Wilcox	492	660	168	Dem.	710	393	317	Dem.	666	376	290	Dem.
	5,656	5,137	519		7,058	4,330	2,728		7,352	4,258	3,094	

Figures for 1855—*Montgomery Advertiser*, Aug. 24, 1853. Official returns give 5293 and 4689 for the totals and 604 for the majority.

Figures for 1857—Totals are official returns; counties, from *Clarke County Democrat*, Aug. 21, 1857.

Figures for 1859—*Clarke County Democrat*, Aug. 18, 1859.

SECOND CONGRESSIONAL DISTRICT

Montgomery and Eufaula District until 1854, then the Eufaula District

	1847	1849				1851			
	Hilliard, H. W. (Whig) No Opposition	Hilliard, H. W. (Whig)	Pugh, J. L. (Ind. Whig)	Majority	Party	Abercrombie, J. (Unionist Whig)	Cochran, John (Secessionist)	Majority	Party
Barbour		992	984	8	Whig	961	1,117	156	Sec.
Butler									
Coffee		302	441	139	Dem.	369	401	32	Sec.
Covington		231	202	29	Whig	316	114	202	Union
Dale		400	647	247	Dem.	565	554	11	Union
Henry		407	637	230	Dem.	543	663	120	Sec.
Lowndes									
Macon		1,393	669	724	Whig	1,395	776	619	Union
Montgomery		1,068	867	201	Whig	1,181	811	370	Union
Pike		1,014	870	144	Whig	1,190	958	232	Union
Russell		963	658	305	Whig	1,078	517	561	Union
		6,770	5,975	795		7,598	5,911	1,687	

Figures for 1849—Mobile *Register and Journal*, Aug. 27, 1849.
Figures for 1851—*Macon Republican*, Aug. 18, 1851..

County	1853 Abercrombie, J. (Union Whig)	1853 Clopton, D. (Democrat)	1853 Majority	1853 Party	1855 Shorter, E. S. (Anti-Know Nothing Democrat)	1855 Alford, J. C. (American)	1855 Majority	1855 Party	1857 Shorter, E. S. (Democrat)	1857 Peterson, B. (American)	1857 Majority	1857 Party	1859 Pugh, J. L. (Democrat)	1859 Sappington, J. E. (Sou. Rights)
Barbour	1,128	1,023	105	Whig	1,436	995	441	Dem.	1,291	859	432	Dem.		
Butler					637	727	90	Amer.	827	746	61	Dem.	945	475
Coffee	532	442	90	Whig	737	414	323	Dem.	778	145	633	Dem.		
Covington	407	102	305	Whig	300	302	2	Amer.	380	222	158	Dem.		
Dale	775	404	371	Whig	1,007	438	569	Dem.	1,105	347	758	Dem.		
Henry	862	401	461	Whig	901	447	454	Dem.	875	423	452	Dem.		
Lowndes					547	828	281	Amer.	763	662	101	Dem.		
Macon	850	1,075	225	Dem.										
Montgomery	787	782	5	Whig										
Pike	1,195	989	206	Whig	1,153	1,339	186	Amer.	1,398	1,050	338	Dem.	1,698	140
Russell	938	620	318	Whig										
	7,474	5,838	1,636		6,718	5,490	1,228		7,417	4,464	2,953			

Figures for 1853—*Macon Republican*, Aug. 25, 1855; the figures are official.
Figures for 1855—*Montgomery Advertiser*, Aug. 21, 1855. Official returns give 6,716 and 5,520 for totals and 1,196 for majority.
Figures for 1857—Original returns.
Figures for 1853—*Macon Republican*, Aug. 25, 1855; the totals are official.

THIRD CONGRESSIONAL DISTRICT

Wetumpka District until 1854, then the Montgomery District

	1847	1849				1851			1853			
	Harris, S. W. (Democrat) No Opposition	Harris, S. W. (Democrat)	Hunter, John (Whig)	Majority	Party	Harris, S. W. (Sec. Dem.)	Mudd, W. S. (Union Whig)	Party	Harris, S. W. (S. R. Dem.)	Moore (Union Whig)	Majority	Party
Autauga		622	486	136	Dem.			S. R.	646	332	314	S. R.
Bibb		589	477	112	Dem.			S. R.	665	193	472	S. R.
Chambers												
Coosa		1,020	620	400	Dem.			S. R.	1,300	182	1,118	S. R.
Dallas		644	795	151	Whig	710	700	S. R.	624	132	492	S. R.
Jefferson		594	377	217	Dem.			S. R.	870	199	671	S. R.
Lowndes		655	801	146	Whig			S. R.	588	274	314	S. R.
Macon												
Montgomery		855	826	29	Dem.			S. R.	842	192	650	S. R.
Perry												
Russell								S. R.	859	118	741	S. R.
Shelby		532	589	57	Whig							
Tallapoosa												
		5,511	4,971	540		4,967	4,385		6,394	1,622	4,772	

Figures for 1849—*Southern Advocate*, Aug. 17, 1849.
Figures for 1851—Original returns.
Figures for 1853—*Montgomery Advertiser*, Aug. 24, 1853; official returns give 5,770 and 1,490 for totals but do not include Dallas County.

	1855				1857				1859			
	Dowdell, J. F. (Democrat)	Watts, T. H. (American)	Majority	Party	Dowdell, J. F. (Democrat)	Judge, T. J. (States Rights Whig)	Majority	Party	Clopton, D. (Democrat)	Judge, T. J. (States Rights Whig)	Majority	Party
Autauga	698	579	119	Dem.	683	548	135	Dem.	605	619	14	Whig
Bibb												
Chambers	1,232	867	365	Dem.	1,139	949	190	Dem.	1,095	1,028	67	Dem.
Coosa												
Dallas												
Jefferson												
Lowndes												
Macon	963	1,265	302	Whig	1,041	1,316	275	Whig	1,213	1,220	7	Whig
Montgomery	949	1,175	226	Whig	1,106	1,256	150	Whig	1,246	1,347	101	Whig
Perry												
Russell	1,017	708	309	Whig	887	955	68	Whig	1,029	993	36	Dem.
Shelby												
Tallapoosa	1,468	1,192	276	Dem.	1,649	1,395	254	Dem.	1,691	1,459	232	Dem.
	6,327	5,786	541		6,505	6,419	86		6,879	6,666	213	

Figures for 1855—*Montgomery Advertiser*, Aug. 14, 1855; official returns give 6,342 and 5,808 and 534 majority.
1857—*Montgomery Advertiser*, Aug. 17, 1857.
1859—*Montgomery Advertiser*, Aug. 17, 1859.

FOURTH CONGRESSIONAL DISTRICT
TUSCALOOSA

	1847				1849				1851			
	Inge, S. W. (Democrat)	Murphy, W. M. (Whig)	Majority	Party	Inge, S. W. (Democrat)	Baldwin, Jos. (Whig)	Majority	Party	Erwin, John (Sou. Rights Dem.)	Smith, W. R. (Unionist)	Majority	Party
Bibb	------	------	------	------	------	------	------	------	------	------	------	------
Fayette	920	225	695	Dem.	1,005	300	705	Dem.	608	630	22	Union
Greene	667	1,059	392	Whig	783	1,047	264	Whig	937	645	292	S. R.
Perry												
Pickens	1,072	1,039	33	Dem.	1,020	952	68	Dem.	1,037	784	253	S. R.
Sumter	1,011	1,001	10	Dem.	988	932	56	Dem.	836	832	4	S. R.
Tuscaloosa	858	1,036	178	Whig	869	1,014	145	Whig	696	1,282	586	Union
Choctaw	------	------	------	------	------	------	------	------	------	------	------	------
	4,528	4,360	168		4,665	4,245	420		4,114	4,173	59	

Figures for 1847—Tuscaloosa *Independent Monitor*, Aug. 17, 1847.
Figures for 1849—Mobile *Register and Journal*, Aug. 27, 1849.
Figures for 1851—*Southern Advocate*, Aug. 27, 1851; official returns give same totals.

	1853			1855				1857				1859		
County	Smith, W. R. (Union Dem.)	Moore, Sydenham (Sou. Rights Dem.)	Hale, S. F. (Whig)	Party	Smith, W. R. (American)	Moore, Sydenham (Democrat)	Majority	Party	Moore, Sydenham (Democrat)	Smith, W. R. (American)	Majority	Party	Moore, Sydenham (Democrat)	Smith, W. R.
Bibb	945			U. D.	694	305	389	Dem.	679	543	136	Dem.		
Fayette	221	266	82	Whig		50 Maj.	50	Dem.	995	592	403	Dem.		
Greene		680	705		726	530	196	Dem.	925	688	237	Dem.	1,007	
Perry	490	673	612	Dem.	952	599	353	Dem.	885	770	115	Dem.	1,027 Maj.	
Pickens	267	604	460	Dem.	757	842	85	Dem.	1,203	654	549	Dem.		
Sumter	989	289	573	U. D.	618	545	73	Dem.	727	531	196	Dem.	641	53
Tuscaloosa	133	462	337	Dem.	1,237	356	881	Amer.	1,018	1,174	156	Amer.		
Choctaw														
	3,045	2,974	2,769		5,034	3,177	1,857		6,432	4,952	1,480			

Figures for 1853—Official returns.
Figures for 1855—*Montgomery Advertiser*, Sept. 22, 1855; official returns give 5,089 and 3,341 for totals.
Figures for 1857—Official returns.
Figures for 1859—Official returns.

FIFTH CONGRESSIONAL DISTRICT
FLORENCE

	1847			1849			1851		
	Houston, G. S. (Democrat)	Hubbard, D. (Democrat)	Majority	Hubbard, D. (Democrat)	O'Neal (Democrat)	Wood (Whig)	Houston, G. S. (Union Democrat)	Hubbard, D. (Sec. Dem.)	Party
Hancock							No Returns		
Franklin	913	662	251	999	360	531		240 Maj.	S. R.
Lauderdale	1,125	332	793	599	316	800	451 Maj.		Union
Lawrence	397	971	574	872	26	552		22 Maj.	S. R.
Limestone	795	319	476	605	262	387	316 Maj.		Union
Marion	270 Maj.			548	381	140	No Returns		
Morgan	696	400	296	557	72	442	170 Maj.		Union
Walker	550	294	256	395	238	232	286 Maj.		Union
	4,746	2,978	1,768	4,575	1,655	3,084	1,223	262	961

Figures for 1847—Southern Advocate, Aug. 20, 1847.
Figures for 1849—Southern Advocate, Aug. 17, 1849.
Figures for 1851—Southern Advocate, Aug. 13, 1851.

	1853	1855	1857			1859		
	Houston, G. S. (No Opposition)	Houston, G. S. (No Opposition)	Houston, G. S. (Democrat)	Hubbard, D. (So. Rts. Dem.)	Majority	Houston, G. S. (Democrat)	Hewlett, W. A. (Democrat)	Majority
Hancock	93		196	189	7	244	263	19
Franklin	763		721	919	198	1,076	665	411
Lauderdale	837		863	642	221	1,146	536	610
Lawrence	569		632	614	18	633	733	100
Limestone			701	367	334	965	441	524
Marion	689		518	587	69	595	716	121
Morgan	540		588	402	186	722	488	234
Walker	531		634	236	398	583	456	127
	4,022		4,853	3,956	897	5,964	4,298	1,666

Figures for 1853: Original returns; there was a scattering vote of 210 in Lauderdale County.
Figures for 1855—Houston received 5,770 votes. Official returns.
Figures for 1857—Official returns.
Figures for 1859—*Southern Advocate*, Aug. 25, 1859.

SIXTH CONGRESSIONAL DISTRICT
HUNTSVILLE

| | 1847 | | | 1849 | | | 1851 | | |
	Cobb, W. R. W. (Democrat)	Acklen, Wm. (Democrat)	Pope, B. F. (Democrat)	Cobb, W. R. W. (Democrat)	Clemens, Jere. (Democrat)	Majority	Cobb, W. R. W. (Union Dem.)	Murphy, Robert (Sou. Rts. Dem.)	Majority
Blount	347	334	210	487	617	130	400 Maj.	---	400
Cherokee	---	---	---	---	---	---	500 Maj.	---	500
DeKalb	526	465	---	915	362	553	1,231	528	703
Jackson	1,072	625	128	1,201	752	449	1,527	371	1,156
Madison	552	762	570	649	1,448	799	950	404	546
Marshall	449	431	174	851	484	367	---	---	---
St. Clair	375	130	202	491	342	149	300 Maj.	---	300
	3,321	2,747	1,284	4,594	4,005	589	4,908	1,303	3,605

Figures for 1847—*Southern Advocate*, Aug. 20, 1847.
Figures for 1849—*Southern Advocate*, Aug. 17, 1849.
Figures for 1851—*Southern Advocate*, Aug. 13, 1851; official returns give 3,625 as the majority.

	1853			1855				1857			1859			
	Cobb, W. R. W. (Union Dem.)	Clay, C. C., Jr. (Democrat)	Majority	Cobb, W. R. W.	Adams, J. M.	Majority	Party	Cobb, W. R. W. (Democrat)	Sanford, Henry (Democrat)	Beaver, H. R. (Democrat)	Cobb, W. R. W. (Democrat)	Snodgrass, Alex. (Democrat)	Wallace, Edwin	Beaver, H. R.
Blount	628	505	123	753	334	419	Dem.	776	376	36	965	270	105	112
Cherokee				1,570	648	922	Dem.	1,236	861	37	802	1,138	324	36
DeKalb	915	462	453	979	408	571	Dem.	923	386	23	815	313	232	85
Jackson	1,296	814	482	1,181	875	306	Dem.	1,101	1,008	21	1,245	224	392	265
Madison	1,125	897	228	1,177	876	301	Dem.	1,109	577	50	1,026	101	554	116
Marshall	755	564	191	600	556	44	Dem.	830	386	56	878	66	278	81
St. Clair	502	502												
	5,221	3,744	1,477	6,260	3,697	2,563		5,975	3,594	228	5,731	2,112	1,885	695

Cobb, 2,152 majority.   Cobb, 1,039 majority.

Figures for 1853—*Southern Advocate*, Aug. 24, 1853.
Figures for 1855—*Sumter County Whig*, Sept. 12, 1855; official returns give 1,460 and 758 as the totals and 702 for the majority
Figures for 1857—*Southern Advocate*, Aug. 27, 1857; official returns give Cobb 2,079 majority.
Figures for 1859—*Southern Advocate*, Aug. 25, 1859.

SEVENTH CONGRESSIONAL DISTRICT

TALLADEGA

	1847					1849				1851			
	Bowdon, F. W. (Democrat)	Rice, S. F. (Democrat)	Phillips	Garrett, Wm. (Democrat)	Party	Bowdon, F. W. (Democrat)	Bradford (Whig)	Majority	Party	White, Alex. (Union Whig)	Rice, S. F. (Sec. Dem.)	Majority	Party
Benton	1,279	739	50	17	Dem.	1,370	556	814	Dem.	633	1,345	712	Sec.
Chambers	551	866	549	7	-------	781	1,218	437	Whig	1,323	792	531	Union
Coosa													
Cherokee	900	512	77	12	Dem.	1,067	747	320	Dem.	1,137	561	576	Union
Jefferson													
Randolph	838	450	35	3	Dem.	938	537	401	Dem.	559	810	251	Sec.
St. Clair													
Shelby													
Talladega	878	723	40	24	Dem.	814	899	85	Whig	1,104	705	399	Union
Tallapoosa	973	734	42	56	Dem.	1,032	938	94	Dem.	988	1,158	170	Sec.
	5,419	4,024	793	119		6,002	4,895	1,107		5,744	5,371	373	

Bowdon, 483 majority.

Figures for 1847—*Southern Advocate*, Aug. 20, 1847.

Figures for 1849—*Mobile Register and Journal*, Aug. 27, 1849.

Figures for 1851—*Macon Republican*, Sept. 25, 1851; official returns give totals same as above.

	1853				1855				1857		
	Dowdell, J. F. (So. Rts. Dem.)	Garrett, T. G. (Ind. Un. Whig)	Majority	Party	Harris, S. W. (Democrat)	Martin, W. B. (Ind. Dem.)	Majority	Party	Curry, J. L. M. (Democrat)	Party	Scattering
Benton	1,749	405	1,344	Dem.	1,031	1,327	296	Amer.	2,026	Amer.	----
Chambers	1,152	819	333	Dem.							----
Coosa					1,241	796	445	Dem.	1,063	Dem.	----
Cherokee	1,220	580	640	Dem.							----
Jefferson					718	322	396	Dem.	775	Dem.	----
Randolph	1,035	579	456	Dem.	1,270	855	415	Dem.	1,281	Dem.	----
St. Clair					801	336	465	Dem.	919	Dem.	----
Shelby					690	707	17	Amer.	1,064	Amer.	89
Talladega	942	817	125	Dem.	1,239	877	362	Dem.	1,183	Dem.	35
Tallapoosa			70 Maj.	Union							
	6,098	3,270	2,828		6,990	5,220	1,770		8,311		124

Figures for 1853—*Montgomery Advertiser*, Aug. 24, 1853; official returns give totals 6,078 and 3,200.
Figures for 1855—*Montgomery Advertiser*, Aug. 22, 1855; official returns give 6,999 and 5,220 for the totals.
Figures for 1857—Official returns.

GUBERNATORIAL ELECTIONS, 1847-59

ELECTIONS FOR GOVERNOR, 1853-1859

	1853				1855		1859	
	Winston (Dem.)	Earnest (Whig)	Nicks (Un. Dem.)	Walker (Whig)	Winston (Dem.)	Shortridge (American)	Moore (Dem.)	Samford (So. Rts. Dem.)
Autauga	565	336	37	31	692	577	668	486
Baldwin	115	90	....	41	54	208	284	111
Barbour	990	297	44	64	1,696	661	948	708
Benton*	1,775	21	384	....	1,711	739	2,291	155
Bibb	651	329	13	....	301	694	847	133
Blount	....	....	....	....	869	253	....	....
Butler	329	101	37	107	699	632	899	685
Chambers	992	325	74	59	1,306	712	1,040	978
Cherokee	1,168	....	584	....	1,670	548	1,776	155
Choctaw**	540	196	1	118	497	442	....	....
Clarke	564	22	6	94	475	274	912	106
Coffee	....	....	....	....	760	283	715	298
Conecuh	....	....	....	....	401	390	534	267
Coosa	1,170	248	150	....	1,214	796	1,311	864
Covington	....	....	....	....	....	....	291	294
Dale	....	....	....	....	1,232	147	....	....
Dallas	599	520	....	....	606	915	913	283
DeKalb	454	....	789	....	1,132	189	....	....
Fayette	....	....	....	....	200 Maj.		1,059	357
Franklin	966	229	80	....	904	860	1,524	284
Greene	657	316	82	74	427	848	979	30
Hancock***	....	....	....	....	270 Maj.		266	91
Henry	....	....	....	....	1,013	347	643	533
Jackson	1,733	....	143	....	2,100	100	1,948	76
Jefferson	787	117	8	....	685	373	1,060	280
Lauderdale	881	184	12	....	1,048	638.	1,174	83
Lawrence	....	....	....	....	602	775	783	122
Limestone	595	82	146	....	548	539	747	114
Lowndes	516	385	....	....	629	808	786	620
Macon	735	840	20	39	950	1,227	1,043	1,126
Madison	945	....	840	....	1,368	632	1,511	29
Marengo	....	....	....	....	636	617	815	289
Marion	751	102	....	....	739	312	921	129
Marshall	475	23	802	....	988	170	....	....

	Winston (Dem.)	Earnest (Whig)	Nicks (Un. Dem.)	Wlker (Whig)	Winston (Dem.)	Shortridge (American)	Moore (Dem.)	Samford (So. Rts. Dem.)
Mobile	1,575	1,230			1,141	1,778	2,047	1,290
Monroe	375			258	543	508	599	261
Montgomery	657	700	5	30	982	1,115	1,225	1,117
Morgan	404	112	277		200 Maj.		1,061	171
Perry	789	256			581	991	1,170	93
Pickens	942	207			916	662	1,267	139
Pike	1,089	294			1,199	1,257	1,388	895
Randolph	943		568		1,288	868	1,423	493
Russell	511	39	686		996	720	960	897
St. Clair	787		117		947	183		
Shelby	699	164	178		424	1,018	1,164	161
Sumter	740	518	3		584	676	625	125
Talladega	841	83	890		1,193	995	1,380	529
Tallapoosa					1,448	1,212	1,647	1,306
Tuscaloosa	753	944	50	10	343	1,267	1,185	456
Walker					578	205	420	229
Washington	155			67	49	73	230	40
Wilcox	649	189	70	76	667	481	814	182
	30,862	9,499	7,096	1,068	42,501	30,715	47,293	18,070

*Benton, name was changed to Calhoun in 1858.

**Choctaw, became a county in 1847.

***Hancock, became a county in 1850; name changed to Winston in 1857.

Figures for 1853 are from *Montgomery Advertiser,* Aug. 13, 1853.

Figures for 1855 are from *Montgomery Advertiser,* Aug. 21, 1855.

Figures for 1859 are from *Montgomery Advertiser,* Aug. 24, 1859.

Collier was reelected in 1851 without regular opposition, receiving a vote of 37,460. B. G. Shields in this election received 5,747; Colonel Terry, 61; Mr. Yancey, 411.—Garret, *Reminiscences of Public Men,* p. 545.

Moore received 41,871 votes in 1857. There were 2,447 scattering votes cast against him, representing twenty-nine counties.—*Journal of the House,* 1857-1858, p. 37-38.

ELECTION OF DECEMBER 24, 1860, FOR DELEGATES TO THE
STATE CONVENTION, JANUARY 7, 1861

Counties	Secessionist Vote	Cooperationist Vote	Majority	Party
Autauga	626	603	23	S
Baldwin	91	1	90	S
Barbour	1,653	....	1,653	S
Bibb	245	....	245	S
Blount	505	805	300	C
Butler	695	....	695	S
Calhoun	1,574	558	1,016	S
Chambers	1,018	665	353	S
Cherokee	1,118	1,139	21	C
Choctaw	463	217	246	S
Clarke	733	170	563	S
Coffee	714	359	355	S
Conecuh	372	399	27	C
Coosa	898	1,126	228	C
Covington	337	229	108	S
Dale	1,007	195	812	S
Dallas	1,015	358	657	S
DeKalb*	....	600 Maj.	600	C
Fayette	432	1,110	678	C
Franklin	348	1,372	1,024	C
Greene	823	530	293	S
Henry	763	....	763	S
Jackson	1,025	263	238	C
Jefferson	574	675	101	C
Lauderdale	505	1,197	692	C
Lawrence*	....	....	....	C
Limestone	314	774	460	C
Lowndes	990	....	990	S
Macon	1,549	258	1,291	S
Madison	404	1,487	1,083	C
Marengo	527	....	527	S
Marion*	255	793	538	C
Marshall	327	906	579	C
Mobile	2,297	1,229	1,068	S
Monroe	515	465	50	S
Montgomery	1,274	158	1,116	S
Morgan	520	627	107	C
Perry	781	19	762	S
Pickens	1,001	300	701	S
Pike	1,571	....	1,571	S
Randolph	1,109	1,303	194	C
Russell	554	....	554	S
St. Clair	499	763	264	C

Shelby	635	588	47	S
Sumter	665	31	634	S
Talladega	993	1,174	181	C
Tallapoosa	983	1,609	626	C
Tuscaloosa	718	1,270	552	C
Walker	143	796	653	C
Washington	64	6	58	S
Wilcox	676	26	650	S
Winston	-------	477	477	C
	36,898	28,631		

Figures are from official returns, in the Alabama Archives and History Department, except for Bibb, Dale, DeKalb, Perry, Pike and St. Clair counties. The *Montgomery Advertiser* of Jan. 6, 1861, gives the election results which are practically the same as the official returns. The vote in DeKalb County is from the *Southern Advocate,* Jan. 2, 1861. No vote was found for Lawrence County.

The Secessionists carried 29 counties by an aggregate majority of 17,891; the Cooperationists carried 23 counties by an aggregate majority of 9,623. The majority of the Secessionists in the state was 8,267.

ROLL OF MEMBERS OF THE LEGISLATURE OF
ALABAMA, 1849-59

MEMBERS OF THE LOWER HOUSE

Autauga
1849, John Wood; Bolling Hall
1851, C. C. Howard; Bolling Hall
1853, Bolling Hall
1855, Crawofrd M. Jackson
1857, Crawford M. Jackson
1859, A. C. Taylor; Daniel Pratt (1860) succeeded Taylor

Baldwin
1849, Reuben McDonald
1851, *William Booth*
1853, *William Wilkins*
1855, *P. C. Byrne*
1857, *Joseph Nelson*
1859, *T. C. Barlow*

Barbour
1849, *Benjamin Gardner; Paul McCall*
1851, John Gill Shorter; John W. W. Jackson
1853, John Cochran; *Paul McCall; J. F. Comer*
1855, John Cochran; M. A. Browder; W. J. Grubbs
1857, H. D. Cayton; M. A. Browder; J. C. McRae
1859, H. D. Clayton; Wm. H. Chambers; W. B. Bowen

Benton
(Name changed to Calhoun in 1858)
1849, *J. N. Young;* Asa Shelton; G. C. Whatley
1851, Wm. P. Davis; Wm. C. Price; Matthew Allen
1853, Wm. P. Davis; Asa Skelton; J. N. Willis
1855, Wm. P. Davis; Isaac P. Moragne; G. C. Ellis
1857, J. H. Caldwell; J. J. Baugh; John H. Wright
1859, Wm. H. Forney; Wm. F. Bush; John H. Wright

Bibb
1849, Oliver S. Quinn
1853, James W. Davis; Chas. P. Findley
1855, *E. H. Bernhard; J. W. Crawford*
1857, Robert Parker
1859, *S. W. Davidson, Jr.*

Blount
1849, Enoch Aldridge
1851, *Thomas W. Staton*
1853, Enoch Aldridge; Wm. P. St. John
1855, Thomas H. Staton; Reuben Ellis
1857, Thomas H. Staton; W. H. Edwards
1859, Enoch Aldridge; A. M. Gibson

Butler
1849, *Edward Bowen;* John S. McMullen
1851, B. W. Henderson; J. S. McMullen
1853, Thomas J. Burnett; *James R. Yeldell*
1855, R. R. Wright; J. S. McMullen
1857, Samuel Adams; *A. B. Scarborough*
1859, Samuel Adams; *M. C. Lane*

Chambers
1849, *J. M. Kennedy; Fortune W. Chisholm;* Josephus Barrow; *Benj. L. Goodman*
1851, *W. W. Carlisle; P. M. Allison; George R. Hendree; Calvin Pressley*
1853, *G. F. Hill; D. S. Robinson; Jesse B. Todd*
1855, Toliver Towles; J. R. Alford; Geo. F. Taylor
1857, G. W. Allen; Samuel Jeter
1859, A. J. Carlisle; Warner F. Meadors

Cherokee
1849, *Thomas B. Cooper;* F. M. Hardwick
1851, *Thomas B. Cooper; John S. Moragne*
1853, James M. Clifton; *G. W. Lawrence; Henry C. Sanford*
1855, E. G. Bradley; Samuel C. Ward; H. C. Sanford
1857, Thomas Espy; L. M. Stiff; A. G. Bennett; W. R. Richardson
1859, Thomas B. Cooper; James M. Clifton; F. M. Hardwick; Dozier Thornton

Choctaw
1849,
1851, Voted with Washington and Sumter
1853, *Edward McCall*
1855, John W. Pennington
1857, John W. Pennington; Ambrose Cullum
1859, James G. Slater; J. G. Fielder

Clarke
1849, Lorenzo James
1851, A. J. Henshaw
1853, E. S. Thornton
1855, James J. Goode
1857, James J. Goode
1859, W. J. Hearin

Coffee

1849, *William Holly*
1851, *William Holly*
1853, Gappa T. Yelverton
1855, A. L. Milligan
1857, Jeremiah Warren
1859, Jeremiah Warren

Conecuh

1849, *William A. Ashley*
1851, *William A. Ashley*
1853, *Andrew Jay*
1855, *Andrew Jay*
1857, John D. Cary
1859, John D. Cary

Coosa

1849, Anderson H. Kendrick; F. F. Foscue
1851, Henry W. Cox; Neil S. Graham
1853, William Garrett; James H. Weaver
1855, George Taylor; N. S. Graham
1857, Geo. E. Brewer; Evan Calfee; Alexander Smith
1859, Calvin Humphries; W. D. Walden; Alex. Smith

Covington

1849, Alfred Holley
1851, *George A. Snowden*
1853, *Alfred Holley*
1855, W. T. Acree
1857, *Alfred Holley*
1859, *Alfred Holley*

Dale

1849, E. R. Boon
1851, E. R. Boon
1853, *James Ward*
1855, James Ward
1857, Elias Register; Haywood Martin
1859, Noah Fountain; W. Griffin

Dallas

1849, *Robert S. Hatcher; George P. Blevins*
1851, *Benj. M. Woolsey;* Hezekiah Bussey
1853, *Robert S. Hatcher; George C. Phillips*
1855, *Benj. M. Woolsey; Robert J. English*
1857, Albert G. Mabry; Thomas E. Irby
1859, Albert G. Mabry; Thomas E. Irby

DeKalb	1849, Madison Hendricks; Robert Murphy
	1851, *Notley M. Warren; Alexander W. Majors*
	1853, M. C. Newman; Robert Murphy
	1855, W. O. Winston; T. J. Burgess
	1857, R. W. Higgins; A. W. Majors
	1859, Seabird Cowan; F. J. Burgess
Fayette	1849, A. J. Coleman; *J. K. McCollum*
	1851, A. J. Coleman; *J. K. McCollum*
	1853, E. W. Lawrence; A. M. Reynolds
	1855, J. C. Kirkland; T. P. McConnell
	1857, A. J. Coleman; James Brock
	1859, A. J. Coleman; James Seay
Franklin	1849, S. Corsbie; Thomas Thorn; *R. S. Watkins*
	1851, *R. S. Watkins; Wesley M. Smith; Wm. H. Peity*
	1853, *R. S. Watkins;* Robert B. Lindsey; Charles A. Carroll
	1855, *L. B. Thornton; Wesley M. Smith; Thos. Thorn*
	1857, A. J. Coleman; James Brock
	1859, William C. Oates; William P. Jack
Greene	1849, *Attaway R. Davis; Alexander Gates*
	1851, Allen C. Jones; *J. D. Webb*
	1853, *Richard F. Inge; A. Benners*
	1855, *Wm. H. Fowler; G. N. Carpenter*
	1857, *Stephen F. Hale;* Robert D. Huckabee
	1859, *Stephen F. Hale;* Robert D. Huckabee
Hancock	1849, Voted with Lawrence and Walker
(Name changed	1851, Voted with Lawrence and Walker
to Winston in	1853, James Vest
1858)	1855, *Absalom Little*
	1857, Absalom Little
	1859, James M. Bibb
Henry	1849, Mathew Perryman; J. J. Sowell
	1851, G. W. Williams; A. J. McAllister
	1853, *Aaron Odom;* J. F. Hays
	1855, *Aaron Odom;* James Pynes
	1857, James Murphy; James Pynes
	1859, P. M. Thomas; B. C. Flake

Jackson

1849, Benj. Franks; Thomas Wilson; J. C. Austin
1851, *Joshua Stephens; Thomas Wilson;* J. C. Austin
1853, Robt. T. Scott; James M. Green; H. C. Cowan
1855, W. R. Larkins; Moses Maples; F. A. Hancock
1857, J. B. Talley; J. S. Eustace; J. M. Cloud
1859, P. C. Griffin; Jonathan Latham; J. M. Huggins

Jefferson

1849, John Camp; Hugh Coupland
1851, *Wm. S. Earnest; S. A. Tarrant*
1853, John Camp
1855, John Camp
1857, O. S. Smith
1859, Alburto Martin

Lauderdale

1849, L. P. Walker; *R. M. Patton;* Jos. Hough
1851, *R. W. Walker; V. M. Benham; O. H. Oates*
1853, L. P. Walker; William Rhodes
1855, R. W. Walker; H. D. Smith
1857, S. A. M. Wood; H. D. Smith
1859, S. D. Hermon; H. D. Smith

Lawrence

1849, *Richard O. Pickett;* O. H. Bynum
1851, *J. Armstrong; W. C. Graham*
1853, *Richard O. Pickett;* David Hubbard
1855, *F. W. Sykes; W. M. Galloway*
1857. *James S. Clarke;* Henry A. McGhee
1859, Wm. C. Sherrod; David Hubbard

Limestone

1849, Nathaniel Davis; *L. Ripley Davis*
1851, *Nathaniel Davis; Nicholas Davis, Jr.*
1853, W. R. Hanserd; W. B. Allen
1855, Thomas H. Hobbs; *Luke Pryor*
1857, Thomas H. Hobbs; Wm. M. Reedus
1859, Thomas H. Hobbs; L. Ripley Davis

Lowndes

1849, *Jasper M. Gonder; W. C. Swanson*
1851, *Jasper M. Gonder; J. S. Williamson*
1853, Walter Cook; *F. C. Webb*
1855, *William Barry; Stephen D. Moorer*
1857, Duncan McCall; James S. Williamson
1859, *James G. Gilchrist; Nathan L. Brooks*

Macon

1849, *Robert F. Ligon; B. W. Walker*
1851, *John Smith; Seaborn Williams*
1853, *Charles A. Abercrombie; T. . V. Rutherford; Sidney B. Paine*
1855, *N. G. Owen; J. W. Echols; J. H. Cunningham*
1857, *Thomas F. Fournoy; J. W. Echols; Benjamin Thompson*
1859, *Thomas S. Tate;* Charles J. Bryan; *William R. Cunningham*

Madison

1849, D. C. Humphries; M. A. King; William Wright
1851, *H. C. Bradford; M. A. King; C. D. Kavanaugh*
1853, D. ᴄ. Humphries; G. W. Laughinghouse
1855, Reuben Chapman; John T. Haden
1857, S. S. Scott; Stephen W. Harris
1859, S. S. Scott; Robert J. Lowe

Marengo

1849, *M. W. Creagh;* Caleb Williams
1851, *Wm. M. Byrd; Benj. N. Glover*
1853, *M. W. Creagh;* F. F. Foscue
1855, *Wm. J. Alston;* James R. Jones
1857, N. B. Leseur
1859, N. B. Leseur

Marion

1849, Woodson Northcut
1851, Kimbrough T. Brown
1853, William A. Musgrove
1855, Kimbrough T. Brown
1857, Kimbrough T. Brown; Leroy Kennedy
1859, K. T. Brown; Wm. A. Musgrove

Marshall

1849, Jas. M. Adams; Jas. Critcher
1851, *Jas. M. Adams; Jas. Critcher*
1853, Frank Gilreath; James Fletcher
1855, Jas. L. Sheffield; Jas. Critcher
1857, Jas. L. Sheffied; Wm. M. Griffin
1859, R. S. Clapp; Wm. M. Griffin

Mobile
1849, *Wm. G. Jones; C. W. Gazzan; E. Lockwood*

1851, Phillip Phillips, Price Williams; C. P. Robinson

1853, Percy Walker; Alexander B. Meek; J. Bell, Jr.; R. B. Owen

1855, *Jones M. Withers* (resigned and succeeded by Charles C. Langdon); *Wm. B. H. Howard; W. M. Smith; J. Battle* (resigned and succeeded by John T. Taylor)

1857, Henry Chamberlain; Wm. G. Jones; T. H. Herndon; H. F. Drummond

1859, Percy Walker; John Forsyth; Alexander B. Meek; G. Y. Overall

Monroe
1849, *Edward L. Smith*

1851, C. McKaskill

1853, Noah A. Agee

1855, Samuel G. Portis

1857, *F. E. Richardson*

1859, H. O. Abney

Montgomery
1849, *Thomas H. Watts; Wm. H. Rives; Charles G. Gunter*

1851, Thomas Caffey; Wm. B. Moss; Francis S. Jackson

1853, *James E. Belser; Thos. J. Judge*

1855, *Jas. E. Belser; Jas. H. Clanton*

1857, *Chas. H. Moulton; James R. Dillard*

1859, *Samuel F. Rice;* Milton J. Safford (resigned and succeeded by M. L. Woods)

Morgan
1849, John D. Rather; John Ryan

1851, *John D. Rather; Wm. H. Campbell*

1853, *Jesse W. Garth, Jr.*

1855, Greene P. Rice.

1857, R. N. Walden

1859, R. N. Walden

Perry
1849, *Henry C. Lee; William Hendrix;* George Goldsby

1851, *Henry C. Lee;* Porter King, George Goldsby

1853, E. G. Talbert; *Jesse G. Cole*

1855, *John C. Reid; W. S. Miree*

1857, Geo. D. Johnston; *A. Q. Bradley*

1859, A. K. Shepard; *A. Q. Bradley*

Pickens   1849, L. M. Stone; A. L. Neal
1851, L. M. Stone; J. B. Gladney
1853, *J. D. Johnson; James Henry*
1855, Z. L. Nabers; S. Williams
1857, Z. L. Nabers; A. L. Neal
1859, A. B. Clitherall; A. L. Neal

Pike   1849, N. McLeod; *Richard Benbow*
1851, *Levi Freeman; Richard Benbow*
1853, W. J. McBryde; *D. H. Horn;* Jas. Farrior
1855, *W. J. McBryde, Duncan L. Nicholson; John F. Rhodes*
1857, John D. Murphree; James Boatright; J. C. Baskins
1859, A. W. Starke; O. F. Knox; *J. B. Goldsmith*

Randolph   1849, R. S. Heflin; C. D. Hudson
1851, Robert Pool; John Reaves
1853, W. P. Newell; *John Goodin*
1855, W. H. Smith; Richard J. Wood
1857, W. H. Smith; A. W. Denman; Isaac S. Weaver
1859, F. A. McMurray; F. M. Ferrill; J. Hightower

Russell   1849, *B. H. Baker; James B. Reese*
1851, *O. B. Walton; S. Bass, Jr.*
1853, *Hiram Nelms; A. T. Calhoun*
1855, W. C. Dawson, Jr.; E. Garlick
1857, S. S. Colbert; Clarke Aldridge
1859, *F. G. Jones;* E. Calhoun

St. Clair   1849, J. M. Edwards
1851, *Albert G. Bennett*
1853, *James Foreman*
1855, G. H. Beavers
1857, Richard F. Hammond, Jr.
1859, Levi Floyd

Shelby   1849, *John S. Storrs;* Thomas H. Brazier
1851, W. L. Prentice; Joseph Roper
1853, A. A. Sterrett; *T. P. Lawrence*
1855, *J. M. McClanahan;* N. R. King
1857, *N. B. Mardis; J. P. Morgan*
1859, D. T. Seal; W. G. Bowdon

Sumter   1849, *R. H. Smith;* T. R. Crews; J. T. Hill
                1851, John C. Whitsett; *J. R. Larkin; Devereux
                Hopkins*
                1853, John C. Whitsett; Benj. P. Portis
                1855, *Jerome Clanton; Wm. J. Gilmore*
                1857, Robert F. Houston
                1859, Bartlett Y. Ramsey

Talladega   1849, *Walker Reynolds; B. W. Groce;* Jacob H. **King**
                1851, *A. J. Liddell, Alves Q. Nicks; Nathan G. Shelley*
                1853, J. L. M. Curry; J. W. Bishop; *N. G. Shelley*
                1855, J. L. M. Curry; J. W. Bishop; D. H. Remson
                1857, James R. Martin; John T. Bell; D. H. Remson
                1859, *Lewis E. Parsons;* John T. Bell; Charles Carter

Tallapoosa   1849, John Rowe; J. L. Simmons
                1851, John Rowe; M. J. Bulger
                1853, *Harry Gillam; R. H. J. Holly; Benjamin Gibson*
                1855, A. G. Petty; Hugh Lockett; J. T. Shackleford
                1857, Henry M. Simpson; M. J. Bulger; James John-
                son
                1859, John J. Holly; O. P. Dark; J. G. Bass

Tuscaloosa   1849, Moses McQuire; *R. Jemison, Jr.; H. Perkins*
                1851, *James B. Wallace; Marion Banks; R. H. Clem-
                ents*
                1853, Joshua L. Martin; Newbern H. Brown
                1855, *Ezekial A. Powell; Newbern H. Brown*
                1857, *Ezekiel A. Powell;* Newbern H. Brown
                1859, *Newton L. Whitfield* Newbern H. Brown

Walker   1849, *James Cain*
                1851, John Manasco
                1853, John Irwin
                1855, John Manasco
                1857, William Reid
                1859, J. M. Easley

Washington   1849, B. L. Turner
              1851, B. L. Turner
              1853, G. W. Gordy
              1855, *James White*
              1857, James B. Slade
              1859, James White

Wilcox   1849, John W. Bridges; Thomas E. Irby
              1851, *David W. Sterrett; Franklin K. Beck*
              1853, Robert H. Ervin; D. J. Fox
              1855, George Lynch; Franklin K. Beck
              1857, Felix Tate
              1859, Felix Tate

MEMBERS OF THE ALABAMA SENATE

District	1849	1851	
1. Autauga (9)			
Coosa (15)	S. P. Storrs	S. P. Storrs	D
2. Barbour (5)	*Jefferson Buford*	E. R. Flewellen	D
3. Benton (20)	Wm. B. Martin	A. J. Walker	D
4 Bibb (13)			
Shelby (21)	*D. E. Waltrous*	*D. E. Waltrous*	W
5. Blount (27)			
Marshall (29)	M. P. T. Brindley	*Enoch Aldridge*	D
6. Chambers (17)	*Charles McLemore*	*Charles McLemore*	W
7. Cherokee (28)			
DeKalb (29)	W. H. Garrett	W. H. Garrett	D
8. Clarke (2)			
Baldwin (2)			
Washington (11)	C. M. Godhold	Lorenzo James	D
9. Dallas (10)	*C. G. Edwards*	*F. A. Saunders*	
10. Fayette (24)			
Marion (24)	Daniel Coggin	*E. P. Jones*	
11. Franklin (25)	B. R. Garland	*R. H. Ricks*	W
12. Greene (12)	*Wm. M. Murphy*	*Geo. G. Perrin*	
13. Henry (4)			
Dale (4)	Elisha Mathews	Elisha Mathews	D
14. Jackson (30)	J. P. Frazier	*J. P. Frazier*	D
15. Lauderdale (33)	J. C. F. Wilson	*R. M. Patton*	W
16. Limestone (32)			
Morgan (32)	Wm. S. Compton	*John N. Malone*	D
17. Lawrence (26)			
Walker (26)	*H. L. Stevenson*	*H. L. Stevenson*	W
18. Lowndes (14)			
Butler (14)	*Thos. J. Judge*	*W. H. Crenshaw*	W
19. Macon (8)	*Geo. W. Gunn*	*Geo. W. Gunn*	W
20. Madison (31)	Wm. Fleming	*Wm. Fleming*	D

Wilcox (10)	*A. R. Manning*	*J. T. Johnson*	
22. Mobile (1)	*G. N. Stewart*	T. L. Toulmin	D
23. Montgomery (9)	*Robert J. Ware*	*B. S. Bibb*	W
24. Monroe (2)			
Covington (3)			
Conecuh (3)	*John Morrisette*	*W. P. Leslie*	
25. Perry (13)	*Jack Cocke*	*Jack Cocke*	W
26. Pickens (23)	J. M. Beckett	J. E. Pearson	
27. Pike (6)			
Coffee (3)	*Jesse O'Neal*	*Jesse O'Neal*	W
28. Randolph (18)			
Tallapoosa (16)	Seaborn Gray	J. T. Heflin	D
29. Russell (7)	*Jas. Abercrombie*	*B. H. Baker*	W
30. St. Clair, (27)			
Jefferson (21)	Moses Kelly	Moses Kelly	D
31. Sumter (11)	J. A. Winston	J. A. Winston	D
32. Talladega (19)	*Leonard Tarrant*	*Leonard Tarrant*	W
33. Tuscaloosa (22)	Dennis Dent	*Robt. Jemison, Jr.*	W

District	1853	1855
1. Mobile (22)	T. B. Bethea	*T. B. Bethea*
2. Baldwin (8)		
Monroe (24)		
Clarke (8)	J. S. Dickinson	Dr. J. S. Jenkins
3. Covington (24)		
Coffee (27)		
Conecuh (24)	*Wm. A. Ashley*	*Wm. A. Ashley*
4. Dale (13)		
Henry (13)	James Searcy	James Searcy
5. Barbour (2)	*Batte Peterson*	Batte Peterson
6. Pike (27)	Harrell Hobdy	Harrell Hobdy
7. Russelll (29)	*Benj. H. Baker*	*Benj. H. Baker*
8. Macon (19)	*N. H. Clanton*	*G. W. Gunn*
9. Autauga (1)		
Montgomery (23)	*Thos. H. Watts*	Adam C. Felder
10. Dallas (9)		
Wilcox (21)	S. R. Blake	*R. S. Hatcher*
11. Sumter (31)		
Choctaw		
Washington (8)	Wm. Woodward	*Thos. Mc C. Prince*
12. Greene (12)		
Marengo (21)	*James D. Webb*	*Jos. W. Taylor*
13. Bibb (4)		
Perry (25)	*Jack F. Cocke*	*Jack F. Cocke*
14. Lowndes (18)		
Butler (18)	*W. H. Crenshaw*	*Dr. F. C. Webb*
15. Coosa (1)	James R. Powell	James R. Powell
16. Tallapoosa (28)	*Allen Kimball*	*Allen Kimball*
17. Chambers (6)	*Chas. McLemore*	Dr. E. J. Bacon
18. Randolph (28)	Henry M. Gay	Henry M. Gay
19. Talladega (32)	J. T. Bradford	J. T. Bradford
20. Benton (3)	Wm. B. Martin	M. W. Abernathy

21. Jefferson (30)		
Shelby (4)	Moses Kelly	H. W. Nelson
22. Tuscaloosa (33)	*Robt. Jemison, Jr.*	*Robt. Jemison, Jr.*
23. Pickens (26)	*John J. Lee*	B. F. Wilson
24. Fayette (10)		
Marion (10)	E. P. Jones	E. P. Jones
25. Franklin (11)	Henry C. Jones	*Henry C. Jones*
26. Lawrence (17)		
Walker (17)	W. A. Hewlett	W. A. Hewlett
Hancock		
27. Blount (5)	M. P. T. Brindley	M. P. T. Brindley
St. Clair (30)		
28. Cherokee (7)	J. M. Hendrix	B. C. Yancey
29. Marshall (5)		
DeKalb (7)	James Lamar	James Lamar
30. Jackson (14)	John P. Frazier	Thomas Wilson
31. Madison (20)	Wm. Acklen	Wm. Acklen
32. Limestone (16)		
Morgan (16)	J. N. Malone	J. N. Malone
33. Lauderdale (15)	*R. M. Patton*	*R. M. Patton*

District	1857	1859
1. Mobile (22)	James S. Deas	T. L. Toumin
2. Baldwin (8) Monroe (24) Clarke (8)	Noah A. Agee	S. B. Cleveland
3. Covington (24) Coffee (27) Conecuh (24)	*D. H. Horn*	*D. H. Horn*
4. Dale (13) Henry (13)	James McKinney	William Wood
5. Barbour (2)	E. C. Bullock	E. C. Bullock
6. Pike (27)	H. B. Thompson	*E. L. McIntyre*
7. Russell (29)	*A. B. Griffin*	A. B. Griffin
8. Macon (19)	*Rev. G. W. Carter*	*W. P. Chilton*
9. Autauga (1) Montgomery (23)	Adam C. Felder	Adam C. Felder
10. Dallas (9) Wilcox (21)	John M. Calhoun	J. M. Calhoun
11. Sumter (31) Choctaw Washington (8)	Wm. Woodward	Wm. Woodward
12. Greene (12) Marengo (21)	Allen C. Jones	Allen C. Jones
13. Bibb (4) Perry (25)	*Jack F. Cocke*	*Jack F. Cocke*
14. Lowndes (18) Butler (18)	T. J. Burnett	T. J. Burnett
15. Coosa (1)	Daniel Crawford	Geo. E. Brewer
16. Tallapoosa (28)	John Rowe	John Rowe
17. Chambers (6)	Robert Mitchell	Robert Mitchell
18. Randolph (28)	Robert S. Heflin	Robert S. Heflin
19. Talladega (32)	George Hill	George Hill
20. Benton (3)	M. W. Abernathy	Thomas A. Walker

21. Jefferson (30)
   Shelby (4)   *John S. Storrs*   H. W. Nelson
22. Tuscaloosa **(33)**   *Robt. Jemison, Jr.*   *Robt. Jemison, Jr.*
23. Pickens (26)   A. B. Clitherall   L. M. Stone
24. Fayette (10)
   Marion (10)   E. P. Jones   E. P. Jones
25. Franklin (11)   R. B. Lindsay   *Wm. M. Jackson*
26. Lawrence (17)
   Walker (17)   O. H. Bynum   O. H. Bynum
   Hancock
27. Blount (5)
   St. Clair (30)   Wm. Thaxton   T. W. Staton
28. Cherokee (7)   S. K. McSpadden   S. K. McSpadden
29. Marshall (5)
   DeKalb (7)   S. K. Rayburn   R. W. Higgins
30. Jackson (14)   Wm. A. Austin   Wm. A. Austin
31. Madison **(20)**   Wm. Fleming   **Wm. Fleming**
32. Limestone (16)
   Morgan (16)   John D. Rather   John D. Rather
33. Lauderdale **(15)**   R. M. Patton   R. M. Patton

Names in italics were Whigs, Unionists, Americans, or Oppositions; names not italicized were Democrats or Southern Rights. The letters after the names of the senators in 1851 indicate the party to which the senator belonged in 1849.

The figures in parenthesis, following each county in the list of the senatorial districts, indicate the number of the new districts into which the counties were placed by the Redistricting Act of 1852.

Choctaw was made a county in 1847.

Hancock was made a county in 1850 and put in a district in 1852; its name was changed to Winston in 1858.

The name of Benton County was changed to Calhoun in 1858.

The *Huntsville Democrat,* Aug. 14, 1851, states that the representatives and the senator from Limestone County in 1851, were Southern Rights men.

Summary of the composition of the lower house:

1847	65 Democrats	35	Whigs
1849	57 Democrats	43	Whigs
1851	88 Southern Rights	62	Unionists
1853	59 Democrats	41	Whigs
1855	61 Democrats	39	Americans
1857	84 Democrats	16	Americans
1859	85 Democrats	15	Opposition

Summary of the composition of the senate:

1849	16 Democrats	17	Whigs
1851	11 Southern Rights	22	Unionists
1853	20 Democrats	13	Whigs
1855	20 Democrats	13	Americans
1857	27 Democrats	6	Americans
1859	27 Democrats	6	Opposition

The party affiliations of the legislators were obtained from the following papers:

1849, *Southern Advocate,* Aug. 24, 1849;

1851, *Alabama Journal,* Aug. 23, 1851;

1853, *Montgomery Advertiser,* Aug. 13, 1853;

1855, *Montgomery Advertiser,* Aug. 21, 1855;

1857, *Montgomery Advertiser,* Sept. 8, 1857;

1859, *Montgomery Advertiser,* Nov. 2, 1859.

DENSITY MAP OF ALABAMA, 1850

☐ 2 to 6 persons a square mile
▨ 6 to 18 persons a square mile
▧ 18 to 45 persons a square mile
O Black counties

U. S. Census, 1880, vol. 1, p. xvii

DISTRIBUTION OF SLAVES IN ALABAMA, 1850

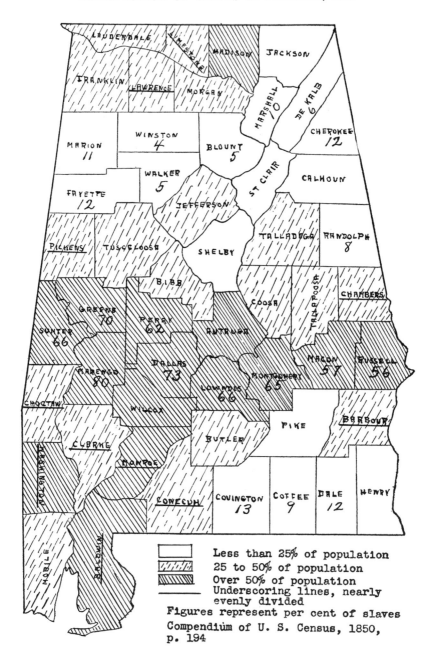

Less than 25% of population
25 to 50% of population
Over 50% of population
Underscoring lines, nearly
   evenly divided
Figures represent per cent of slaves
Compendium of U. S. Census, 1850,
   p. 194

NATIVE STATES OF THE PEOPLE OF ALABAMA, 1870

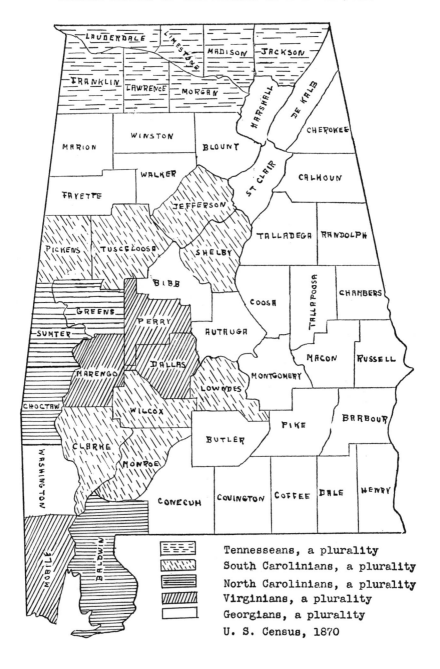

Tennesseans, a plurality
South Carolinians, a plurality
North Carolinians, a plurality
Virginians, a plurality
Georgians, a plurality
U. S. Census, 1870

PRESIDENTIAL ELECTION IN 1848

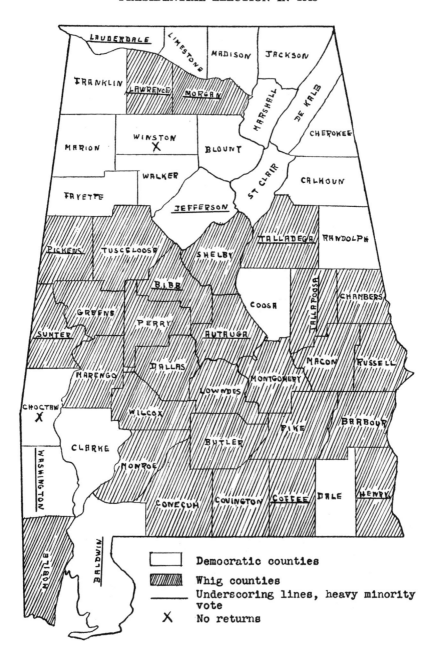

CONGRESSIONAL ELECTIONS IN 1851

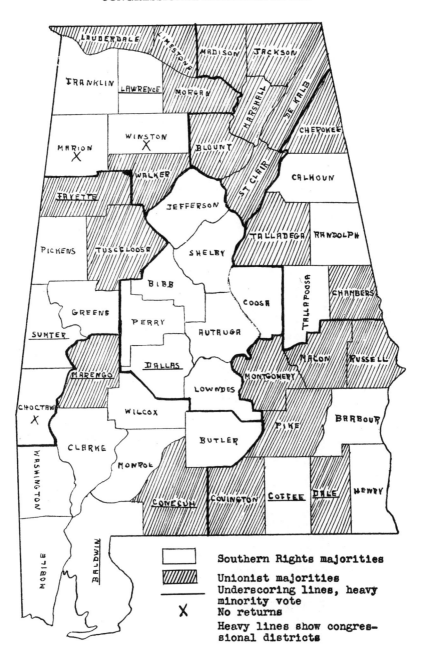

Southern Rights majorities

Unionist majorities

Underscoring lines, heavy minority vote

X No returns

Heavy lines show congressional districts

COMPOSITION OF THE LOWER HOUSE IN 1851

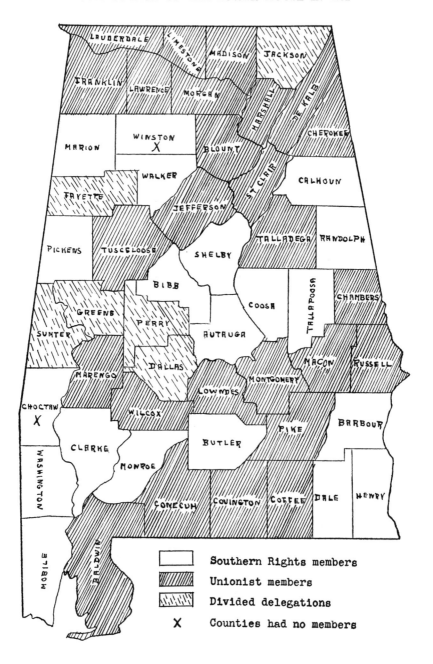

PRESIDENTIAL ELECTION IN 1852

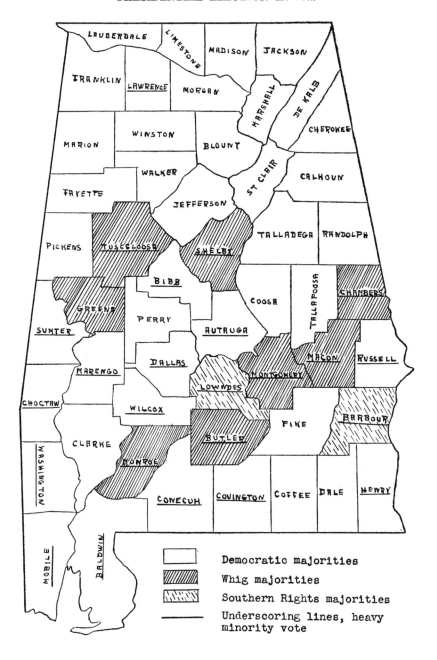

Democratic majorities

Whig majorities

Southern Rights majorities

Underscoring lines, heavy
minority vote

VOTE IN THE SENATE ON THE WHITE BASIS, 1854

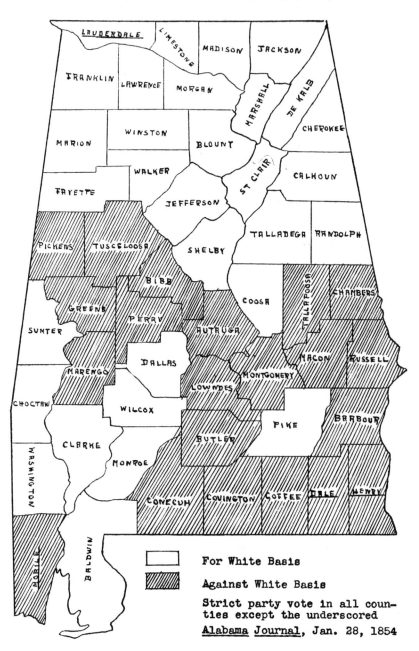

For White Basis

Against White Basis

Strict party vote in all counties except the underscored
Alabama Journal, Jan. 28, 1854

GUBERNATORIAL ELECTION IN 1855

Democratic majorities

American majorities

Underscoring lines, heavy minority vote

VOTE IN LOWER HOUSE FOR U. S. SENATOR, 1855

For Fitzpatrick (Democrat)

For Pryor (American)

Divided vote

Journal of the House, 1855-56,
pp. 44-46

PRESIDENTIAL ELECTION IN 1856

PRESIDENTIAL ELECTION IN 1860

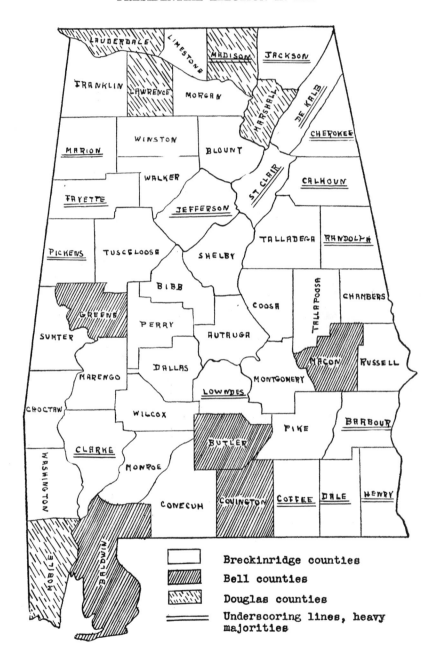

ELECTION FOR DELEGATES TO THE SECESSION CONVENTION

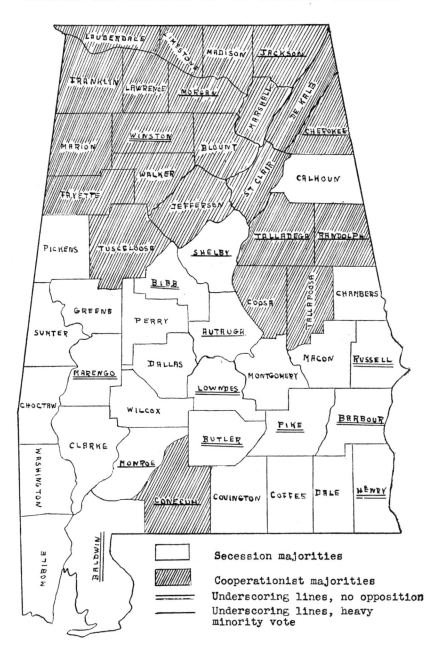

Secession majorities

Cooperationist majorities

Underscoring lines, no opposition

Underscoring lines, heavy
minority vote

BIBLIOGRAPHY

I. SOURCE MATERIALS

Acts of the General Assembly of Alabama, 1849-59.

Journal of the Senate of Alabama.

Journal of the House of Alabama. Neither the Supreme Court library at Montgomery nor the State Archives Department has the Journals for 1853-54.

Code of Alabama, 1852.

United States Census Reports for 1850, 1860, 1870.

Census for the State of Alabama, 1855. This census was made in pursuance of an act of the legislature of 1854, which established the public school system of the state. These returns give the names of heads of families, number of children in families, number of slaves, and the free negroes who had white guardians.

V. Gayle Snedecor, *A Directory for Greene County for 1855-56,* Mobile, 1856.

W. C. Tharin, *A Directory for Marengo County for 1860-61,* Mobile, 1861.

"Correspondence of John C. Calhoun," edited by J. F. Jameson, in *Annual Report of the American Historical Association for 1902,* vol. 2, Washington, 1902.

II. MANUSCRIPT LETTERS AND PAPERS

M. P. Blue Papers. Blue was an associate editor of the *Montgomery Advertiser* in the early fifties and was later appointed postmaster at Montgomery by President Pierce. These papers were collected by Blue for the purpose of writing a history of Alabama. They contain much material, largely statistical, from the various counties.

Clay Papers. This collection contains papers of Governor C. C. Clay and his son, C. C. Clay, Jr., who was United State senator from 1853 and who played an important part in political affairs in the state. The collection was in possession of Mrs. Bettie V. Adams, of Gurley, Alabama, until acquired by Duke University in 1931.

Thomas B. Cooper Letters. Cooper was a Whig member of the legislature from 1849 to 1853. These letters were written to his wife and describe political trading in the legislature.

Bolling Hall Papers. Hall was a prominent Democratic planter of Autauga County and an intimate friend of Benjamin Fitzpatrick and the other Black Belt political leaders, whom their Whig opponents called the "Montgomery Regency."

W. R. King Papers. There are only a few papers in this collection and they are not of great importace for the politics of this period.

A. J. Pickett Papers. Pickett was a prominent Democratic planter of Autauga and Montgomery counties. He was allied with Fitzpatrick and his group. He was mentioned for governor in 1853. Most of these papers are not political, but relate to his *History of Alabama.*

W. L. Yancey Papers. Mainly newspapers which contain speeches made by Yancey.

John J. Seibels Letters. These letters were written by John T. Seibels, from Columbia, South Carolina, to his son, J. J. Seibels, who was editor of the *Montgomery Advertiser.* They show the South Carolina influence upon Alabama in the early fifties. They are in possession of Emmett Seibels, Montgomery, Alabama.

All of the above mentioned papers and letters, with the exception of the Clay Papers and Seibels Letters, are in the Alabama Archives and History Department at Montgomery.

III. NEWSPAPERS

Auburn, Macon County (now Lee County), *Southern Era,* Feb. 21, 1860-Dec. 1860.

Cahaba, Dallas County, *Dallas Gazette,* Jan. 5, 1854-Dec. 30, 1859. Democratic and later Southern Rights.

Clayton, Barbour County, *Clayton Banner,* May 31, 1860-April 25, 1861. Edited by Jefferson Buford, secessionist.

Eufaula, Barbour County, *Eufaula Democrat,* July 4, 1848-June 22, 1852; sundry numbers from May 8, 1855 to June 24, 1861. The name was changed to the *Spirit of the South* on Oct 22, 1850; under this name it was strongly Southern Rights. It exercised much influence over the people in the southeastern counties which were often spoken of as the "Cow" counties.

Florence, Lauderdale County, *Florence Gazette,* Oct. 1, 1858-July 10, 1861. Democratic.

Gainesville, Sumter County, *Gainesville Independent,* Nov. 18, 1854-Sept. 23, 1865. Was said to have been set up as the organ of Governor John A. Winston.

Greensboro, Greene County, (now Hale County), *Alabama Beacon,* Jan. 4, 1851-Dec. 1855; Jan. 2, 1857-through 1860.

Greenville, Butler County, *Southern Messenger,* March 16, 1859-Dec. 19, 1860. *South Alabamian,* April 7, 1860-Dec. 22, 1860.

Grove Hill, Clarke County, *Clarke County Democrat,* Jan. 31, 1856-through 1860. Democratic.

Huntsville, Madison County, *Southern Advocate,* complete for the period. Edited by W. B. Figures and influential in the Tennessee Valley. It was Whig up to 1850; Unionist in 1851; opposed Know Nothingism in 1855 and 1856, and supported Douglas in 1860. *Huntsville Democrat,* Oct. 11, 1848-Oct. 1852; Oct. 1858-Sept. 1860. Strongly Democratic; edited by J. Withers Clay, a brother of Senator Clay. It did not carry much news of state politics but is good for comments on national politics. It quotes much from the *Charleston Mercury* and other Democratic papers.

Jacksonville, Calhoun County, *Jacksonville Republican,* complete for the period; Democratic.

Livingston, Sumter County, *Sumter County Whig,* April 22, 1851-April 16, 1856; Whig.

Mobile, Mobile County, *Herald and Tribune,* 1847-March 30, 1851. *Register and Journal,* Jan. 1, 1849-Oct. 31, 1849.

Monroeville, Monroe County, *Southern Champion,* April 6, 1860-April 26, 1861.

Montgomery, Montgomery County, *Advertiser and State Gazette*, complete for the period. The *Advertiser* was the leading Democratic paper of the state. It was ably edited and was generally considered the organ of the Democratic Party in the state. It was closely identified with Fitzpatrick and the "Montgomery Regency." Contrary to a popular belief, it was not the organ of W. L. Yancey, and opposed Yancey during much of the period. *Alabama State Journal*, 1849-1856. The *Journal,* edited by John A. Bates, who was born in Boston, was a leading Whig paper until it ceased publication in 1858, upon the death of Bates. It reluctantly supported the Know Nothing candidates in 1855 and 1856, and attempted to revive the Whig Party after 1856.

Montgomery Weekly Mail, May 1854 through 1855. Established by J. A. Holifield, a preacher and temperance reformer, and J. J. Hooper, an old Whig. Hooper had become a strong Southern Rights man by 1855, and began to claim that the Democratic Party would not protect the rights of the South as long as the Alabama Democrats continued to cooperate with the northern branch of the party, and thus put party allegiance above Southern Rights. This paper was the most important Know Nothing paper in the state.

Montgomery Daily Post, April 7, 1860 through 1860. Supported Bell in 1860.

Montgomery Confederation, June 8, 1860-Jan. 11, 1861. Edited by J. J. Seibels, who had been editor of the *Montgomery Advertiser,* in 1850-51. Was a Douglas paper in 1860.

Moulton, Lawrence County, *Moulton Democrat,* Jan. 20, 1855-through Dec. 1858.

Selma, Dallas County, *Alabama State Sentinel,* 1855. Edited by John Hardy; was Know Nothing in 1855.

Dallas Gazette.

Troy, Pike County, *Independent American,* 1855-1860. Established in 1855 as a Know Nothing paper; it was for Southern Rights and supported Breckinridge in 1860.

Tuscaloosa, Tuscaloosa County, *Tuscaloosa Monitor,* complete 1850-1860. Was an important Whig paper.

Crystal Fount, June 6, 1851-May 28. 1852; official organ of the Sons of Temperance.

Tuskegee, Macon County, *Macon Republican,* Nov. 8, 1849-Dec. 8, 1859. Edited by Daniel Sayre and one of the most influential Whig papers in the eastern Black Belt.

Wetumpka, Coosa County, (now Elmore County), *Daily State Guard,* Jan. 2, 1849-Dec. 31, 1849.

Dorsey's Dispatch, Sept. 5, 1856-July 10, 1857; was Democratic in 1856.

Wetumpka Spectator, Nov. 14, 1856-Oct. 6, 1857; sundry numbers for 1857.

All of the papers listed above were weeklies except the *Montgomery Advertiser,* the *Alabama Journal,* the *Montgomery Mail,* and the *Wetumpka State Guard,* which were dailies. The files are in the State Archives Department, except the *Clayton Banner,* which is in the court house in Clayton, Alabama; the *Montgomery Advertiser* and the *Alabama Journal,* which are in the files of the *Montgomery Advertiser;* and the *Montgomery Mail,* which is in the Carnegie Library, at Montgomery.

IV. SPECIAL STUDIES

Seven monographs prepared by members of the seminary of the Alabama Polytechnic Institute, under the direction of Professor George Petrie, and printed in *Transactions of the Alabama Historical Society,* 1899-1903, volume iv. The titles are as follows: W. L. Fleming, "The Buford Expedition to Kansas;" S. H. Roberts, "Benjamin Fitzpatrick and the Vice-Presidency;" Miss Toccoa Cozart, "Henry W. Hilliard;" Miss E. B. Culver, "Thomas Hill Watts;" J. E. D. Yonge, "The Conservative Party in Alabama, 1848-60," George Petrie, "What will be the final Estimate of Yancey," and "William F. Sanford, Statesman and Man of Letters." A reprint of these papers was made at Montgomery, 1904.

A. C. Cole, "The South and the Right of Secession in the Early Fifties," in *Mississippi Valley Historical Society,* I. 379-99.

C. P. Denman, *The Secession Movement in Alabama,* Montgomery, 1933. This is a doctoral dissertation. Much of the material was taken from manuscripts in private possession. It was painstakingly and excellently done and is a valuable work.

V. GENERAL SECONDARY WORKS

Brant and Fuller, compilers, *Memorial Record of Alabama,* Madison, Wisconsin, 1893. Largely biographical.

Willis Brewer, *Alabama: Her History, Resources, War Record, and Public Men,* 1540-1872, Montgomery, 1872. This work contains valuable material for all the counties and sketches of prominent men.

W. G. Brown, *A History of Alabama,* University Publishing Company, 1900. A text-book.

J. W. DuBose, *Life and Times of Yancey,* Birmingham, 1892. DuBose was an admirer of Yancey, but this work contains a great deal of valuable material. It overemphsizes Yancey's influence in state politics, however. A satisfactory life of Yancey has not been written.

William Garrett, *Reminiscences of Public Men in Alabama for Thirty Years* (about 1840 to 1872), Atlanta, 1872. Garrett was an important political Democratic leader during the fifties. He was speaker of the house, 1853-54, and later secretary of state, which enabled him to compile much valuble material in this work. It is largely biographical.

Joseph Hodgson, *The Cradle of the Confederacy,* Mobile, 1876.

A. B. Moore, *History of Alabama and her People,* The American Historical Society, Chicago, 1927, three volumes. The first volume of this work is the most complete history of the state which has been undertaken since Pickett's work. It is an excellent work.

Thomas M. Owen, *History of Alabama and Dictionary of Alabama Biography,* four volumes, Chicago, 1921. This is the best collection of materials on Alabama History. Dr. Owen worked for years in collecting this material and it is invaluable to the student and research scholar in the field of Alabama History.

Smith and DeLand, Publishers, *Northern Alabama,* Birmingham, 1893. Principal value is biographical sketches.

J. E. Saunders, *Early Settlers of Alabama,* New Orleans, 1899. Largely biographical.

All of these works are in the Alabama Archives and History Department at Montgomery.

VI. COUNTY AND LOCAL HISTORIES

Reverend T. H. Ball, *Clarke County and Its Surroundings,* 1882.

E. C. Betts, *Early History of Huntsville, Alabama,* Montgomery, 1909, revised 1916.

M. P. Blue, *History of Montgomery, Alabama,* 1909. This work is of some value.

John Hardy, "History of Autauga County," in the *Daily State,* August 10, 1867.

John Hardy, *Selma, her Institutions and her Men,* Selma, 1879.

Shadrach Mims, *History of Autauga County* Twenty-three pages, typewritten.

John B. Little, *History of Butler County, Alabama,* Cincinnati, 1885.

George Powell, "History of Blount County," in Alabama *Hist. Soc. Publications,* 1855.

B. F. Riley, *History of Conecuh County, Alabama,* Columbus, Georgia, 1881.

Nelson F. Smith, *History of Pickens County, Alabama,* Carrollton, Alabama, 1856.

W. E. W. Yerby, *History of Greensboro, Alabama,* Montgomery, 1908.

These histories are of little value, for the most part, for party politics. They are largely chronicles of the early settlers of towns or counties, and were written from reminiscences or traditions. All of them are in the Alabama Archives Department.

VII. MAPS

La Tourrette's *Map of Alabama,* 1856, Published by D. H. Cram.

Colton's *Atlas of the World,* New York, 1856. Alabama is map number 31 in this Atlas.

INDEX

Abercrombie, James, 56-58, 60, 77, 87-88.

Abolitionists, 100, 163.

Acklen, William, 24, 93.

Adams, James M., 122.

Alabama Journals news service in 1855, 19-20; favors maintaining the Union Party, 68, 70, 71-72; 72-73; opposes senatorial apportionment law, 73-74; defends Yancey in 1852, 79-80; opposes the White Basis, 97-98; opposes the congressional redistricting act of 1854, 99; opposes a fusion of the Whigs with the Know Nothings, 104; supports the Know Nothings in 1855, 107, 116; supports Filmore for President in 1856, 127 ceases publication in 1857, 138.

Alabama Beacon, editorial on success of the Union Party in 1850-51,61-62.

Alabama legislature:

Acts and resolutions; on slavery extension in 1847, 38-39; Ga. Platform, 70-71; senatorial districts in 1852, 73-74; to thank King and Clemens in 1852, 74; on White Basis in 1854, 97-98; congressional reapportionment act in 1854, 98-99; Nebraska question, 99; on a state convention, 142-143; for a military corps and state convention, 152.

Composition of; in 1847, 28; in 1849, 37; in 1851, 54-55; 1853, 91-92; 1855, 122-123; 1857, 141; 1859, 151.

Election of U. S. Senators: D. H. Lewis in 1847, 28-29; W. R. King in 1849, 39; J. Clemens in 1849, 41-42; attempt to elect Clemens in 1851, 69-70; B. Fitzpatrick in 1855, 123-124; Winston's candidacy in 1857, 142; Yancey's candidacy in 1857, 152-153.

Alabama in 1850; Geographical divisions, 11-13; density, 13-14; immigrants, 14-15; towns, 15; foreign population, 15; sectionalism, 16; transportation, 16-18; newspaper and editors, 18-20.

"Alabama Platform,' 27, 29-30, 125, 129, 169, 172.

Alford, Julius C., 119-120.

Alston, William J., 35.

American national convention of 1856, 126.

American Party: origin, 101; local successes, 103; campaign in 1855, 106; attracts Southern Rights men, 111-113; abolishes secrecy, 125; split over national platform in 1856, 126; campaign of 1856, 133-134; in election of 1857, 139-141.

Armstrong, James, 77.

"Avalache counties," 24, 31, 116.

Bacon, E. J., 117, 129.

Bagby, Arthur P., 39, 49.

Baker, Alpheus, 36.

Baker, Robert A., 104-105, 134.

Baldwin, Marion A., 59, 70.

Banks, E. A., 158.

Baptist Chuch, 166.

Barbecues, 131.

Barr, John G., 129.

Battle, C. A., 155.

Bell, John, 159-160, 164.

Belser, James E., 33, 35, 99, 125.

Bethea, T. B., 117.

Bibb, B. S., 125.

Blevins, G. P., 96-97.

Bradford, J. T., 153, 157.

Bragg, John, 55, 135.

Breckinridge, John C., 162, 163, 164.

Brittan, P. H. 103.

Brooks, Preston, 127.

Brooks, William M., 34, 154.

Buford, Jefferson, 36, 79, 130.

Bullock, E. C., 36, 152-153, 155.

Bush, Floyd, 156.

Bynum, O. H., 158.

Byrd, W. M., 70.

Buchanan, Pres. James, 135, 139, 143, 154

Calhoun, John C., 27, 29, 31, 32, 33, 38, 43-44, 97.

Campbell, John A., 29, 30, 61, 167.

Cass, Lewis, 42.

Cato, L. I., 36.

Cato, Sterling G., 36.

Catholics, 101, 110, 113-114.

Chapman, Reuben, 27, 33, 37-38, 39, 117, 157.

Chilton, W. P., 14, 151, 152.

"Chivalry,' 29.

Clanton, J. H., 125.

Clay, C. C., 95-96, 132.

Clay, Senator C. C., Jr., 33, 37,77, 81-82, 91, 93-96, 130-131, 133, 135, 147, 157.

Clay, J. Withers, 20, 91.

Clay-Clopton, Mrs. Virginia, 59.

Clayton, Henry D., 36, 155, 156.

Clemens, Jeremiah, 36-37, 41-42, 48, 68 69-70, 75, 80-81, 92-95, 117, 126, 130-131.

Clopton, David, 88.

Cloud, N. B., 146.

Cobb, Howell, 32, 34.

Cobb, R. W., 155.

Cobb, W. R. W., 24, 36-37, 58-59, 91 ff., 166.

Cochran, John, 34, 36, 56-58, 61, 70, 101, 137-138.

Cocke, Jack F., 151.

Cole, A. C., 62, 81.

Collier, Henry W., 34, 51-52, 65, 70, 73, 76.

Comer, John F., 137.

Compromise of 1850: 43, 48, 49-50, 51-52, 76, 77. See also *Georgia Platform.*

Congressional districts: description and political affiliations, 20-26; redistricting of in 1854, 98-99.

Congressional elections: see *Elections, congressional.*

Conner, H. W., 33.

Constitutional Union Party, 159-160.

Conventions, national: see *American; Democratic; Whig.*

Cooper, Dr. Thomas, 15.

Cooper, Thomas B., 28, 74.

Cooperationists, in election of Dec. 24, 1860, 167-168.

Cottrell, J. L. F., 84-85.

"Cow" counties, 13, 21, 120.

Curry, J. L. M., 129, 141, 151, 155.

Davis, Nathaniel, 69, 70.

Davis, Capt. Nicholas, 24, 28.

Davis, Nicholas, 123, 155, 158.

Democratic national conventions; Charleston of 1848, 27, 29, 31; in 1852, 77; Charleston in 1860, 156-157; Richmond in 1860, 156, 158, 160; Baltimore in 1860, 159.

Democratic Party: strongholds, 13, 14; two wings in party in 1847, 27; Southern Rights wing gets leadership, 43-48; party goes into Southern Rights movement, 49-51; defeated in 1851, 55-60; reorganization in 1851-52, 65-68; two wings unite in election in 1852, 81; cooperates with national Democratic Party in 1856, 128-135; supports the policies of the Buchanan administration, 138-139; opposes Yancey's efforts to break with the Northern Democrats, 143-149; split with the Northern Democrats over support for S. A. Douglas for President, 154-159; divided in the campaign of 1860, 162-164; summary of the history of, 170-171.

Douglas, S. A., 154 ff., 163.

Dowdell, James F., 77, 91, 120-121, 135, 139-140, 156.

Earnest, William S., 86-87.

Elections:

Congressional summary of, 21-25; of 1847, 28; of 1849, 35-37; of 1851, 55-60; of 1853, 87-91; of 1855, 119-122; of 1857, 139-141; of 1859, 149-151.

Gubernatorial: of 1847, 27-28; of 1849, 33-35; of 1851, 51-52; of 1853, 82-87; of 1855, 104-119; of 1857, 137-139; of 1859, 148-149.

Members of the Alabama legislature: see *Alabama legislature, Composition of.*

Mayors of Mobile and Montgomery in 1859, 103.

Presidential: of 1848, 29-31; of 1852, 77-81 of 1856, 125-135; of 1860, 154-164.

U. S. Senators: see *Alabama legislature, election of U. S. Senators.*

Election of delegates to the secession convention, Dec. 24, 1860, 167-168.

Elmore, John A., 33, 49, 53, 79.

Erwin, John, 58.

"Eufaula Regency," 36, 47, 101, 119, 137.

Eufaula *Spirit of the South*, organ of the 'Eufaula Regency," 22; analysis of defeat of secession in 1851, 63-64.

Filibustering, 146.

Fillmore, President Millard, 77.

'Fire-eaters," 47, 70, 73.

Fitzpatrick, Benjamin, 33, 38, 4!-42,52, 53, 65, 70, 81, 93-96, 114, 123-124, 129, 135, 146, 152-153, 158, 166, 167, 172.

Florence Gazettes favors uniting north Alabama with Tennessee, 16.

Forsyth, John, 20, 11, 145, 151, 158.

Forney, W. H., 155.

Frasier, J. P, 92

French Revolution, 102

Garrett, Thomas G, 91

Garrett, William, 65, 92, 158.

Gayle, George W,, 161

Georgia, influence on Alabama, 14-15, 48, 55

Georgia Platform, 55-60, 70-71, 76 See also *Compromise of 1850*

Gerrymanders, 26, 73-74, 98-99.

Gilchrist, J. G., 79.

Goldthwaite, George, 33, 49.

Hale, Stephen F., 91, 122, 151.

Hall, Bolling, 53, 64, 84, 88-90, 158, 172.

Hansford, C. R., 103.

Hardy, John 80, 89-90, 104-105.

Harris, S. W., 22, 58, 84-85, 88-90, 122.

Herbert, Hilary A., 155.

Helms, Rev. Moses W., 110.

Herndon, Thomas H., 155.

Hilliard, Henry W., 22, 35, 36, 44, 55-56, 100, 104, 130, 132-133, 134, 137, 138, 140, 159, 160.

Hodgson, Joseph, 50.

Holifield, J. A., 112.

Hooper, J. J., 20, 34-35, 36, 60-61, 66, 112, 125, 160.

Hopkins, Arthur F., 28, 39, 41, 125, 126.

Houston, George S., 23, 31-32, 34, 36, 58, 91, 122, 133, 135, 140-141, 151, 158, 166.

Hubbard, David, 34, 36, 58, 99, 137-138, 140-141.

Humphreys, D. C., 158, 159.

"Hunkers," 29, 30.

Hunter, R. M. T., 157.

Irish laborers, 117.

Internal improvements, 75, 82-83, 87. See also *State aid*.

Jackson, Andrew, 14, 128.

Jackson, Crawford M., 53.

Johnson, Gov. Andrew, 133.

Jones, A. C., 156.

Judge, Hilliard M., 32-33, 43.

Judge, T. J., 139-140, 150, 160.

Kansas-Nebraska question, 100.

Kansas, Southern emigration to, 126-127.

Kennedy, J. S., 156.

King, William R., 27, 28-29, 34, 39-41, 48, 53, 65, 68, 73, 75, 76, 77.

Know Nothing : see *American Party*.

Kossuth, Louis, 75-76.

Langdon, C. C., 55, 125, 126, 158.

Lawyers, political influence of, 172.

Leagues of United Southerners, 143-145.

Lee, C. W., 34, 77.

Legislature : see *Alabama legislature*.

Lewis, Dixon H., 27, 28-29, 33, 39.

Liddell, A. J., 69.

Lindsay, Robert B., 159.

Lockwood, E., 87.

"Loco Focos," 104.

Longstreet, A. B., 110.

Lyon, F. S., 65, 77, 155.

McIntyre, E. L., 120.

McLemore, Charles, 69, 74.

Manly, Basil, 166.

Manning, A. R., 74.

"Marseillaise,' 114-115.

Martin, William B., 92, 122.

Meek, A. B., 129, 151, 155.

Methodist conference and secession, 166.

Middleton, Lewis A., 109.

'Minute Men," 162, 167.

Ministers, in politics, 109-11, 133.

Mobile Register : opposes secession in 1851, 50-51; used by clubs as a text-book in 1856, 128.

Montgomery Advertiser : circulation in 1855, 19, organ of the "Montgomery Regency," 22; advocates a Southern

Rights party, 46, 48; favors a reorganization of the Democratic Party, 65;
supports Sen. Ging for the presidency,
65; advocates fewer laws, 75; editorial
on J. A. Winston, 85; attacks the Know
Nothings, 102, 113, 114; change in
ownership, 142, 146; considered the organ of Winston, 142; supports Yancey
for U. S. senator, 146, 147; attacks Sen.
Fitzpatrick, 146.

Montgomery Mail, established as a Know
Nothing paper 112; favors Southern
Rights in 1855 112.

"Montgomery Regency," 34, 41, 53, 65,
89, 98-99, 129, 147, 158, 171.

Moore, A. B., 64, 137-138, 148-49 164.

Moore, John E., 137-138, 157.

Moore, Sydenham 91, 121-122, 140.

Morgan, John T., 17, 155, 156.

Mudd, W. S., 58.

Murphy, Robert, 58.

Nashville convention, 43-48.

Newspapers, from other states read in
Alabama, 20.

Nicks, A. Q., 86-87.

Norman, F. G., 157.

North Carolina, influence on Alabama,
14-15.

Oates, W. C., 156.

O'Neal, E. A., 155.

Opposition Party, 11.

Parsons, L. E., 125, 158.

Parties, political: see *American Party,
Constitutional Union Party, Democratic
Party, Opposition Party, Southern
Rights Opposition Party, Union Party,
Whig Party.*

Patton, R. M., 123, 134, 159.

Phelan, John D., 74, 149.

Phillips, Philip, 75, 87.

Pickett, A. J., 104.

Pierce, Pres. Franklin, 77, 78.

Plank roads, 82.

Planters, political influence of, 172.

Political songs, 57, 80, 115, 124.

Porter, B. F., 126.

Powell, N. B., 155.

Pratt, Daniel, 125.

Primitive Baptists, 110-111, 133.

Pryor, Luke, 117, 123, 126.

Pryor, R. A., 144.

Pugh, James L., 35-36, 120, 129, 150.

Quitman, John A., 79 ff.

Railroads, 16-18, 82-83, 117, 151.

Rather, John D., 69, 129.

"Red Warriors," 115.

Rhodes, James F., 62.

Rice, S. F., 53, 59, 117, 151, 161.

Riots in Mobile in 1854, 103-104.

Ritchie, Thomas, 57.

Rose, Howell, 47.

Sag Nichts, 115.

Saffold, M. J., 153.

Samford, William F., 20, 137, 144, 147,
148-149, 155.

Sappington, J. E., 150.

Saunders, James E., 34, 77, 78, 158.

Sayre, Daniel, 72.

Scott, Winfield, 78 ff.

Secession convention, Jan., 1861, 168-169.

Secession newspapers; in 1851, 51, 63; in
1852, 76, 81.

Secession sentiment; in 1850-51, 46-48, 56,
57, 59-60; in 1860, 162; after the election of Lincoln, 164-167.

Secessionists, in election of Dec. 24,
1869, 167-168.

Seibels, John J., 20, 47, 49, 50, 52, 65,
80-81, 129, 138, 145, 153, 158.

Seibels, John T., 47-48.

Sellers, C. C., 35.

Semple, Henry C., 154.

Shepherd, F. B., 149-150.

Shields, B. G., 51, 61-62.

Shorter, Eli S., 20, 34, 36, 119-120 155.

Shorter G. H., 146.

Shorter, John Gill, 36 155.

Shortridge George D., 90, 104, 106 ff.,
126, 161.

Slavery Agitation___ over Wilmot Provis-
ion 27-29; "Alabama Platform,' 30-31;
Calhouns "Southern Address," 31-32;
Gov. Chapmans message to the legisla-
ture in 1849, 37-38; resolutions of the
legislature on slavery extension, 38-39;
Senator King's views on Southern
Rights, 40-41; Nashville convention,

43-48; Compromise measures in Congress in, 43-48; Sen. King on Southern Rights, 40-41; issue in elections of 1851, 51-60; resolution of legislature on in 1854, 99; excitement over Kansas-Nebraska bill, 100.

Slave areas in 1850, 12, 13, 14.

Slave trade, attempt to reopen, 146.

Sons of Temperance, 83, 86.

South Carolina College, 59.

South Carolina, influence upon Alabama, 14-15, 38, 43, 44, 47-48, 49. 50, 57, 65, 167.

"Southern Address," of Calhoun, 31-32.

Southern Rights Party; organization, 49; attitude towards the Compromise measures, 50-51; in the elections of 1851, 51 ff.

Southern Rights Opposition Party, 161-162.

Smith, William R., 23, 58, 91, 117, 121-122, 140.

Stallworth, J. A., 119, 149-150.

State aid: political issue in 1853, 82-83; issue in 1855, 104, 107, 108, 109, 116-117; issue in 1859, 151. See also *Internal improvements*.

Stephens, Alexander H., 48.

Stone, Lewis M., 77.

Sumner, Charles, 127.

Taylor, Pres. Zachary, 35, 42.

Temperance reform, 82-83, 107, 110, 111, 118.

Tennessee, influence upon Alabama, 4-15, 128.

Thorington, W. H., 102.

Toombs, Robert, 48, 140.

Troup, George, M., 79 ff.

Union Pary; organization, 1849; supports B. G. Shields for governor in 1851, 51; in election of 1851, 51 ff.

"Vigilance Committees," 114.

Virginia, influence upon Alabama, 14-15.

Walker, L. Pope, 93, 104, 129, 155, 157.

Walker, Percy, 79, 104, 117, 119, 126, 151.

Walker, Richard W., 24, 86, 104, 117, 123.

Walker, R. J., 138-139.

Walker, Thomas, A., 59, 84-85.

Walker, William, filibusterer, 146.

Wallace, Edward, 156.

"War of the Roses,' 35, 36.

Watts, Thomas H., 50, 52, 100, 114, 120-121, 125, 134, 160, 162, 165.

Weakley, S. D., 155.

Webb, James, 164.

Whig Party: strongholds 13; Whig press 20; defeat in 1847-49, 27 ff., goes into Unionist movement, 44ff.; reorganization of, 68, 72-73; decline after 1851, 77-80; defeats in 1853, 85-88, 91-92; opposes White Basis, 25-26, 96-98; opposes congressional redistricting act in 1854, 98-99; embarrassed by Northern Whigs, 35, 77, 80, 100; goes into the Know Nothing movement, 100, 106 ff.; supports Bell in 1860, 159-160; summary of history, 170-171.

Whig national convention: Baltimore in 1852, 77; in 1852, 77.

White, Alexander, 22, 59, 60, 77-78, 91, 126, 158.

White Basis principle 25-26, 96-98 142.

Wiley, J. McCaleb, 120.

Williams, Jere N., 36.

Williams, Price, 78.

Williams, Thomas, 49.

Winston, John A., 70-71, 77, 83 ff., 86-87, 103 ff., 142, 147, 158, 159, 165.

Withers, Jones M., 126.

Woolsey, B. M., 125.

Woods, C. R., 130.

Worthy, A. N., 120, 130.

Yancey, B. C., 123, 129.

Yancey, William L., 20, 22, 27, 30-31, 33, 34, 35-36, 45, 46, 48, 49, 50, 51, 53, 55-56, 61, 76, 78-80, 102, 123, 128, 129, 131-133, 135, 139, 140, 143 ff., 152-153, 154-155, 172-173.

Yelverton, Cappa T., 90.